12 -

Volume 74   Number 4   December 2002

American Literature

Contents

Wai Chee Dimock and Priscilla Wald

Preface
Literature and Science: Cultural Forms,
Conceptual Exchanges

In his Rede Lecture of 1959, the English scientist and novelist C. P. Snow coined the phrase "two cultures" to describe a disjunction between the sciences and the humanities that, he believed, both signaled and produced grave social problems. Four years later he explained that his primary objective in the lecture was to sharpen "the concern of rich and privileged societies for those less lucky." But what amazed, angered, or amused his ever broadening audience, and subsequently became the chief legacy of the piece, was his claim that "the intellectual life of the whole western society is increasingly being split into two polar groups." Humanists and scientists, he argued, have nothing in common: from their assembled data to their research methods, from the way they think to the way they talk, "a gulf of mutual incomprehension" divides them. They inhabit, in an anthropological sense, two cultures.[1]

The accuracy of Snow's comments is not our concern in this special issue. We are interested more in what Jay Clayton, in his essay in this volume, calls a "convergence." On the one hand, scientific specializations have moved at such a pace that the untrained are virtually illiterate. On the other hand, the practical impact of this specialized knowledge—from reproductive technologies to electronic archives, from bioterrorism to gene therapy—makes science illiteracy no longer an option. Scholars in the humanities simply have to come to terms with these forces of change. Unpersuaded by the language of crisis with which some cultural observers have responded to the current situation, we see an opportunity for creative and productive responses to the emergence of new forms of knowledge, of cross-disciplinary

American Literature, Volume 74, Number 4, December 2002. Copyright © 2002 by Duke University Press.

conversations and collaborations, all born of the necessity to address the growing entanglement of culture, technology, and science. As our cover art suggests, science can quite literally generate new art forms that at once register and promote new conceptual exchanges across and within traditional disciplines.

We do not argue in this special issue that there is a revolution in the making. Sociologist of science Steven Shapin reminds us that the word *revolution* is not neutral, that to speak of a revolution is to subscribe to the absoluteness of "a radical and irreversible reordering developed together with linear, unidirectional conceptions of time."[2] This unidirectionality can be contested. Rather than putting the sciences and the humanities in linear narratives, we have tried to keep in mind that they are both language systems and that the problem of translating from one language to another merits renewed and ongoing attention. We depart from Shapin in focusing less on the social genealogies of science than on the current intersections among the disciplines, intersections productive of large-scale changes across the entire institutional landscape.[3] This volume grows out of our commitment to that project.

The questions that motivated our call for papers are both familiar and pressing: How should the humanities come to terms with changes in our experience of the world and in the new forms of knowledge and conceptual exchanges now emerging? How do these changes affect our objects of study, our methodologies, our habits of thought? And how, conversely, can literary and cultural critics formulate a set of questions to evaluate these new developments? In this issue of *American Literature*, we bring together scholars who try to imagine what literary and cultural studies would look like if science and technology were seated at the table. We see them as dynamic partners rather than unwelcome guests or hereditary enemies, not always congenial but necessarily in dialogue. In these new convergences, the keyword for us is *and*, a copula meant not to eliminate the distance between literature and science or to suggest an easy harmony but, rather, to map out a contact zone, a few interrogatory points, as it were, through which one discipline might put pressure on the other, might generate frictions that illuminate.[4]

We want to bear down on the sciences, holding them accountable for issues not necessarily expressible through their disciplinary language and not necessarily highlighted for their practitioners. At the same time, and with no less urgency, we want to bear down on the humanities, holding them accountable in just the same way. Like the sciences, the humanities have fields of inquiry naturalized by convention; these institutional domains appear as if they were objective facts. That problem is as acute now as it was fifty years ago. Most of us, professionalized into our respective fields, tend to do our work according to set protocols, unstated but tacitly obeyed, and largely invisible to us. We tend to cite the same theoretical texts, apply them to similar archives, derive from them the same analytic lexicon, the same periodization, the same set of questions to be addressed. Using the language of Thomas Kuhn, we can say that the humanities, no less than the sciences, are paradigm-dependent, paradigm-legitimated, and paradigm-normalizing.[5] As institutional artifacts, both are dedicated to regulating their output and reproducing their practitioners in a recognizable mold. It is against this shared normativity—against the mechanisms of regulation and reproduction at work in both disciplines—that we hope to mobilize one against the other, the better to disturb fixed protocols in each.

Four sets of questions are brought into relief by this interdisciplinary contact. First, on the most immediate level, how are the humanities affected by new technologies such as the Internet and electronic archives? How have these technologies changed the methods and the very materials of our research? The digitized library not only allows broad access to multimedia databases but also unglues the packets of information built into "standard editions," generating new kinds of evidence and making the infrastructure of research more experimental, more open to scrutiny, and more hospitable to collaborative work. How might the humanities, currently an atomic enterprise rewarding the highly stylized work of individual "stars," respond to these pressures for access, for democratization of the profession, for public accountability?

Even as digitized archives transform the nature of work in the humanities, inscription technologies intervene from a different direction. Donna Haraway has written of the cyborg as a composite of organism and machine.[6] The same analysis might be extended to the novel, a print genre inherited from the eighteenth and nineteenth centuries, now turning into hypertext in the twenty-first century—a multilevel and multipathway network, its very form a function of readerly decision. Can we still speak of authorial intention (or authorial consciousness) when the literary text is operationally defined by its physical properties: unconventional page design, different types of fonts, the recycling and redeploying of material from other representational media, as well as a repertoire of indexical activities demanded of the reader? Do we still read at the same pace, with the same distribution of attention, the same license and constraint? What kind of readerly subjectivity is being generated?

Meanwhile, science and technology are not just forces of change. They are themselves human vehicles, not given but made, and thus belong to that world of motivated means and ends that is the province of the humanities. The discourse of science is *literature*, which was how the word was understood in the fourteenth and fifteenth centuries, a usage recently enlarged upon by Michel Serres and Bruno Latour.[7] This broad definition suggests that science literacy is a birthright and perhaps also an obligation for those of us in literature departments. J. M. Coetzee, Evelyn Fox Keller, and Richard Lewontin have all called attention to the metaphors of science and the way this metaphoricity qualifies science's claim to being an objective, numerical discipline.[8] Perhaps there is no such thing as a natural science, since the very articulation of a scientific concept takes it away from the realm of nature into the realm of human speech, where it carries all the cultural baggage of humanity. This is especially visible now in discussions about and cultural representations of genes, an almost inescapable nodal point for discourses about identifiable, ownable, and transmissible personhood.

Science, in this way, becomes "evidence" in the humanities archive. But not without asking some hard questions about the scope and rationale of that archive, especially in light of its counterparts in the sciences. The archives for astrophysics and evolutionary biology comprise large-scale phenomena, traceable only across extended duration: 14 billion light years in the case of the former, a few hundred million years in the case of the latter. What sort of phenomena should the humanities explore, and what is the scale on which the evidentiary domains should be constructed? What difference would it make if the humanities were to adopt, say, the scale of ecological disasters—the scale of nuclear accidents or global warming—to map out the space and time coordinates of their discipline? What analytic lexicon would emerge? What sequences of events would show up in humanities narratives?

■ ■ ■

The first four essays in this issue focus primarily on the way fiction registers scientific thought, while making clear that this is hardly a one-way street. All four demonstrate how conceptual changes in the sciences are accompanied by cognitive shifts that they simultaneously precede, accompany, and augment. Fiction both reflects and fosters those changes. All four essays, implicitly or explicitly, advocate an activist role for fiction in shaping responses to a changing environment and shifting ideas about our places within it.

In tracing the connections between the late-nineteenth-century literary movement known as realism and historically contemporary developments in neurology and brain biology, for example, Randall Knoper illustrates their mutual impact. In so doing, he offers a nuanced understanding not only of realism but also of the history of science in the United States. The preeminence of Freud has obscured other models of cognition and consciousness that continue subtly to shape cultural assumptions about subjectivity and experience. By attending to the impact of late-nineteenth-century neuroscience on some of the most influential writers of the period, Knoper encourages a new consideration of some of those obscured assumptions as well as the active part literature played, not only in registering but also in fostering conceptual change.

While Knoper chronicles the historical development of a literary form of cognition, Ursula Heise calls attention to the current need for new literary forms and genres that respond to analogous changes. In her study of the relationship of narrative form to risk analysis and ecological disaster, she argues that while literary treatments of that topic register the emergence of new subjectivities, writers' reliance on familiar narrative forms protect readers from the instabilities and uncertainties that the characters face. The result, she argues, is a retreat from precisely the conceptual challenges that writers such as Don DeLillo and Richard Powers ostensibly advocate. Contemporary fiction, she observes, must find new forms—perhaps new media— through which to capture the challenges of new subjects and new subjectivities.

For N. Katherine Hayles, those forms have already begun to emerge. In response to the literary challenge of how to reconcile mainstream readers' desire for coherent characters with the (variously) fragmented subjects of philosophy, science, and literary criticism, Hayles offers Mark Danielewski's *House of Leaves* as a work predicated on the "new storytelling media" for which Heise calls. In his endlessly refracted tales within tales, Danielewski makes use of "remediation," in which material presented in one media reappears in another. This re-presentation, which calls attention to the specificities of each of the media involved in the transposition, underscores (in this case) the new roles for print in a digital age. If we consider disciplines as having corresponding media for the presentation of data, remediation may provide a useful conceptual frame for understanding the rich, though complicated, relationships among science, technology, fiction, and literary criticism.

Those relations are currently shifting, according to Jay Clayton, who sees a subgenre (and accompanying synergy) emerging out of their productive flux. In the particular imaginative writing about science that he dubs "geek novels," Clayton identifies a convergence that, like all such phenomena, is at once immensely creative and profoundly rough-edged. Emergencies, notes Clayton, promote cross-disciplinary communication, but habits of thought (such as disciplines) prove recalcitrant. "The trick," he contends, "is to find ways of turning effective responses to 'the present emergency' . . . into permanent critical strategies," and the archetype for such strategies is the development of the literature-about-science subgenre that he chronicles in his essay.

Two observations from Clayton's essay could serve as epigraphs for Martha Nell Smith's pivotal account of the genesis and contribution of the Maryland Institute of Technology in the Humanities, which she directs. "Prophecy courts the ridicule of time," writes Clayton, "and those who dream of tomorrow often wake to laughter." Smith indeed recalls her colleagues' bemused skepticism when news of her intention to integrate new media technologies into her research and scholarship became known. But Clayton also insists that "a critical engagement with technology, not withdrawal, is the best hope for what were once called humanist values," and indeed Smith demonstrates how that engagement is setting new standards and opening new possibilities for editorial and scholarly work in the humanities. At the same time, she insists, this technology can promote productive and unprecedented collaboration in the humanities, not only among coauthors or co-editors but also among readers, authors, and editors. Using primarily the example of the Emily Dickinson archives, Smith shows how new media technologies can upset ossified (and profoundly racialized and gendered) assumptions about authorship and shift the orientation of textual editing and literary criticism.

The remaining three essays reverse the direction of the first group as they use rhetorical analysis to show how humanities archives might complicate and unsettle our understanding of science. Legal discourse, film, and poetry are not just passive indexes of technological development. They have something to say in return.

For Robyn Wiegman, the custody battle over a boy born as the result of the accidental in vitro implantation of the fertilized eggs of a black couple in a white woman illustrates the heady brew of cultural assumptions mixed into new reproductive technologies. By juxtaposing the media accounts of the custody battle and the contemporary popular film *Made in America*, Wiegman foregrounds the unresolved and contradictory meanings of race that emerge in these discussions and that, in turn, "make legible the messiness of affect, personhood, property, and kinship." Wiegman notes the evident destabilizing that emerges as these technologies challenge formerly meaningful and unquestioned categories. Popular culture thus bears witness to a struggle between the familiar narratives of white liberalism and masculinity that find utopian expression as the desire for multiracial kinship and the "messy" details to which Wiegman calls our attention. She asks that we consider the consequences both for the (social) understanding of the case and for the practice of science when "genetics replaces gestation as the foundational language of property-as-life, and maternal affect is rerouted in the language of the law from the discourse of the body to the property life of the gene."

Similarly, Stephanie Turner is interested in how two popular narratives, *Jurassic Park* and its sequel, *The Lost World*, show how the field of molecular biology created habits of thought about DNA largely through metaphors that continue to govern not only popular but also scientific understandings of the DNA molecule. Arguing that these metaphors "laid the foundation for our present 'bioinformatics economy,' in which the marriage of biology and information technology in postcapitalism has transformed the life sciences into a global network of commodity biological information," Turner illustrates the development and consequences of what she calls "a surplus of meaning associated with the 'master molecule.'" Placing cloning at the center of her

inquiry, she shows how literary analyses of popular narratives potentially challenge even as (or maybe because) they reproduce the often
obscurantist structuring assumptions of reprogenetics.

The volume concludes with an essay that turns to poetry to articulate a new conception of time, both humanist and scientific. For Wai
Chee Dimock, the modern world is ruled by Newtonian mechanics,
in turn governed by the "jurisdiction of number," which is especially
powerful when it serializes the world in the form of dates. To the
extent that a national chronology rests on a fixed sequence of dates,
it is very much a Newtonian artifact. Against this serialization of the
national within the numerical, Dimock argues for an alternative, non-
Newtonian time, traceable to Aristotle and Einstein, and recoverable
through the reading of poetry. Robert Lowell's uses of Roman history
during the Vietnam war—juxaposing the year 65 with the year 1965—
put this non-Newtonian time to work.

As these essays make clear, we experience the world through space
and time coordinates that are naturalized (almost) beyond inspection
by conventions of language and habits of thought. These space and
time coordinates determine what counts as data in both the humanities and the sciences. But it has also been a stated goal in both disciplines to interrogate the evidentiary domains so constituted. The idea
of "two cultures" assumes a mutual defensiveness that makes this
interrogation difficult. Pointing, as in fact Snow did, to the potential for
communication across disciplines, we try to experiment here with a
variety of languages that, we hope, will loosen up protocols currently
reproduced with too much normative force. Our goal is to encourage
both the sciences and the humanities to estrange themselves from
themselves, seeing with the shock of recognition that comes only
when we take up residence in a different archive, a different body of
knowledge mapping the idea and experience of humanity. The essays
that follow take on the task of making visible the contours of the obvious—what we overlook when what we see is beyond question.

Yale University
Duke University

Notes

1   C. P. Snow, *The Two Cultures* (1959; reprint, Cambridge, Eng.: Cambridge
     Univ. Press, 1993), 3, 4. For critical responses to Snow, see *The Two Cul-*

tures: The Significance of C. P. Snow, ed. F. R. Leavis (New York: Pantheon, 1963); and more recently, *One Culture: Essays in Science and Literature*, ed. George Levine (Madison: Univ. of Wisconsin Press, 1987); and *The One Culture*, ed. Jay A. Labinger and Harry Collins (Chicago: Univ. of Chicago Press, 2001).

2   Steven Shapin, *The Scientific Revolution* (Chicago: Univ. of Chicago Press, 1996), 3.

3   We do not mean, however, to draw a stark line between our project and science studies. An emerging field, science studies is both broad and flexible, and several of the contributors to this volume have been (and remain) central to its formation and development.

4   Even an instance of interdisciplinary hostility such as the Sokal Hoax can be illuminating; see Alan D. Sokal, "Transgressing the Boundaries: Toward a Transformative Hermeneutics of Quantum Gravity," *Social Text* 46–47 (spring–summer 1996): 217–52; Sokal, "A Physicist's Experiments with Cultural Studies," *Lingua Franca* 6 (May 1996): 62–64; Andrew Ross and Bruce Robbins, "Mystery Science Theatre," *Lingua Franca* 6 (July 1996): 54–57; and Ross and Robbins, "The Sokol Hoax: A Forum," *Lingua Franca* 6 (July 1996): 58–62. These essays, along with responses published in the *New York Times*, the *New York Review of Books*, and the *Times Literary Supplement*, have been collected in *The Sokol Hoax: The Sham That Shook the Academy*, ed. the editors of *Lingua Franca* (Lincoln: Univ. of Nebraska Press, 2000). For a vigorous objection to cultural studies as confusing an antirealist epistemology with a radical politics, see John Guillory, "The Sokal Affair and the History of Criticism," *Critical Inquiry* 28 (winter 2002): 470–508.

5   Thomas S. Kuhn argues that "normal science" is unified and legitimized by a tacitly obeyed paradigm, until a scientific revolution comes along and causes a "paradigm shift" (*The Structure of Scientific Revolutions*, 2d ed. [Chicago: Univ. of Chicago Press, 1970]). For an important response to Kuhn, see Mary Hesse, *Revolutions and Reconstructions in the Philosophy of Science* (Bloomington: Indiana Univ. Press, 1980).

6   See Donna J. Haraway, "The Cyborg Manifesto: Science, Technology, and Socialist Feminism in the Late Twentieth Century," in *Simians, Cyborgs, and Women: The Reinvention of Nature* (New York: Routledge, 1991), 149–81.

7   As Raymond Williams points out, the word *literature* came into the English language in the fourteenth century (from French, *littérature*, and Latin, *litteratura*), and its fifteenth-century adjectival form was the word *literate* rather than the word *literary*, which did not enter the language until the seventeenth century. For Williams's illuminating discussion, see *Keywords: A Vocabulary of Culture and Society* (New York: Oxford Univ. Press, 1976), 150–54. For Michel Serres's analysis of information theory as a linguistic system, see "The Origin of Language: Biology, Information

Theory, and Thermodynamics," in *Hermes: Literature, Science, Philosophy*, ed. Josue V. Harari and David F. Bell (Baltimore: Johns Hopkins Univ. Press, 1982), 71–83. For Bruno Latour's analysis of science as literature, see *Science in Action* (Cambridge: Harvard Univ. Press, 1987), 21–62.

8   See J. M. Coetzee, "Newton and the Ideal of a Transparent Scientific Language," *Journal of Literary Semantics* 11 (April 1982): 3–13; reprinted in *Doubling the Point: Essays and Interviews*, ed. David Attwell (Cambridge: Harvard Univ. Press, 1992), 181–94; Evelyn Fox Keller, *Refiguring Life: Metaphors of Twentieth-Century Biology* (New York: Columbia Univ. Press, 1995); and Richard Lewontin, *The Triple Helix: Gene, Organism, and Environment* (Cambridge: Harvard Univ. Press, 2000).

Randall
Knoper

American Literary Realism and
Nervous "Reflexion"

American literary realism flourished in the late nineteenth century along with rapid developments in the sciences of the brain and nervous system. The literature that was so devoted to accurate representation, in other words, grew in tandem with the science devoted to explaining how humans perceive and apprehend the world. While we have long assumed the importance of science to realist movements, the primary connection has been drawn rather narrowly, between scientifically objective observation and realist aspirations to truthfulness in representation. Scholarship has not attended to realist writers' interest in sciences of the brain and nervous system or explored the effect of rapid developments in neurology and brain biology on these writers' conceptions of mimesis. But there *was* an effect. As "mental physiology" intruded upon realist aesthetics, some of the writers we most associate with realism loosened their allegiance to the model of the detached observer and opened their conception of literary production to a biological model of image transmission. New ideas about the apprehension of reality—such as the indexical reception of reality-impressions in neural tissue or the furrowing of memory pathways in brain circuits—dislodged the image of the cool, untouched, representing consciousness. And ultimately the model of unconscious brain and nervous system processes as the manufacturers of literature challenged that of the conscious reporter.

My history here of the intersection between literature and neuroscience in the late nineteenth century is offered partly as a rethinking of American literary realism, in order to put back into the cultural configuration that includes literary realism the physiological psychol-

American Literature, Volume 74, Number 4, December 2002. Copyright © 2002 by Duke University Press.

ogy that was more or less dashed from view in the early twentieth century by behaviorism and psychoanalysis.[1] But this is also a more general story of relationship and exchange between literature and science, in which both scientists and literary authors worked to crystallize common cultural concerns; the preoccupation they all shared with questions of identification and duplicity, for example, replays familiar nineteenth-century anxieties about identity and dissimulation, and about signification itself, in urbanizing and modernizing societies. The profound way that gender colors conceptions of both the nervous system and literary creation—with effects we have come to criticize—also connects the scientific and literary cultures. My interest here, however, is more with the way the authors engage science and its discoveries, incorporate science in their thinking and their work, adopt its mistakes, and explore the implications of its conceptions. Most important, this is a story of how science complicated and changed these authors' ideas about the representation of reality, ultimately making "naïve realism" impossible. Moving beyond the ways these authors were affected by science, this story shows too how they departed from scientific modes of thinking, probing the implications of the supposed workings of the nervous system, bringing home the unconscious operations and the fallibilities of perception that the scientists themselves managed to identify and then quarantine in their patients.

What follows, first, will be a tracing through nineteenth-century neurophysiology of the idea that imitation and mimesis, and finally literary representation, are natural and biological functions, effects particularly of the nervous system and the brain. The territory includes not only American neurophysiology but also British psychophysiology and French neurology, which seem to be the sources upon which American writers drew most heavily. Several questions preoccupied scientists in these fields. They wondered, for one thing, if mimetic impulses, or a mimetic faculty, might be automatic and unconscious, the result of natural bodily systems that operate independently of consciousness and the will. (Theories of imitation as reflex action of the nerves were central to this conception.) Of interest too was the question of whether such unconscious mimesis might be more accurate or truthful than mimesis influenced by consciousness, with its capacities for dissimulation and misdirection. But they also wondered whether such mimesis might be the effect of disease, whether its imitations might therefore be hallucinatory distortions, and whether it required such absolute identification—erasure of self—or suspension of reason and the will that it should bear the name of a morbid condition. Scientific investigators had to wonder, that is, whether the hysterics, somnambulists, hypnotized subjects, cataleptics, and spiritualist mediums, who were their main objects of study, displayed natural or diseased mimetic impulses. Potentially at stake, of course, was the very nature of artistic mimesis, so after this initial attention to neurophysiology, I will look at the interweavings of neurological conceptions of literary creation and representation with the literary theorizing and practice of Oliver Wendell Holmes, Mark Twain, and William Dean Howells. Holmes, a kind of protorealist novelist as well as a professor of physiology, had the most full-fledged ideas about literary creation as "reflex action of the brain."[2] And his writing and ideas clearly influenced Twain and Howells. The latter two writers explored the interconnections of the nervous system, mental representations, and literary representation, and their explorations caused these two central figures of American literary realism to question and rethink their ideas about fictional representation. They opened realism to the uncertain processes of the organism.[3]

Sympathy, Reflexion, and Representation

In its most general, longstanding conception, which nineteenth-century fiction writers would still have held, the nervous system was characterized as an avenue for representations. Stimuli entered the body through the senses, and the images formed traversed the body to produce mental, emotional, physical, or behavioral states, responses, or symptoms. This process was facilitated by the nerves; that is, the nervous system was the medium by which the world was pictured to consciousness—and the medium, too, through which the body represented its various parts to one another.[4] Seventeenth- and eighteenth-century researchers had elaborated the ancient concept of sympathy, the involuntary mechanism by which organs not visibly connected reflected one another and through which, especially, an organ could respond to the diseased state of another.[5] Robert Whytt, one of the eighteenth-century physiologists who gave the nervous system the central role in the body and, in most accounts, helped develop the concept of reflex response, described the "sympathy of the nerves," by which the smell of food makes saliva flow, an irritation in the windpipe causes coughing, or, because of oversensitive nerves, irritation of the uterus or ovaries causes hysteria.[6] Such notions of sympathetic nervous connections, often involving mysterious and immaterial resonances between body parts, persisted through the nineteenth century.[7]

Late in the century, from a decidedly materialist point of view, Henry Maudsley in his influential *Body and Mind* (1885) still declared that "all parts of the body, the highest and the lowest, have a sympathy with one another more intelligent than conscious intelligence can yet, or perhaps ever will, conceive." This means, he wrote as part of his argument for the physical basis of the mind, that the material circuits of the nervous system establish sympathetic connections not only between the digestive organs and those of taste, the respiratory organs and those of smell, and the organs of smell and those of sexual feeling but also between the brain and the heart, the lungs, and the abdominal organs. Through the nervous system, maladies of the lower organs could be sympathetically reproduced in the brain, causing mental disorders.[8] And, of course, the mind recorded itself in the body, automatically, unconsciously. The nineteenth-century history of this idea ranged from early-nineteenth-century phrenological signs, marks of mind and brain on the surface of the head, to cases of neurasthenia and hysteria in the last years of the century, the sort of cases of mind-body interaction to which Maudsley gave special attention. The human organism was thought to have an astonishing interconnectivity, in other words; throughout the century, the body was taken as a model communications network.

Maudsley's clinching examples of intrabody nervous communication, and especially of the effect of organs on the mind, come from the sexual system. Patently clear, he writes, are the mental influences of masturbation, menstruation, lactation, pregnancy, menopause, and irritation of the ovaries or uterus.[9] In 1899 the American gynecologist Charles A. L. Reed reasserted this point, using the metaphor of the nervous system as a telegraphic system that was so often adopted in the nineteenth century to characterize nerve pathways and their means of electrical communication. The great sympathetic nerve, he writes, "furnishes an abundant supply of branches directly to the womb, the ovaries, the vagina and the external genitalia." The significance is that "the genital organs of women . . . are nothing more or less than a central telegraphic office, from which wires radiate to every nook and corner of the system, and over which are transmitted messages, morbific or otherwise, as the case may be; and it should be remembered right here that telegraphic messages travel both ways over the same wire; that there are both receiving and sending offices at each end of the line."[10] The metaphor of the telegraphic system, whose central office was usually located in the brain, is notably upended here, a reversal that of course conveys a familiar message about nineteenth-century conceptions of women, and female hysterics, as governed by their bodies and reproductive systems rather than their minds. But it also reemphasizes communication that takes place between the far-flung parts of the body, quite independently of the brain. Interorgan communication was, again, a process of transmitting, or registering, representations—pictures in one part of the body of conditions in another. Dyspepsia could be the stomach's version of mental distress, its mimesis of the mental landscape, its translation of brain storm into gastroenterological upset. The difficulty of diagnosing, or interpreting, the sign in one part of the body of a malady in another part did not seem immediately to raise the question of the reliability of the nervous system as a medium.

The representation of one body part in another, and the connection between the rest of the body and the brain, which was naturally the most interesting and complicated instance of such nervous system telegraphy, inevitably had ramifications for understanding self-expression and artistic representation. It was the reflex-arc theory of nerve action, I will suggest, that especially established the importance of the nervous system as a channel for literary writing among late-nineteenth-century American literary realists. Emerging from the theories in the seventeenth and eighteenth centuries about the sympathetic rapport between parts of the body, the theory of the reflex made explicit the process of representation in nervous communication. For the reflex was, exactly, a matter of reflexion, by which a sensory impression was reflected, as by a mirror, into a motor nerve, causing a muscular contraction. Also like a mirror because it was automatic, unconscious, and unwilled, the reflex was thought to work throughout the body, and even to affect mental processes, though in the 1830s Marshall Hall influentially, and temporarily, separated mechanical and material reflex responses from higher centers of consciousness.[11] Simply put, what Hall called the reflex arc named the circuit of a sensory nerve linked by the central spinal cord or the lower brain regions to a motor nerve. Through it, a stimulus produced a movement without mediation or direction from consciousness or from the cerebral hemispheres.[12] This conception of sensorimotor acts initially served to explain automatic, instinctual, and some emotional actions—all as functions of the lower nervous system, matters of the spinal cord and brain stem. Although these reflex actions could to some extent be controlled by the will, they were distinct from the cerebral hemispheres, distinct from mental life and consciousness.[13] And as mental life had no bearing on reflex response, so the concept of the reflex, in Hall's understanding, had no pertinence to such mental functions as writing and literary creation.

Hall's duality between the lower-level reflex and the mental life of the brain was challenged, however, by various researchers. Most of these challengers insisted on a continuity of function between nerve cells of the spinal cord and those of the brain. Some even suggested that the conscious mind itself operated through a principle of reflexion, as images came to consciousness and were then reflected into action.[14] Notably, beginning in 1838 with his inquiries into spiritualist mediums, British physiologist Thomas Laycock published a series of studies that extended the idea of reflex function to complex mental operations.[15] The reflex arc, for Laycock, was not only the basic unit of the nervous system but also a fundamental principle of its operation, and even the brain operated accordingly. The brain could be the end point of the reflex arc, or its beginning—that is, a lower-nervous-system stimulus (say, uterine irritation) could reflexively effect a mental response, but the brain's own activity could also reflexively effect further *mental* activity, and that mental activity could effect complex motor responses, quite apart from consciousness, attention, or the will.[16] Impelled partly by the puzzling phenomenon of people who could accomplish complex tasks while seemingly unconscious of what they were doing—spiritualist mediums but also hysterics, somnambulists, people who had been mesmerized or hypnotized, people who committed heinous murders in a supposedly mechanical and uncomprehending way, in short, people whose bodies seemingly acted in ways not directed by the will—Laycock, Maudsley, William B. Carpenter, T. H. Huxley, and others applied the idea of the reflex, as an automatic nervous mechanism independent of consciousness, to everything from walking a habitual route or playing the piano to writing a great work of literature.[17]

Especially important for two of the authors I will be considering, Oliver Wendell Holmes and Mark Twain, were the ideas of British professor of physiology William Carpenter. A prolific writer about physiology and the nervous system from the 1830s onward, in the fifth edition of his *Principles of Human Physiology* (1855) and more fully in *Principles of Mental Physiology* (1874), Carpenter elaborated and extended Laycock's idea that brain activity is subject to reflex action. Carpenter made two basic arguments central to the history I am tracing here: first, that many of our mental processes are automatic, proceeding in an uncontrolled manner by suggestion and association along ingrained nervous pathways and are therefore aptly called "reflex action of the Cerebrum"; second, that this reflex action takes place not only within the brain but can also operate between an idea (or an emotion or sensation) and a motor nerve; that is, an idea, by reflex action and apart from the will, can cause purposive movement through an "ideo-motor" response.[18] To exemplify the first category of cerebral reflex action, Carpenter points not only to the normal trains of thought that proceed involuntarily when one's attention is released (*PMP*, 251–55) but also to processes that operate unconsciously— dreaming, for example, or the experience of giving up on solving a problem or remembering a name only to find that the solution or the name spontaneously surfaces later (*PMP*, 469, 519, 522, 532–39). He calls such reflex activity "unconscious cerebration" (*PMP*, 469). Ideo-motor responses are exemplified by the somnambulist who unconsciously finds his way about the house or the hypnotized woman who acts out the experimenter's suggestion. But Carpenter extended the phenomenon to telegraph operators or piano players, whose complex actions can proceed without conscious direction (*PMP*, xxv–xxvi); to dousers with divining rods, which dip toward water without the douser's conscious intent; and to spiritualist mediums, who sincerely believe that their automatic, planchette writing comes from the spirit world and not from their own minds (*PMP*, 279–81, 284–89, 292, 302–4). These people's actions are reflexively governed either by habitual chains of thought or by ideas otherwise implanted in their minds, say by hypnotic suggestion.

The instances of seemingly automatic, unwilled reflex operation do not stop there. Orators can speak, Carpenter observes, and musicians can play, lawyers can write litigation, poets can versify, math problems can be solved, and reasoning can go on while people are in somnambulistic states, "and it is a very remarkable fact that their purely Automatic action in this state will frequently evolve conclusions which Volitional exertion has vainly striven to attain" (*PMP*, 591, 594). Moreover, quite apart from somnambulistic states, a host of mental operations proceed automatically, the effect of nervous system circuits, of brain pathways. Once triggered, memory progresses through mechanical associations (*PMP*, 429–30, 434) and "is essentially an automatic form of Mental activity," relying on "the mechanism by which past states of consciousness spontaneously reproduce themselves" (*PMP*, 465). Reasoning, analysis, synthesis, comparison, generalization, abstraction, and judgment can also go on largely automatically (*PMP*, 261–62). Imaginative conception, or the reproduction of "the mental 'idea' or representation of an object formerly perceived through the senses," can happen automatically too, as can the processes of the constructive imagination as it fashions images (*PMP*, 487–489). Indeed, Carpenter concludes, the "work of the Imagination is itself purely automatic," though "the Will can both set it going and keep it going by the fixation of the attention" (*PMP*, 512–13). It may come as no surprise, then, that Carpenter characterizes writing as automatic; the mind can become "engrossed with the subject," and the writer's habitual mode of operation will take over, the ideas flowing and "clothing themselves in words," with this "automatic action" continuing "uninterruptedly for hours" (*PMP*, 263). Finally, Carpenter declares that the operations of genius are "essentially automatic," possible to call into play by the will but apt to operate thenceforth "beneath the consciousness" (*PMP*, 510).

Poetry as Spasm, Paroxysm, and "Mental Neuralgia"

For Oliver Wendell Holmes, novelist and poet but also Harvard professor of anatomy and physiology, these developments in mental physiology and the claims made about art as a function of the nervous system had a special resonance. Reflex action, what he still referred to as "the mechanical sympathy . . . of distant parts," was especially important.[19] Holmes had probably met Marshall Hall in the 1830s in Paris, when Holmes was a medical student; he reported on Hall's work then, and he later helped prepare for press the first American edition of Hall's *Principles of the Theory and Practice of Medicine* (1839).[20] But following Carpenter and Laycock, Holmes extended the concept of the reflex well beyond Hall's conception. This "doctrine of reflex action," he writes, which "started from the fact of the twitching of a decapitated frog's hind legs, has grown to such dimensions that it claims to solve some of the gravest questions in psychology."[21] And in the persona of the unnamed "professor" in *Elsie Venner*, Holmes declares: "Automatic action in the moral world; the reflex movement which seems to be self-determination," needs to be studied "as Marshall Hall has studied reflex nervous action in the bodily system."[22] At the more modest end, Holmes writes of "reflex vision," by which reflexion transfers "impressions from one retina to the other."[23] More grandly, in *The Autocrat of the Breakfast Table* (1858), Holmes declares that physiologists are becoming more and more interested in "the automatic and involuntary actions of the mind," and then, invoking William Carpenter, he notes that such automatisms range from the unconscious processes by which an idea deposited in the intellect establishes relations with other ideas, or a name is remembered after we have turned our attention to other matters, to the "spasmodic cerebral action" that issues in poetic expression. "A man abandons himself to a fine frenzy," he writes, "and the power which flows through him . . . makes him the medium of a great poem or a great picture. The creative action is not voluntary at all, but automatic; we can only put the mind into the proper attitude, and wait for the wind, that blows where it listeth, to breathe over it. Thus the true state of creative genius is allied to *reverie*, or dreaming." It is "poets and artists" who "exercise those faculties of the mind which work independently of the will, . . . who follow their imagination in their creative moments, instead of keeping it in hand as your logicians and practical men do with their reasoning faculty."[24] The imagination works unconsciously, independent of the will. Literary art is automatic, the effect of a nervous mechanism. Poetic inspiration is like a spasm, and therefore like a hysteric's convulsion.

In *The Professor at the Breakfast Table* (1860), Holmes returns to the issue of the "hidden spring of reflex action," declaring that it may even control the will, while we think we are self-determining.[25] And in *The Poet at the Breakfast Table* (1872) he compares poetry to *tic douloureux*, a kind of "mental neuralgia," characterizing poetic expression as physiological: "You can't order these organic processes," he declares, "any more than a milliner can make a rose." When the orator's brain is aflame, or the poet's heart in tumult, "it is something mightier than he and his will that is dealing with him!"[26] However, it was in the talk he gave before the Phi Beta Kappa Society at Harvard in June 1870, "Mechanism in Thought and Morals," that he most pointedly addressed these matters of the nervous system and literary creation and brought poetry and art distinctly into the realm of the reflex function. Referring to Laycock's "On the Reflex Function of the Brain" and to Carpenter's work—but noting the contributions of Maudsley, James Mill, W. E. H. Lecky, Eneas Sweetland Dallas, and others—Holmes declared unconscious cerebration to be a doctrine that "seems almost to belong to our time" ("MTM," 278). Much in the manner of these other thinkers, he likens unconscious "mechanisms" of thought to breathing, a reflex response that, like our chains of mental association, can be affected but not stopped by the will ("MTM," 261, 267). He notes the emblematic examples of unconscious mental processes—when a memory returns to us after we have given up on it, when the brain solves problems while we are asleep, when people knit or play the piano without having to think about these actions ("MTM," 279–81). And then he characterizes the process of writing poetry as similarly "automatic and imperceptible" ("MTM," 282). The poet's emotion, he writes, comes without being willed and it changes in unexpected ways. Such "strange hysterics of the intelligence," he asserts, are "as automatic, involuntary, as entirely self-evolved by a hidden organic process, as are the changing moods of the laughing and crying woman. The poet always recognizes a dictation ab extra; and we hardly think it is a figure of speech when we talk of his inspiration." That is, poetic inspiration comes from automatic, unconscious, reflexive operations of the brain and nervous system, the same sort of sources that cause symptoms of hysteria; the poet must keep his mind "passive to the influx from without," though ready actively to seize out of the eruptions from the unconscious only what will suit his poetic purpose ("MTM," 286).

When Holmes called his first two novels "Studies of the Reflex Function in its higher sphere" and declared his intent to "follow the automatic machinery of nature into the mental and moral world," his primary aim was to portray characters whose nervous-system biology in some way determined their moral or immoral behavior.[27] The narratives, however, can be readily understood, too, as stories of reproduction and representation, and as such they crystallize problems that emerge from the juncture of art and the nervous system. Elsie Venner, whose nervous system was poisoned by snake venom while she was still *in utero*, cannot sing, or play music, or even give articulate voice to her underlying, true, human, feminine inner life, because the natural impulses that would issue in such manifestations are inhibited by her "ophidian tendencies," by the snake-nature grafted into her nervous system (*EV*, 341–42, 418, 434–35). Elsie does need, however, to express herself through a snakely "fierce paroxysm" (*EV*, 388), and she does this especially by dancing. Abandoning herself to a "dancing frenzy that seized upon her," she winds her arms, undulates her body, and rattles her castanets (all secretly watched by her doctor) (*EV*, 147–48). If her true, or human, nature is obscured, without representation, her ophidian nature seemingly achieves full expression, as if, indeed, the reflex response can unconsciously, guilelessly, and transparently express *this* nature. Holmes suggests that Elsie's "dancing paroxysm" is a lower form of expression than poetry or music—with the implication that her dancing is a kind of reflex spasm of the lower spinal cord, or merely the kind of instinctual nervous response that a snake would experience. Apparently for Holmes, in much the same way that one's biology could be defective and issue in immoral action, or highly evolved and issue in moral action, so one's biology could reflexively express itself, in higher or lower forms of art, depending on one's makeup. But where, then, on this continuum, do we place female hysteria, or the "frenzy" and "hysterics" to which the poet abandons *him*self? Are there strata of unconscious reflexion? Higher and lower levels of unconscious cerebration? Do hierarchies of gender, of consciousness, of reason pertain here? Holmes poses but doesn't resolve the question of whether the automatisms, spasms, and hysterics that issue in art are somehow lower than the aesthetic fabrications of consciousness. Nor finally does he fix the status of cerebral reflex action itself.

Focusing again on a female with mixed inheritance in *The Guardian Angel* (1867), Holmes attributes the medium-like visions Myrtle Hazard experiences to a number of possible causes—all seemingly biological and neurological. It may be that her ancestors, Puritan and Indian, are reproducing themselves, in her body, in her multiple personalities, in her mystical visions. Her trauma of near-drowning may be producing hysterical hallucinations. And she may have visions induced by hypnotic suggestion. Quite a medium, in other words, Myrtle invokes conceptions of the unconscious artist, the representer of other beings and other scenes. And it is significant that Holmes chose to focus this novel, like *Elsie Venner*, on a young female character who might possibly be diagnosed as a hysteric. Hysteria, for so many of the psychophysiologists I have mentioned, was the exemplary case of reflex cerebration *and* of mediumistic mimicry and reproduction. It is also significant that, in *The Guardian Angel*, Holmes brings hysteria together with inheritance (often thought to be the root of hysteria) and hypnosis (thought by some, such as Jean-Martin Charcot, to be especially effective, or *only* effective, on hysterics). Joining inheritance, hysteria, and hypnosis as biological conditions for involuntary mental representations provided Holmes with a topical and controversial combination. But the combination also brings to the foreground the abiding question of reflexion as a reliable mirroring, a question that lurks in any discussion of hysterical mimesis or hypnotic mimicry. What, for example, is one to make of the supposedly direct, faithful, passive reproduction of a hypnotic suggestion next to, say, the wildness of a hysterical hallucination? It is, indeed, primarily in Holmes's fictions that questions of the nervous system and fidelity of representation surface, and in both *Elsie Venner* and *The Guardian Angel*, disease, especially hysteria, becomes the ground for the question of truthfulness in the bodily, nervous-system registration of reality. Does disease, does hysteria, create morbid conditions of oversensitivity and heightened imagination that distort reality? Or do these states heighten capacities of registration, recording, mimesis? Are "sick" women peculiar in their capacity to represent, or do they evince a tendency all humans have? These questions, engaged but suspended by Holmes, have a particular background in nineteenth-century neurophysiology.

Nervousness, Hysteria, and "Instinctive Imitative Propensities"

Hysteria, of course, has been characterized as the mimetic disease par excellence.[28] As Jean-Martin Charcot undertook his task of describing, classifying, and understanding the various disorders diagnosed as hysteria at the Salpêtrière, the first task was to distinguish hysteria from epilepsy, a job made doubly hard because, as he came to understand it, so many hysterics at the hospital skillfully mimicked epileptics.[29] As the definition of the disease settled into the now-familiar conversion disorder, its distinguishing trait came to be a malady of representation—the real problem, whatever it might be, disguising itself as something else. But the 1870s and 1880s saw a much more widely ranging discussion of nervous mimicry, its causes and implications.

In 1875 the English physician Sir James Paget, for example, coined the term *neuromimesis* as a more precise replacement for the catch-all term *hysteria* when speaking of a patient's involuntary imitation of a disease.[30] For Paget, neuromimesis is situated somewhere between the mind and the reflex, between consciousness and simple automatism—a formulation that understandably results in contradiction. On the one hand, he repeatedly insists that neuromimesis is not a disorder of the brain but instead "a disorder of other nervous centres," in which such centers are "too alert," excited, and sensitive, so that any impression on them is "too . . . vehemently reflected" ("NM," 236, 249, 186, 176). This is a version of involuntary, reflexive imitation, not involving the mind at all. On the other hand, he acknowledges that some mimicries might be "essentially mental," due to imagination, or fear, or abnormally focused attention ("NM," 183). It is as if Paget's distinction means to resurrect Hall's division between lower-level reflex and cerebral function, except that Paget situates neuromimesis as a middle term. But whether the mimicry involves lower or higher nervous centers, its primary feature is a malady of the will, a loss of control over nervous sensitivity or imagination. While this imitative disorder is typical of hysterics, and of anyone with a deficit of will—such as the subjects of mesmerism and spiritualism, who unconsciously conform themselves to another's idea—even people with "good nervous systems" are naturally susceptible to neuromimesis, so everyone has to cultivate the all-purpose cure, the training of the controlling will ("NM," 249). The paradox Paget offers is that forsaking the will can yield truthful representation; this illness of "vehement reflection" may not be a distortion of mimesis but, rather, a perfection of it. The confusion Paget poses is that by situating the conscious will on one side, he crucially mingles on the other side the uncontrolled and potentially distorting imagination and the automatic reflexion of neuromimesis; they exist in the uncertain territory where "cerebration" and reflex meet, where hallucination bleeds into involuntary imitation.[31]

In the United States, S. Weir Mitchell—physician, nerve specialist, novelist, friend of Holmes, acquaintance of Howells, and generally influential figure—makes similar generalizations about nervous mimicry in the two chapters he wrote on the topic for his *Lectures on Diseases of the Nervous System, Especially in Women* (1885). Mitchell situates nervous mimicry on a continuum from normal tendencies to hysterical disease, and in a range from involuntary and mechanical reproduction to conscious and highly duplicitous simulation. Thus, he explains, among the root causes of nervous mimicry are natural instincts to imitate, which "are deeply human, and exist in all of us in varying amount."[32] Each of us naturally has "a tendency to automatic and unconscious imitation which is the parent of a good deal of mimicry of disease." For example, a physician looks at a "case of unilateral grimace" and unconsciously imitates it. A physiologist has diarrhea when about to give his first lecture, then has it every time before lecturing, for a year; he finally describes the problem to a physician, who adopts the same symptom before *his* lectures. People cough when forced to listen to someone else coughing for a long time. A husband of a pregnant woman vomits, in a case of sympathetic morning sickness ("MD," 61–63). These automatic mimeses are natural responses of the nervous system. But in states of "general nervousness," or in hysteria, "the qualities which we all possess are apt to take on a morbid development, and to get out of the limits of rational control" ("MD," 57). First, that is, there is a morbid oversensitivity; these subjects become highly sensitive registering and reproduction devices, for whom even the slightest hint can evoke a new symptom. Second, like Paget, Mitchell sees loss of control over identification and instinctual mimicry as the problem; he adds a notable twist by warning of the potential collapse of rational resistance against the "pleasure in giving way to instinctive imitative propensities" ("MD," 70). The danger of succumbing to this pleasure is a kind of loss of the sense of the real: the patients' "power to reason on the phenomena of the senses leaves them," Mitchell writes, "and what they conceive to be the case takes the place of that which is" ("MD," 65). We might say, differently, that the subject's reproduction of another's reality is so powerful and full that it displaces an accurate sense of her own. Paradoxically, while this unwilled and uncontrolled imitation—this automatic identification with what the patient sees or hears—is one version of the malady of nervous mimicry, so too is the case of the hysteric who willfully acts out disease symptoms for an audience, in order to gain sympathy or attention, or to fool her caretakers. As Mitchell puts it, there is a range, from "simulation, not consciously imitative, to conscious unresisted simulation, and at last dissimulation" ("MD," 81). The natural, innocent form of unconscious imitation, of mistaking oneself for another, gathers a more positive aura about it than conscious mimicking of symptoms. But finally the prescription is to steer between two dangers: conscious duplicity, on one hand, and, on the other, the unconscious loss of the self in the imitated image.

Finally, Alfred Binet and Charles Féré, experimenters at the Salpêtrière, went farthest in characterizing hysterical neuromimesis as a kind of accurate mechanism of reproduction. As Charcot's colleagues, they were interested in hypnosis and hysteria and in hypnotic states of catalepsy, somnambulism, and other altered states of consciousness, as effects of "reflex cerebral action."[33] Their book, *Animal Magnetism* (1888), is really about these topics and not about Mesmer's mysterious fluid; indeed, they reiterate the judgment by the Parisian commission that discredited Mesmer—that his supposedly mesmerized subjects, especially the women with their "more mobile nerves" and excitable imaginations, were simply imitating the actions and symptoms that they saw around them, through "the mechanical imitation which involuntarily impels us to repeat that which strikes our senses" (*AM*, 17).[34] Hysteria rather than animal magnetism was their quarry, and they note that the imitation of Mesmer's patients is akin to "the well-known contagious effect of example in all hysterical manifestations" (*AM*, 15). But Binet and Féré invest hysteria with extraordinary qualities. "It should be known," they write, "that some hysterical subjects become when hypnotized so sensitive and such delicate reagents, that no word or gesture escapes their notice; they see, hear, and retain everything, like registering instruments" (*AM*, 192). Somnambulists and hypnotized persons, too, have heightened senses, and improved memories (they can recall what conscious persons can't), which can enhance their capacities for imitation (*AM*, 134–37). On the one hand, this behavior is akin to the simple automatism of a cataleptic, a person reduced to a personality-less state, who will imitate "the experimenter" mechanically and will "echo" utterances "as if he were transformed into a phonograph" (*AM*, 283–84, 143). Like the cataleptics, hysterics and hypnotized subjects may mechanically imitate what strikes their senses—though, unlike cataleptics, they retain signs of personality and judgment, even in an unconscious state. But they also move beyond cataleptics in their capacities, for they are unusually sensitive recorders and reproducers. When hypnotized they surpass conscious people in these abilities. And truly unconscious, they are truly truthful, for deception and simulation occur only as consciousness and the intellect are brought into play (*AM*, 188). Such mechanical propensities for the accurate and truthful reproduction of reality, accomplished by biology and without the biases and interference of consciousness, posed an allure, I suggest, for realist writers.

Unconscious Cerebration, Memory, Writing, and Truth

Oliver Wendell Holmes on unconscious cerebration and the French neurophysiologists on automatic mimesis—these two sources provide the right reference points, I believe, for Mark Twain's conception of involuntary and unconscious mental processes of representing reality. For Twain not only knew Holmes's writings thoroughly—and as a subscriber to *Atlantic Monthly* would have kept abreast of Holmes's thinking—he also knew of "Charcot's pupils & disciples"[35] and "French" experimenters in hypnosis and "somnambulic sleep."[36] Susan Gillman suggests that the work on hypnosis and multiple personality done by Charcot and Pierre Janet at the Salpêtrière and by Ambroise Auguste Liebeault and Hippolyte Bernheim at Nancy "constituted perhaps *the* body of knowledge crucial to Twain's later years."[37] But a more general interest associating reflex responses with the revelation of the truth seems to be present at least by the early 1880s. Huck Finn, disguised as Sarah Williams, brings his legs together to catch a lump of lead and reveals himself as a boy. And Tom Canty's learned reflex, his idiosyncratic startle response—to shield his eyes when surprised—reveals him, to his mother, as the pauper in prince's clothing. Jubiter Dublap, also in disguise in *Tom Sawyer, Detective*, reveals himself as the murderer by his unconscious, idiosyncratic, reflexive gesture of drawing a cross on his cheek.[38]

These sensorimotor-like responses that expose truth are of a part, I suggest, with Twain's moments of unconscious cerebration. Tom Sawyer talks in his sleep and quite possibly reveals to his brother Sid his secret knowledge of the murder of Doc Robinson. Pudd'nhead Wilson falls asleep and finally solves the problem of whose fingerprints are on the knife that killed Judge Driscoll.[39] Perhaps Mr. X, the somnambulist riverboat pilot in *Life on the Mississippi* who steers his boat at night through treacherous waters, functioning better than if he were awake, is the best example. Twain says generally of the "pilot's memory," "how unconsciously it lays up its vast stores, hour by hour, day by day, and never loses or mislays a single valuable package of them all!"[40] That is, the process of registering the reality of the river, including Mr. X's detailed and most accurate remembering, is automatic, unconscious. Mr. X's piloting, in turn, is a cerebral reflex action, an unconscious, "ideo-motor" response, to borrow William Carpenter's conception. I would suggest that this process of automatic registration, followed by a reflex piloting that is in effect a precise tracing of the river on the inky blackness of night, provides an analogy for Twain's understanding of his writing process.

"Unconscious plagiarism," the concept Twain borrowed from Holmes, exemplifies the process still further. In his speech at Holmes's 70th birthday dinner in 1879, Twain said that his dedication in *The Innocents Abroad* was "unconsciously plagiarized" from Holmes's dedication in his book of poems, *Songs in Many Keys*. He further explained that a couple of years before publication of *Innocents Abroad* (1869), he had been stuck in the Sandwich Islands with nothing to read but Holmes's book of poems, which he read and reread until his "mental reservoir was filled up with them to the brim." He then "unconsciously stole" the dedication.[41] In a 1904 autobiographical dictation, he further explained that having realized the plagiarism three years after *Innocents* appeared but still ignorant of the "mysteries of the human mind," he had guiltily written Holmes an apology. He got back a gracious answer, he reports, in which Holmes said that everyone unconsciously plagiarizes every day; all of our phrasings come from our readings, none is original with us, and even when we think we are fresh, we at best just stamp the familiar with our personal style.[42]

Twain's adoption of the concept of unconscious plagiarism demands attention for several reasons. First, it is a model of unconscious replication, a representation channeled involuntarily from the senses, into the "mental reservoir," and then onto the page. Second, it is a perfect example of Holmes's "unconscious cerebration" or "cerebral reflex action." Notably, Twain would have read some of Holmes's remarks on unconscious plagiarism as a cerebral reflex response before receiving Holmes's gracious letter—specifically, when he read *The Autocrat of the Breakfast Table* and shared it with his wife, Livy, in 1869.[43] He would also have had the chance to read about unconscious plagiarism in Holmes's 1862 essay in the *Atlantic Monthly*, "My Hunt after 'the Captain.'"[44] And he would have had the chance to read about it as a kind of automatism in Holmes's essay on "Mechanism in Thought and Morals," also published in the *Atlantic Monthly*, in 1871.[45] The concept could have been developing latently in Twain for a long time.

In light of the equivalence Holmes makes between unconscious plagiarism and cerebral reflex action, the similarity between Twain's account of the plagiarism and his accounts of his writing process as "unconscious cerebration" seems all the more important. More than once Twain uses the same image of a mental reservoir or tank, and always as a resource that replenishes itself through what he calls the never idle "machinery" of "U.C.," or "unconscious cerebration." (He famously employs this image to explain how he finally finished *Tom Sawyer* after having run dry.)[46] This must be paired with Twain's equally well-known pronouncements that when he wrote he felt "like a mere amanuensis, . . . merely writing from dictation." He said repeatedly that he would let every book of his "write itself," and he would take dictation. But when the book "tried to shift to *my* head the labor of contriving its situations, inventing its adventures, and conducting its conversations, I put it away and dropped it out of my mind."[47] In other words, his remarks on his own writing process conform to notions of writing as a cerebral reflex, as an unconscious "hysterics of the intelligence," which registers sensory impressions and operates as a kind of automatic mimesis. There is the persistent sense in Twain's reflections on the writing process that this automatism, this pleasurable surrender, we might say, to a biological propensity for mimesis, yields something truer, more authentic, something free from the contrivances of consciousness.

But if it is science that, for Twain, shifts the possibility for fidelity to reality from a separate representing consciousness to a mechanical, unconscious brain, it is also brain science that undoes that hope. We see the glimmer of this shift in *Life on the Mississippi* (1883). There, the ideal process for learning the river, the mode of the accomplished pilot, is for the brain, with its trained faculties, to "instantly photograph" the details of the river—such as change of depth and bearings—and then store "the important details for future reference without requiring any assistance from him in the matter" (*LM*, 65). That is, the pilot's consciousness need not participate. And then, like Twain's writer-amanuensis, the pilot recognizes treacherous waters and steers the boat through them "instinctively," automatically—as Mr. X was able to do (*LM*, 46). But to some degree the perfect, involuntary, unconscious registration of every detail of the river in the brain is undone by the material flowing of the river itself, with its shifting sandbars, caving alluvial banks, moving snags, cut-off oxbows, and new channels. And the metaphorical insight begins to dawn that the river "that's in your head" (*LM*, 40), as Bixby says, behaves in the same way as the river outside, undergoing a constant process of physical mutation and rechanneling. It is very plausible that Twain would have read two influential essays by Frances Power Cobbe, "The Fallacies of Memory," published in the *Galaxy* in 1866 shortly before Twain began to work for that paper, and the even better-known "Unconscious Cerebration" (1870). The latter essay proclaims the unconscious brain as extremely "veracious"; unconscious cerebration can photograph and reproduce scenes; and forgotten or suppressed truths, retained in all their detail in brain tissue, can come out under hypnosis, or while drunk, or in delirium.[48] This would support a Twainian idea of mental automatism, or cerebral reflex, as a mechanism that both records and reproduces images with fidelity to reality. But Cobbe's essay on memory stresses its "habitual mendacity," its mutability.[49] Memory, she writes, is like a finger-mark on shifting sand, obliterated by the river of our days if left unrenewed, and if renewed, modified, not the same. In her conception, memories are perpetually lost thanks to the very processes of registration, of flows, of pathways forged in our gray matter. Her two seemingly contradictory essays crystallize the division that Twain seems to have felt.

Any thought that looks new and fresh to us, Holmes writes as a way of explaining unconscious plagiarism, is really the result of "long trains of thought" and unconscious recombinations of ideas, of mutations and modifications (*A*, 31). In a metaphor that appears to invoke a neurological model, Holmes suggests that an idea can nestle into the brain and, if left by itself—if one has no occasion to think of it or refer to it for "an hour, a day, a year"—it will eventually have "domiciliated itself, so to speak,—become at home,—entered into relations with . . . other thoughts, and integrated itself with the whole fabric of the mind" (*A*, 134). An idea is "an impression made on a living tissue," which changes and grows when one "is least conscious of it" ("MTM," 56). Through this process, the brain generates ideas that look unfamiliar. By the end of his life, in *What Is Man?* (1906), Twain has fully turned this brain process into a generator of hodgepodge. His Old Man declares that anyone's opinions, thoughts, writings (even Shakespeare's) are involuntarily and automatically forged, second-hand, from odds and ends unconsciously gathered from books, conversations, and so on; we can't even claim credit for putting the borrowed materials together, because the brain, our mental machinery, does that without consciousness or reflection.[50] In this melange, realism, in the sense of accuracy and fidelity, has gone by the wayside.

Intimations of the Organism

It is Howells, the theorist of realism, who perhaps puts most explicitly the questions that emerge from these crossings of neurophysiology and literature. In particular, he grapples directly with the question of whether unconscious cerebration might yield a more reliable account of reality than consciousness does, with its dodges and self-deceptions. As part of this question, he engages the matter of whether the mimetic representations of unconscious cerebration are effects of disease, and whether they are instinctive but "brute" impulses loosed by a relaxed or diseased will.[51] My focus will be on his novella, *The Shadow of a Dream* (1890), a fiction that marks the beginning of his inward-turning period, when, students of Howells generally agree, the author became preoccupied with what he eventually named, in a *North American Review* essay, "A Psychological Counter-Current in Recent Fiction."[52] From 1890 through his last writings, Howells produced a range of stories focused on what we might call "psychical physiognomies," to borrow one of his phrases.[53] These include several that can only be described as fictions of neurophysiology, especially those collected in *Between the Dark and the Daylight: Romances* (1907). There we find stories of memory disorders ("A Sleep and a Forgetting" and "A Memory That Worked Overtime"), a story of hallucinations ("The Eidolons of Brooks Alford"), and a story that might be one of hysterical mimesis ("A Case of Metaphantasmia"). *The Shadow of a Dream* and *Between the Dark and the Daylight* mark years in which Howells's thinking was influenced by his research into dreaming, his reading of William James, his interest in the Society for Psychical Research, and his study of French neurology. The neurophysiology of mental representations became a pivotal concern.

In 1880 Howells described "unconscious cerebration" as "the scientific term for dreaming,"[54] and it was in terms of dreams that he explored this supposed reflex action of the brain. In his fullest statement, "True, I Talk of Dreams" (1895), he forcefully characterizes dreams as the product of a lower self, animal-like, primitive, unmoral, "merely natural man." Although the "mind keeps on working" in dreams, the "supernal criticism" that operates when we are awake, that sits in evaluation of our mental processes and flights—and that comes from consciousness, or conscience, or the soul—is absent. This bears directly on the question of unconscious cerebration and literary creation, for, as Howells says in this essay, an imagination uncontrolled by consciousness and conscience is like the unbridled imagination in dreams; rather than doing "great things," it accomplishes only "little things, foolish and worthless things" ("T," 840). In fact, Howells says finally, "[T]here is no analogy . . . between the process of literary invention and the process of dreaming. In the invention, the critical faculty is vividly and constantly alert; in dreaming it seems altogether absent" ("T," 841). Or, he says later, "The two kinds of inventing, the voluntary and the involuntary, seem absolutely and finally distinct" ("T," 843). While this point of view might not mesh at all with that of Howells's friend Mark Twain, or with that of Holmes, both of whom put great artistic stock in involuntary processes of the nerves and the brain, it clearly does resonate with the views of Howells's acquaintance S. Weir Mitchell, who emphasized the importance of conscious evaluation of the real and rational control over the instinctive mimetic propensities. However, near the end of his essay, Howells notes: "I have verified in my own experience the theory of [Théodule] Ribot that approaching disease sometimes intimates itself in dreams of the disorder impending, before it is otherwise declared in the organism" ("T," 843). This may look at first like a small concession to the idea that unconscious cerebration may apprehend realities consciousness misses. And it is only a momentary countercurrent in Howells's general discounting of dreams and their unconscious brain processes. But it harks back importantly to *The Shadow of a Dream*, which invokes the same idea from Ribot but can be read more fully, I believe, as an engagement of Ribot's ideas about psychophysiology, and as a serious treatment of the unconscious recording and expression of a truth that eludes the "supernal critic."

Ribot, professor at the Collège de France and author of immensely influential books on diseases of the personality and memory (books translated into English), was very much a physiological psychologist.[55] Like the physiologists who wrote of reflex actions in the brain, or of unconscious cerebration, Ribot characterizes human beings as composites of nervous-system processes, some conscious, most not. "The brain is a sort of busy workshop where ten thousand different operations are going on at once," he writes. "Consciousness is the narrow wicket through which a very small portion of all this work becomes visible to us."[56] In this conception, as with Laycock, Carpenter, and Holmes, higher-order mental processes, operating as mechanically reflex-like functions, can take place without consciousness. Ribot notes that poetic and scientific inventions can burst into consciousness—after having been developed in unconscious cerebration. Solutions to problems long studied can come unexpectedly, automatically, from the brain's unconscious workshop. Obscure ideas can be ordered.[57] Passions, such as love or hatred, can develop unconsciously, ignorant of themselves, and burst suddenly into consciousness ("T," 836–45). Ribot credits fully the creative richness of cerebral processes that take place outside of consciousness.

These ideas provide the perfect framework for thinking about Howells's *The Shadow of a Dream* (1890), a work, I will argue, that is concerned about whether organic and automatic processes of the mind can discern, register, and reproduce in dreams a reality that eludes consciousness. In this narrative, Basil and Isabel March, from whose point of view the story is told, pay a visit to Douglas Faulkner, a heart disease victim troubled by a recurrent dream. Although Faulkner doesn't tell the dream to the Marches, they surmise that it is a jealous dream about the relationship between his wife, Hermia, and his friend Jim Nevil, who has been staying with the couple. In a conversation about dreams, Faulkner suggests that instead of meaningless emanations from a savage unconscious, dreams can be a source of revelation. Then he invokes the same passage from Ribot's *The Diseases of Personality*, to which Howells's essay refers, in which Ribot writes of people whose dreams tell them of physical diseases they have. A man dreams of being bitten by a dog, Faulkner reports, and wakes up with a malignant ulcer on the spot of the bite; he dreams of an epileptic, and wakes to have his first fit; he dreams of a deaf-mute, and wakes with a palsied tongue. These are, Faulkner explains, "intimations of calamity from the recesses of the organism to the nerve centres, which we don't notice in the hurly-burly of conscious life."[58] Why shouldn't such unconscious sensings, and their revelation in dreams, he asks, extend beyond bodily illness, to the moral realm?

This is the question I want to foreground as the special concern of this narrative. Can the organism's unconscious nerve processes work more sensitively than consciousness, apprehending realities and reproducing them in dreams? Faulkner's physician, the nervous specialist Dr. Wingate, says no. Dreams *are* signs, he says, but only of mental disturbance, in this case caused by Faulkner's heart disease; they are not otherwise representations of reality.[59] But Wingate's close-mindedness clearly discredits him. After Faulkner dies (of a heart attack, while fending off the ministrations of his anxious wife), the question is thrown onto the drama of Hermia and Jim, which is mediated by the interpretations of Basil and Isabel March. When Jim and Hermia get engaged, suspicion is raised, and the possible truth of Faulkner's dream gains credibility. But when Dr. Wingate finally tells Hermia her dead husband's dream, the guilt she and Jim suffer, and their subsequent renunciation of each other (after a desperate and passionate kissing embrace), make Basil March think instead that with the shadow of this dream over them and their relationship, they've wrongly convicted themselves of unconscious lust and unfaithfulness. Basil and Isabel eventually learn the exact details of the dream from Faulkner's mother: Hermia and Jim are waiting for Faulkner to die so they can get married, and when he does die, the funeral and the marriage take place at the same time, in the same church, with Faulkner unable to stop it. The Marches, however—who from the start have felt drawn to Jim and Hermia and obviously want to give them the benefit of a doubt—finally deny that the dream has any substance, and Isabel in particular refuses to think that the pair could have secretly, unconsciously, loved each other, because she will not accept that our feelings are not at our bidding. Howells, it appears, sets the Marches up; their stretched interpretations and denials are too much, and the exertions of their consciousness undermine its credibility. Although Howells leaves the story pointedly ambiguous, the only conclusion we can draw, I think, is that in line with Ribot's ideas about passions we don't realize, Jim and Hermia were indeed in love, and in accord with Ribot's ideas about the unconscious apprehension of reality, Douglas's dream *was* a revelation.

More than once, Ribot compares consciousness to the shadow that accompanies the steps of a traveler—a concomitant, a tagalong with other, unconscious nervous system processes, an ineffectual epiphenomenon.[60] While I don't want to assign it too much weight, the metaphor does resonate nicely with Howells's title. While the shadow of Faulkner's dream has traditionally been equated with its tragic effect on Douglas, Hermia, and Jim, it also arguably refers to consciousness—the thing that dogs the unconscious cerebration of the dream, the various interpretations that swirl around the primary, unconscious process of the dream. A powerful suggestion lurks that the process of unconscious cerebration, resulting in the dream, is the more reliable apprehension and representation of the reality. The shadow of consciousness is the dim reflection, the convoluted cloud, that obscures the primary meaning.

This story was only a start in Howells's grappling with the intersection of neurophysiology and representation. But it lucidly poses the questions at stake. Were such mental representations as Faulkner's merely the effect of disease, manifestations of a mental distress that arose in sympathy with physical illness but that otherwise were not representations of reality? Or did these organic, neural processes operating outside consciousness issue in mimed realities whose truth surpassed conscious apprehension? Was "unconscious cerebration" a lower-nervous-system phenomenon, perhaps only savage and meaningless, and hence not worth attention? And, by analogy, should a literary artist, a realist writer, credit those neural processes as circuits for literary representation, or should one insist that only the separate representing consciousness, the "supernal critic," is capable of cleaving to the truth, capable of distinguishing tricks of fancy from insights into the real?

The pursuit of questions posed by an emergent neuroscience brought Holmes, Twain, and Howells to different endpoints, or to different questions. Holmes, the scientist himself, was the most thoroughgoing in theorizing poetry and imaginative writing as "hysterics of the intelligence," or as an unconscious cerebration that lay in mutable brain tissue. And yet when he examined hysterics of the intelligence in his novels, they not only had highly ambiguous status as expressive means but they also were situated in young women, who were watched over by detachedly observant, wise, protective males, and whose stories were told as case studies, in the voice of reason and scientific scrutiny—from a stance unaffected by the neurophysiological processes at work outside the wicket of narrative consciousness. Science more radically pushed Twain's pursuit of representation, I would suggest, from the stance of the observer to the neurally embodied circuit. At first, he most fully entertained the idea that reality was more surely grasped by plain impressions on tissue, by the physical circuits of unconscious cerebration. But the stability of this circuit was eroded by its sheer materiality: the mutability of the body, including its brain and nerve cells, introduced contingency. If Howells never relinquished the "supernal critic" as fully as Twain did, for him, the unconscious cerebration of dreamwork was at least momentarily credited, in *The Shadow of a Dream*, with a fidelity to reality that the dodges and denials of interpretive consciousness precluded.

In 1883, Twain and Howells collaborated on a play called *Colonel Sellers as a Scientist*, which was designed to capitalize on the popularity of the main character in Twain's dramatization of *The Gilded Age*. Among its various farcical elements is a phonograph that, as Sellers explains, "if . . . [left] open, and all set," will "eavesdrop, so to speak— that is to say, it will load itself up with any sounds that are made within six feet of it."[61] Such a phonograph remarkably resembles the mechanism of unconscious cerebration, with its promise of accurately recording *everything*, through a process of undistorted physical registration, and then, in effect, reflexively playing it back. But Sellers's phonograph is an occasion for burlesque, as it eccentrically mixes sounds up, plays back fragments in collage, and juxtaposes the serious with the low. Its operation eerily foreshadows the workings of the brain as understood by Twain's Old Man, as the machine of unconscious cerebration jumbles and mutates impressions and memories into mental hash. And it resonates with the "unconscious plagiarism" of Holmes and Twain, pressing it to the point that any sense of the origin of thoughts and impressions is lost amidst neural recombinations and crisscrossings. If Howells did not follow Twain to this breakdown of literary realism and representation itself, and instead clung by a thread to his "supernal critic" even as he allowed conscious apprehension to be challenged and transformed by unconscious cerebration, both these writers must be credited with crystallizing problems that mental science was generating. While scientists probed more and more into the biological vicissitudes of imitation and representation, tracing what they thought to be neural mechanisms of registration but preserving still their objectivity and observational integrity above such vicissitudes, these American writers rethought their own observation and realistic representation in terms of this nervous-system biology. They put themselves in the place of the neuromimetic subject and let their conception of the human biological transmitter dislodge the detached observer. In the process, they advanced literary realism to its precipice, and they used science to think themselves to a place well beyond the conceptions of scientists themselves.

University of Massachusetts

Notes

1 Jonathan Miller gives an excellent introduction to this psychology, and an account of its suppression, in his essay "Going Unconscious," in the aptly named volume *Hidden Histories of Science,* ed. Robert Silvers (New York: New York Review of Books, 1995), 1–35.

2 Oliver Wendell Holmes, "Mechanism in Thought and Morals," *Pages from an Old Volume of Life: A Collection of Essays, 1857–1881,* in vol. 8 of *The Works of Oliver Wendell Holmes* (Boston: Houghton Mifflin, 1892), 277. Further references to this essay will be to this edition and will be cited parenthetically as "MTM."

3 I should note here the similarity between my argument and that of Jonathan Crary in *Techniques of the Observer: On Vision and Modernity in the Nineteenth Century* (Cambridge: MIT Press, 1990). One of Crary's main points is that during the nineteenth century the disembodied and decorporealized observer became reembodied; the observer thus became an object of observation, and the processes of vision were relocated in human flesh and tissue. Once situated in the unstable physiology of the body, vision had to give up conceptions of transparent reflection, and the way was paved for modernist subjectivism. In a Foucaultian way, however, Crary thinks of science and art as parts of a pervasively interlocking field of knowledge and practice. My more particular history here accommodates more possibilities, conflicts, and players.

4 See George Frederick Drinka, *The Birth of Neurosis: Myth, Malady, and the Victorians* (New York: Simon and Schuster, 1984), 30.

5 On theories of sympathy, see Ruth Leys, "Background to the Reflex Controversy: William Alison and the Doctrine of Sympathy before Hall," *Studies in History of Biology* 4 (1980): 1–66; and Edwin Clarke and L. S. Jacyna, *Nineteenth-Century Origins of Neuroscientific Concepts* (Berkeley and Los Angeles: Univ. of California Press, 1987), 102.

6 Robert Whytt, *Observations on the Nature, Causes and Cure of Those Disorders Which Have Been Commonly Called Nervous, Hypochondriac or Hysteric: To Which Are Prefaced Some Remarks on the Sympathy of the Nerves,* 3d ed. (1764; reprint, Edinburgh: printed for T. Becket and P. A. De Hondt; and J. Balfour, 1767), v, 1. On Whytt, see Leys, "Background," 9–10.

7 See Clarke and Jacyna, *Nineteenth-Century Origins,* 151. Whytt himself

believed that sympathy was the effect of an immaterial soul that pervaded the nervous system (see Leys, "Background," 9).

8   Henry Maudsley, *Body and Mind: An Inquiry into Their Connection and Mutual Influence, Specially in Reference to Mental Disorders*, rev. ed. (New York: Appleton, 1885), 36, 37, 83, 85, 87–88. On the ideas of Maudsley and others concerning reproductive organ disorders as causes of hysteria and mental problems, see Roy Porter, "The Body and the Mind, the Doctor and the Patient: Negotiating Hysteria," in *Hysteria beyond Freud*, ed. Sander L. Gilman, et al. (Berkeley and Los Angeles: Univ. of California Press, 1993), especially 251–55.

9   Maudsley, *Body and Mind*, 78–82. And on Maudsley, see Elaine Showalter, *The Female Malady: Women, Madness, and English Culture, 1830–1980* (New York: Pantheon, 1985), 112–25.

10   Charles A. L. Reed, "The Genital Factor in Certain Cases of Neurasthenia in Women," *Gaillard's Medical Journal* 70 (1899); quoted in F. G. Gosling, *Before Freud: Neurasthenia and the American Medical Community, 1870–1910* (Urbana: Univ. of Illinois Press, 1987), 98.

11   See Marshall Hall, "On the Reflex Function of the Medulla Oblongata and Medulla Spinalis," *Philosophical Transactions of the Royal Society of London* 123 (June 1833), 635–65, and *Lectures on the Nervous System and Its Diseases* (London: Sherwood, Gilbert, and Piper, 1836). On the history of the reflex, see Clarke and Jacyna, *Nineteenth-Century Origins*, 102–56; see also Leys, "Background," and Stanley Finger, *Minds behind the Brain: A History of the Pioneers and Their Discoveries* (New York: Oxford Univ. Press, 2000), 221. The standard history is Franklin Fearing, *Reflex Action: A Study in the History of Physiological Psychology* (Cambridge: MIT Press, 1970).

12   See Roger Smith, *Inhibition: History and Meaning in the Sciences of Mind and Brain* (Berkeley and Los Angeles: Univ. of California Press, 1992), 68–69.

13   See Smith, *Inhibition*, 69; and Clarke and Jacyna, *Nineteenth-Century Origins*, 128. See also Leys, "Background."

14   See Clarke and Jacyna, *Nineteenth-Century Origins*, 133–39; see also W. F. Bynum, "The Nervous Patient in Eighteenth- and Nineteenth-Century Britain: The Psychiatric Origins of British Neurology," in *The Anatomy of Madness: Essays in the History of Psychiatry. Volume 1: People and Ideas*, ed. W. F. Bynum, Roy Porter, and Michael Shepherd (London: Tavistock, 1985), 94–95.

15   Thomas Laycock makes the argument that hysteria is a disorder of the nervous system and that it operates by reflex transmission of ovarian irritation to the brain (see *A Treatise on the Nervous Diseases of Women; Comprising an Inquiry into the Nature, Causes, and Treatment of Spinal and Hysterical Disorders* [London: Longman, Orme, Brown, Green, and Longmans, 1840]). Later Laycock makes his argument about "the automatic

and unconscious action of the cerebral hemispheres on the muscular system" in two works: *Mind and Brain*, 2 vols. (1860; reprint, New York: Arno Press, 1976), 2:10; and "On the Reflex Function of the Brain," *British and Foreign Medical Review* 19 (January 1845): 298–311. For a general discussion of Laycock, see Kurt Danziger, "Mid-Nineteenth-Century British Psycho-Physiology: A Neglected Chapter in the History of Psychology," in *The Problematic Science: Psychology in Nineteenth-Century Thought*, ed. William R. Woodward and Mitchell G. Ash (New York: Praeger, 1982), 122–28.

16 See Danziger, "Mid-Nineteenth Century British Psycho-Physiology," 127–28.

17 Ibid., 124, 125, 127, 129; and L. S. Jacyna, "The Physiology of Mind, the Unity of Nature, and the Moral Order in Victorian Thought," *British Journal for the History of Science* 14.47 (1981): 109–32, especially 111–17. Danziger notes that Carpenter's "ideo-motor" conception is actually an elaboration of James Mills's declaration that ideas and sensations can produce movements apart from volition (129), and Johannes Müller put the idea forth not long after Mill; still, it was Carpenter who popularized the idea.

18 William B. Carpenter, *Principles of Mental Physiology, with Their Application to the Training and Discipline of the Mind, and the Study of Its Morbid Conditions*, 4th ed. (1874; London: Henry S. King, 1876), 105, 515, 130, 120–21; further references to this source will be to this edition and will be cited parenthetically in the text as *PMP*.

19 Oliver Wendell Holmes, "Border Lines of Knowledge in Some Provinces of Medical Science," *Currents and Counter-Currents in Medical Science, with Other Essays* (Boston: Houghton Mifflin, 1892), 246–47.

20 See Eleanor M. Tilton, *Amiable Autocrat: A Biography of Dr. Oliver Wendell Holmes* (New York: Henry Schuman, 1947), 119–20, 157–59. See also the indispensable essay by Charles Boewe, "Reflex Action in the Novels of Oliver Wendell Holmes," *American Literature* 26 (November 1954): 303–19. Boewe's essay is focused on Holmes's "physiological psychology" and his conviction that reflex responses enter into the mental and moral realm and may diminish moral responsibility.

21 Oliver Wendell Holmes, "Crime and Automatism," *Atlantic Monthly*, April 1875, 469.

22 Oliver Wendell Holmes, *Elsie Venner: A Romance of Destiny*, vol. 5 of *The Works of Oliver Wendell Holmes* (Boston: Houghton Mifflin, 1892), 227; further references to this source will be to this edition and will be cited parenthetically in the text as *EV*.

23 Oliver Wendell Holmes, "Reflex Vision," *Proceedings of the American Academy of Arts and Sciences* 4 (February 1860): 374.

24 Oliver Wendell Holmes, *The Autocrat of the Breakfast Table*, vol. 1 of *The Works of Oliver Wendell Holmes* (Boston: Houghton Mifflin, 1892), 134–35, 189, 191, 187; further references will be to this edition and will be cited parenthetically as *A*.

25 Oliver Wendell Holmes, *The Professor at the Breakfast Table; with "The Story of Iris,"* vol. 2 of *The Works of Oliver Wendell Holmes* (Boston: Houghton Mifflin, 1892), 34–35.

26 *The Poet at the Breakfast Table*, vol. 3 of *The Works of Oliver Wendell Holmes* (Boston: Houghton Mifflin, 1892), 101, 46.

27 Oliver Wendell Holmes, introduction to *The Guardian Angel*, vol. 6 of *The Works of Oliver Wendell Holmes* (Boston: Houghton Mifflin, 1892), viii–ix.

28 This is still the way recent studies of hysteria characterize the disorder; see, for example, Elaine Showalter on hysteria as a "mimetic disorder" in which the unconscious mind "mimics culturally permissible expressions of distress," in *Hystories: Hysterical Epidemics and Modern Culture* (New York: Columbia Univ. Press, 1997), 15.

29 See Stanley Finger, "Jean-Martin Charcot: Clinical Neurology Comes of Age," in *Minds behind the Brain*, 194; and Ilza Veith, *Hysteria: The History of a Disease* (Chicago: Univ. of Chicago Press, 1965), 230.

30 James Paget, "Nervous Mimicry," in *Clinical Lectures and Essays*, ed. Howard Marsh (London: Longmans, Green, 1875), 172; further references to this essay will be cited parenthetically as "NM."

31 On Paget, and neuromimesis in general, see Athena Vrettos, *Somatic Fictions: Imagining Illness in Victorian Culture* (Stanford, Calif.: Stanford Univ. Press, 1995), 81–90.

32 S. Weir Mitchell, "Mimicry of Disease," in *Lectures on Diseases of the Nervous System, Especially in Women* (Philadelphia: Lea Brothers, 1885), 56; further references to this source will be cited parenthetically as "MD."

33 See Alfred Binet and Charles Féré, *Animal Magnetism* (New York: Appleton, 1888), 175; further references to this source will be cited parenthetically in the text as *AM*.

34 Despite this discrediting, of course, mesmerism persisted into the nineteenth century and gained a new prominence in the 1840s, accommodating and even promoting, this time around, the idea that mesmerized subjects have a special capacity for imitation. Asserting that mesmerized subjects will echo the gestures of the mesmerizer with whom they are in rapport, and will even mimic his movements if he is in another room or otherwise out of sight—transmitting pictures of his movements via mesmeric fluid—antebellum-era mesmerists named this phenomenon "traction," or "simulated motion" (see Alison Winter, *Mesmerized: Powers of Mind in Victorian England* [Chicago: Univ. of Chicago Press, 1998], 53, 73).

35 Samuel L. Clemens to Olivia Langdon Clemens, January 1894, *Mark Twain-Howells Letters: The Correspondence of Samuel L. Clemens and William Dean Howells, 1872–1910*, ed. Henry Nash Smith and William M. Gibson, 2 vols. (Cambridge: Belknap Press of Harvard Univ. Press, 1960), 2:659.

36 Samuel Clemens, notebook entry, 7 January 1897, *Mark Twain's Notebook* (New York: Harper and Brothers, 1935), 349.

37 Susan Gillman, *Dark Twins: Imposture and Identity in Mark Twain's America* (Chicago: Univ. of Chicago Press, 1989), 47.

38 See Mark Twain, *Adventures of Huckleberry Finn*, ed. Walter Blair and Victor Fischer (Berkeley and Los Angeles: Univ. of California Press, 1988), 72; *The Prince and the Pauper* (Berkeley and Los Angeles: Univ. of California Press, 1979), 115–17, 304; and *Tom Sawyer, Detective*, in *The Adventures of Tom Sawyer; Tom Sawyer Abroad; Tom Sawyer, Detective* (Berkeley and Los Angeles: Univ. of California Press, 1980), 412.

39 See Twain, *Adventures of Tom Sawyer*, 90; and Mark Twain, *Pudd'nhead Wilson and Those Extraordinary Twins* (New York: Norton, 1980), 104.

40 Mark Twain, *Life on the Mississippi* (New York: Bantam, 1956), 65; further references to this edition will be cited parenthetically in the text as *LM*.

41 Mark Twain, "Unconscious Plagiarism," *Mark Twain's Speeches*, ed. Albert Bigelow Paine (New York: Harper and Brothers, 1923), 77–79.

42 *Mark Twain's Own Autobiography: The Chapters from the North American Review* (Madison: Univ. of Wisconsin Press, 1990), 181–82.

43 For the account of this reading, see Alan Gribben, *Mark Twain's Library: A Reconstruction*, 2 vols. (Boston: G. K. Hall, 1980), 1:317–18. Holmes's discussions of unconscious plagiarism are in *Autocrat of the Breakfast Table*, in *Works*, 31, 144–45.

44 Oliver Wendell Holmes, "My Hunt after 'the Captain,'" *Atlantic Monthly*, December 1862, 738–64; reprinted in Holmes, *Soundings from the Atlantic* (Boston: Houghton Mifflin, 1880), 24–123. For the discussion of unconscious plagiarism, see *Soundings*, 72.

45 Oliver Wendell Holmes, "Mechanism in Thought and Morals," *Atlantic Monthly*, May 1871, 653–54; see also "MTM," *Pages from an Old Volume*, 260–314.

46 Samuel Clemens, autobiographical dictation, 30 August 1906, *Mark Twain in Eruption: Hitherto Unpublished Pages about Men and Events*, ed. Bernard DeVoto (New York: Harper and Brothers, 1940), 197; also see Twain's letter to Emily G. Hutchings, 14 November 1902, in *Mark Twain the Letter Writer*, ed. Cyril Clemens (Boston: Meador, 1932), 25. Twain might have adopted "unconscious cerebration" as phrase and concept from Holmes, Carpenter, William Lecky, or Frances Power Cobbe (see Cobbe's "The Fallacies of Memory," *Galaxy* 1 [May 1866]: 149–62, and "Unconscious Cerebration" [1870], in *Darwinism and Morals and Other Essays* [Boston: George H. Ellis], 324–55).

47 "Mark Twain on Thought-Transference," *Journal of the Society for Psychical Research* 1 (October 1884): 166–67; quoted in Gillman, *Dark Twins*, 139; see also *Mark Twain in Eruption*, ed. DeVoto, 243, 196.

48 Cobbe, "Unconscious Cerebration," 345, 343.

49 Cobbe, "The Fallacies of Memory," 156.

50 Mark Twain, *What Is Man?*, in *What Is Man? and Other Philosophical Writings*, ed. Paul Baender (Berkeley and Los Angeles: Univ. of California Press, 1973), 128–30, 148, 176–83.

51 William Dean Howells, "True, I Talk of Dreams," *Harper's Monthly*, May 1895, 840; further references to this source will be cited parenthetically as "T."

52 See William Dean Howells, "A Psychological Counter-Current in Recent Fiction," *North American Review*, December 1901, 872–88. On this period in Howells's life and fiction, see especially the work of John W. Crowley, both *The Mask of Fiction: Essays on W. D. Howells* (Amherst: Univ. of Massachusetts Press, 1989), particularly part 2, and "Miracles of the Inner World," the last chapter of *The Black Heart's Truth: The Early Career of W. D. Howells* (Chapel Hill: Univ. of North Carolina Press, 1985), 150–60. Although my stress on Howells and psychophysiology goes in the opposite direction from Crowley's psychological and psychoanalytical framework, I am indebted to his research.

53 See William Dean Howells, "Editor's Easy Chair," *Harper's Monthly*, October 1908, 798.

54 William Dean Howells, "Contributor's Club," *Atlantic Monthly*, June 1880, 859.

55 On Ribot, see Laura Otis, *Organic Memory: History and the Body in the Late Nineteenth and Early Twentieth Centuries* (Lincoln: Univ. of Nebraska Press, 1994), 14–16, 23. See also Michael S. Roth, "Remembering Forgetting: *Maladies de la Mémoire* in Nineteenth-Century France," *Representations* 26 (spring 1989): 49–68; and John L. Brooks, "Philosophy and Psychology at the Sorbonne, 1885–1913," *Journal of the History of the Behavioral Sciences* 29 (April 1993): 123–45.

56 Théodule Ribot, *The Diseases of Memory*, trans. J. Fitzgerald (New York: J. Fitzgerald, 1883), 9.

57 Ibid., 8.

58 William Dean Howells, *The Shadow of a Dream*, in *"The Shadow of a Dream" and "An Imperative Duty"* (Bloomington: Indiana Univ. Press, 1970), 32–33.

59 Ibid., 34, 46–47.

60 See Ribot, *The Diseases of Personality* (Chicago: Open Court Publishing, 1891) 14; and *Memory*, 2.

61 Mark Twain and W. D. Howells, *Colonel Sellers as a Scientist*, in *The Complete Plays of W. D. Howells*, ed. Walter J. Meserve (New York: New York Univ. Press, 1960), 209.

Ursula K. Heise

Toxins, Drugs, and Global Systems: Risk and Narrative in the Contemporary Novel

Much work in the field of ecocriticism, established in American literary studies during the 1990s, assumes that the natural world is endangered, and that some of the human activities that threaten nature also put human health and life at risk. But while this assumption explicitly shapes a good deal of environmentalist politics and implicitly underlies most, if not all, ecocritical research, the concept of risk has so far rarely been subjected to theoretical discussion in ecocriticism. This omission is all the more remarkable considering that risk theory and risk analysis constitute a well-developed field of study in the social sciences, encompassing more than three decades of research. Perhaps because this field is not committed to the same environmentalist concerns that interest ecocritics, it has so far attracted little attention in ecological criticism. One exception is the work of Lawrence Buell, which engages some studies of risk in the analysis of what Buell calls "toxic discourse," textual and visual representations of exposure to hazardous chemicals. But even in his work, the notion of risk and the social scientific theories that have evolved around it play only a relatively minor role.[1] My essay will discuss connections among ecocriticism, risk theory, and narrative to suggest, on one hand, that a focus on the notion of risk as a literary theme can substantially sharpen and shift standard interpretations of some contemporary texts and, on the other hand, that a consideration of risk and the kind of narrative articulation it requires has potentially important implications for the analysis of narrative form.

My argument focuses on a particular type of risk—exposure to chemical substances—but similar analyses could be carried out, with

American Literature, Volume 74, Number 4, December 2002. Copyright © 2002 by Duke University Press.

some modifications, for literary representations of other ecological and technological hazards. This focus allows me to foreground how my argument builds upon Buell's earlier analyses of toxic discourse but also how contemporary novelists use chemical substances as a trope for the blurring of boundaries between body and environment, public and domestic space, and harmful and beneficial technologies. My analysis begins with Don DeLillo's postmodern classic *White Noise*, whose exploration of a local risk scenario by means of satire raises complex questions about the role of realism and hyperbole in risk perception and representation. The second section lays out the theoretical background of this analysis in more detail by giving an overview of some important approaches and insights in risk theory. The third section returns to the literary representation of risk through a very different novel, Richard Powers's *Gain*, which examines risk in the context of complex global systems and thereby raises the question of how such systems can be effectively captured in narrative. These readings of particular texts may point the way toward some of the implications risk theory might have not only for a thematic study of literature but, beyond that, for the consideration of literary form.

"Unreliable Menace": *White Noise*

DeLillo's *White Noise* was published in January of 1985, only a little over a month after a toxic gas accident at a Union Carbide plant in Bhopal, India, killed at least two thousand people and injured thousands more. The coincidence was not lost on the novel's first reviewers, who pointed out the eerie echoes between the Bhopal accident and the toxic gas incident in the novel's middle chapter.[2] This "airborne toxic event" (*WN*, 117), as the media euphemistically call it, occurs in the Midwestern college town of Blacksmith, where professor of Hitler studies Jack Gladney lives with his wife, Babette, and their family. After an accident at a train depot, the gas Nyodene Derivative, a byproduct of pesticide manufacture, leaks from one of the wagons and forms a large cloud over Blacksmith, whose inhabitants receive the order to evacuate. En route to the evacuation camp, Jack Gladney is briefly exposed to the toxic gas. When the evacuees' health data are recorded at the camp, Gladney realizes that even this short exposure might have potentially serious consequences for his health. During his interview with one of the health technicians, the following conversation unfolds:

"Am I going to die?"

"Not as such," [the technician] said.

"What do you mean?"

"Not in so many words."

"How many words does it take?"

"It's not a question of words. It's a question of years. We'll know more in fifteen years. In the meantime we definitely have a situation."

"What will we know in fifteen years?"

"If you're still alive at the time, we'll know that much more than we do now. Nyodene D. has a life span of thirty years. You'll have made it halfway through."

"I thought it was forty years."

"Forty years in the soil. Thirty years in the human body."

"So, to outlive this substance, I will have to make it into my eighties. Then I can begin to relax."

"Knowing what we know at this time."

"But the general consensus seems to be that we don't know enough at this time to be sure of anything."

"Let me answer like so. If I was a rat I wouldn't want to be any-where within a two hundred mile radius of the airborne event."

"What if you were a human?"

He looked at me carefully. . . . "I wouldn't worry about what I can't see or feel," he said. "I'd go ahead and live my life. Get married, settle down, have kids. . . ."

"But you said we have a situation."

"I didn't say it. The computer did. The whole system says it. It's what we call a massive data-base tally. Gladney, J.A.K. I punch in the name, the substance, the exposure time and then I tap into your computer history. Your genetics, your personals, your medi-cals, your psychologicals, your police-and-hospitals. It comes back pulsing stars. This doesn't mean anything is going to happen to you as such, at least not today or tomorrow. It just means you are the sum total of your data. No man escapes that." (*WN*, 140–41)

This conversation, and others like it, has generated a good deal of criti-cal comment on how it makes death appear both real and vague, and how Gladney's existential concern is transformed, not without a con-siderable amount of humor, into a simulacrum of computer data.[3] Such a transformation is hardly surprising, many critics would argue, in a novel in which even the starkest realities seem to disappear behind multiple layers of representations and simulations. In *White Noise*, disaster victims feel unable to relate to their own situation unless it is amply covered by the media; Adolf Hitler and Elvis Presley appear side by side in an academic lecture on their relationship to their mothers; and the Nyodene D. accident turns into a mere prelude to the simulated evacuations rehearsed by Advanced Disaster Management, a company relying on the philosophy that such simulations not only prepare for but actually prevent real disasters. Gladney discovers his own nine-year-old daughter impersonating a victim in one of these simulations and remarks to the manager, perhaps sarcastically, perhaps seriously: "'Are you people sure you're ready for a simulation? You may want to wait for one more massive spill. Get your timing down'" (*WN*, 204). The abundance of Baudrillardesque scenes such as these has led many critics to interpret *White Noise* as a narrative showcase of the postmodern culture of the simulacrum, a novel in which simulation systematically takes precedence over whatever might be left of the real.[4]

DeLillo's undeniable emphasis on representation as reality has led critics to dismiss the novel as a serious engagement with the problem of technological risk. A. O. Scott, for example, claims that "DeLillo's 'airborne toxic event' is freighted with symbolism: it's a projection of the ambient dread that pervades the social and emotional lives of his characters, and its source as a physical occurrence is thus irrelevant to the novel's purposes."[5] Even as eminent an ecocritic as Buell has argued recently that "*White Noise*'s framing of th[e] toxic event as, chiefly, a postmodern symbol of inauthenticity" reduces it "to the status of catalyst to the unfolding of the [protagonist's] culturally symptomatic vacuousness."[6] Hence, in Buell's view, a different disaster with no ecological implications would have served the plot just as well. Such arguments, however, have validity only if one isolates the Nyodene D. incident from the rest of the novel as the only point of engagement with technological risk scenarios. A diametrically opposed picture emerges when one traces *White Noise*'s thematic engagement with risk more systematically and pursues some of the implications of risk theory for its narrative form.

As a motif, the Nyodene D. spillage is far from the only risk scenario that threatens the Gladney family. On the contrary, the novel abounds in pointed or casual references to the multiple technologically generated risks that the average American family encounters in daily life. Early on, for example, the Gladney children's school has to be evacuated because of toxic fumes, possibly caused, as the reader is told, by the "ventilating system, the paint or varnish, the foam insulation, the electrical insulation, the cafeteria food, the rays emitted by microcomputers, the asbestos fireproofing, the adhesive on shipping containers, the fumes from the chlorinated pool, or perhaps something deeper, finer-grained, more closely woven into the basic state of things"; whatever their origin, these fumes are lethal enough to kill one of the members of the school inspection team (*WN*, 35, 40). At another point, Jack Gladney worries over his son Heinrich, who is beginning to lose hair even though he is only fourteen, and Gladney wonders whether this might be caused by exposure to chemical waste or polluted air (22). The father of Gladney's stepdaughter Denise drops by on his way to a fundraiser for the "Nuclear Accident Readiness Foundation," which he refers to as a "[j]ust in case kind of thing" (56). And not only the adults are aware of risks; Heinrich details the dangers of electromagnetic radiation emanating from electrical wires and appliances: "'The real issue is the kind of radiation that surrounds us every day. Your radio, your TV, your microwave oven, your power lines just outside the door, your radar speed-trap on the highway. . . . Forget spills, fallouts, leakages. It's the things around you in your own house that'll get you sooner or later'" (174–75). Less eloquently, Babette's daughter Steffie points out to her mother the carcinogenic additives in chewing gum (41–43), and her daughter Denise insists that Babette use sunscreen during her runs so as to avoid skin cancer (264). In fact, the children at times appear to take risk more seriously than the adults: "'Every day on the news there's another toxic spill. Cancerous solvents from storage tanks, arsenic from smokestacks, radioactive water from power plants. How serious can it be if it happens all the time? Isn't the definition of a serious event based on the fact that it's not an everyday occurrence?'" Babette asks at one point (174), outlining an entire "riskscape" surrounding the family even as she denies its dangers.[7] At another point, she similarly dismisses a radio injunction to boil water before consuming it as just another fad (34). But her perception that such occurrences are frequent, at any rate, seems to be accurate: several months after the poison gas incident, Blacksmith is once again overwhelmed by airborne substances, this time in the form of chemical smells drifting into town from across the river (270–71). Along somewhat different lines, risks associated with car accidents and plane crashes are mentioned frequently in the novel, and I will comment presently on those associated with pharmaceutical products. These examples show that the "airborne toxic event" at the center of the plot is by no means exceptional but simply a threat that is (or appears to be) much larger than other hazards in the Gladneys' universe, where environmental risks ranging from the trivial to the deadly surround the average citizen. DeLillo's novel, then, is not so much about an ordinary family's encounter with one exceptionally dangerous technological accident as about the portrayal of life in what German sociologist Ulrich Beck calls the "risk society" of the late twentieth and early twenty-first centuries.[8]

From the beginning, Jack Gladney's experience of risk is intertwined with his self-perception as a member of the middle class. In the novel's first scene, Gladney observes the students as their parents bring them to campus at the beginning of the academic year: the fathers are "content to measure out the time, distant but ungrudging, accomplished in parenthood, something about them suggesting massive insurance coverage" (*WN*, 3). The bourgeois establishment, in his view, is defined by its possession of time and insurance against risk—two assets that Gladney no longer has, or thinks he no longer has, after the poison gas accident. But at the beginning of the Nyodene D. crisis, Gladney still seems to believe that being part of the middle class is a sort of insurance against risk. When his family expresses increasing concern that they might be affected by the gas, Gladney claims:

> "These things happen to poor people who live in exposed areas. Society is set up in such a way that it's the poor and the uneducated who suffer the main impact of natural and man-made disasters. People in low-lying areas get the floods, people in shanties get the hurricanes and tornados. I'm a college professor. Did you ever see a college professor rowing a boat down his own street in one of those TV floods? We live in a neat and pleasant town near a college with a quaint name. These things don't happen in places like Blacksmith." (*WN*, 114)

Whether Gladney himself believes his statement or primarily wants to reassure his family, he relies on the conviction that exposure to risk follows established lines of social stratification. As I will show in more detail presently, Beck argues precisely the opposite, namely, that new kinds of risk will create new types of social structure characteristic of a different form of modernity. In Beck's terms, Gladney here attempts to portray his own position in the risk society by means of categories that derive from an earlier type of modernity; significantly enough, he bases his argument on natural disasters such as floods and hurricanes, not on human-made crises like the one in which he is already immersed. That his assertions about the relationship between class and risk are at that moment part of a rather obvious denial strategy lends support to the claim that in *White Noise*, DeLillo is concerned with the way in which new kinds of risk have invaded the lives of even those citizens that might earlier have had reason to believe themselves safe from their most dire consequences.

Buell argues that the Gladneys' death obsession, on which the novel's final chapter focuses, is "no more than tenuously linked" to the poison gas accident, further evidence, in his view, that this event is nonessential to the plot, a mere "supporting metaphor."[9] In "Dylarama," the last chapter, Gladney discovers that Babette has obtained experimental drugs designed to suppress fear of death, in exchange for sexual favors to one of the psychopharmaceutical company's representatives. He becomes obsessed with finding and killing this man and with obtaining a supply of the pills to fight his own chronic fear of dying. What he finds, however, is a man devastated by the side effects of an overdose of these pills. Gladney first attacks and injures him, but then, in a complete reversal of his plan, rescues him by taking him to a hospital. Critics other than Buell have also argued that this sequence of events does not seem to make sense within a novelistic plot.[10] But if *White Noise* is a narrative portrayal of the technological risk society, the plot is not as incoherent as it seems. The Gladneys' desperate hunt for a drug that might alleviate their existential fear, regardless of its experimental status and unknown side effects, is simply the narrative inversion of the risk scenario that was portrayed in the previous chapter. While the description of the poison gas accident revolves around an individual's involuntary exposure to potentially lethal risk from a chemical substance, "Dylarama" portrays the same character's voluntary acceptance of risk from another chemical substance that he hopes will counteract the effects of the first one.

That Nyodene D. and Dylar are meant to point to the complementary sides of exposure to powerful chemicals is marked quite clearly in the text. Nyodene D. forces people out of their homes, and Gladney is exposed to it outdoors, while Dylar foregrounds the penetration of chemicals into the domestic sphere. For this reason, the health technician's advice to Gladney to ignore his health prospects and "[g]et married, settle down and have kids" is doubly ironic (*WN*, 141): not only is this piece of advice given by a young man to a college professor in his fifties who has been married four times and has three children and two stepchildren, but it also projects the domestic sphere as a way out of the uncertainties of chemical risk assessment. As it turns out, however, the family home exposes the individual to its own array of chemical hazards. When Gladney casually remarks, early in the novel, that Babette's medicine cabinet contains "[b]lood pressure pills, stress pills, allergy pills, eye drops, aspirin. Run of the mill," he gives a first glimpse of the multiple therapeutic chemicals that form part of daily routine even for a homemaker (*WN*, 62). The question that surfaces in this early scene, as to what side effects such drug combinations might have, only unfolds in its full significance later, when Gladney discovers the nature of the new pills his wife has been taking. But even at this early moment in the novel, it becomes clear that the family homestead offers no refuge from chemical exposure. If Nyodene D. threatens the community and the public sphere, Dylar signals the presence of chemical hazards in the privacy of the domestic realm.

Both substances, moreover, have effects on the human body that are only partially known but potentially lethal. During the evacuation, Heinrich comments: "'In powder form [Nyodene D.]'s colorless, odorless and very dangerous, except no one seems to know exactly what it causes in humans or in the offspring of humans. They tested for years and either they don't know for sure or they know and aren't saying'"(*WN*, 131). Similarly, Babette explains, official tests of the drug Dylar were suspended because the company considered them too fraught with risk: "'I could die. I could live but my brain could die. The left side of my brain could die but the right side could live. . . . Mr. Gray wanted me to know the risks'" (*WN*, 193). The side effects of the two substances that actually manifest themselves in the novel are symmetrical inversions of each other: déjà vu, an unexpected onslaught of memory, is the most lasting observable after-effect of Nyodene D. in Blacksmith, while Babette suffers from memory lapses after taking Dylar. Gladney, finally, articulates the complementarity of the two chemicals quite explicitly as he reflects on Dylar: "Would it ever work. . . ? It was the benign counterpart of the Nyodene menace . . . releasing benevolent chemicals into my bloodstream, flooding the fear-of-death part of my brain. . . . Technology with a human face" (*WN*, 211). The plot of *White Noise*, then, not only juxtaposes the deadly and life-giving facets of technology but also confronts the protagonist's fear of lethal risk in one case with his willingness to accept the same risk in another. Similarly, the novel points up the implicit contradiction between Babette's attempts to lose weight for health reasons and her reckless acceptance of as serious a health risk as losing half her brain capacity.

Because it is difficult to justify these protagonists' decisions rationally, DeLillo may well be drawing a satirical portrait of the paradoxes to which risk awareness can lead. But as many critics have noted, the Gladneys' fear of death seems irrational in the first place, not justified by any acute danger. This is true if, once again, one takes the poison gas accident to be the only instance of a real hazard in the novel; admittedly, Gladney's fear of dying precedes rather than originates in his exposure to the gas, which merely confirms and reinforces it. But if the narrative aims at the broader portrayal of a society in which individuals and communities are exposed to multiple risks, many of which are completely new and at least partially unknown in their effects, then the Gladneys' existential fear may not be as unfounded as it seems: it is precisely the fact that so many of these risks are not yet known that justifies it. In other words, the portrayal of the risk society in *White Noise* is based on two dimensions: on one hand, the novel refers not just to one technological disaster but to a range of risks from the trivial to the lethal; on the other hand, this wide spectrum of risk scenarios hints that there might be many others hidden in plain sight of ordinary life, dangers that simply have not yet been detected. If, as Beck has argued, risk awareness is based not only on experience and second-hand experience but also on "second-hand non-experience," that is, on the expectation of risks that no one has consciously experienced yet, then the Gladneys' fear of dying no longer appears unmotivated.[11]

One might object that this analysis amounts to reading *White Noise* as a realist novel, a documentary of the risk society. Clearly, such an interpretation cannot hold true in any simple sense. *White Noise* is above all a satire of the contemporary, juxtaposing painfully realistic details from the world of supermarkets, credit cards, and brand-name advertising with absurd, hyperbolic, or humorous elements: a department of Hitler studies chaired by a professor who does not speak

German, a tourist attraction called "The Most Photographed Barn in America," pills that cause one to take words for objects, nuns who admit they do not believe in God but make believe they do for the sake of nonbelievers. To the extent that my analysis of the importance of risk for the plot is accurate, one might argue that DeLillo mocks contemporary risk perceptions rather than engaging them seriously. Undeniably, to the extent that the Gladney family's daily life is an object of satire in the novel, so are their experiences of risk. Yet the text is quite a bit more complex than that. Even calling it a satire and identifying its realistic and hyperbolic elements relies on the assumption that we as readers know what the real world is like, and how DeLillo's narrative universe differs from it. But in practice, the line between realism and hyperbole turns out to be often difficult to draw: we may agree that a department of Hitler studies sounds implausible, but how about scholars who study narratives on cereal boxes and offer courses on car-crash scenes in American movies? Pills that make one take words for things do not sound realistic, yet we all know something about effects of psychopharmaceuticals that would have seemed quite unlikely a few decades ago. The description of media coverage of the Nyodene D. accident with its gradually intensifying euphemisms is undoubtedly very funny, but it would be easy to come up with comparable examples of media obfuscation from the "real" world. *White Noise* certainly functions as a satire at one level, therefore, but at another level, it puts into question the reader's ability to distinguish the real from the fake and the hyperbolic.[12]

The ontological uncertainty that results from this deployment of the satiric mode has been theorized by Brian McHale in a broader context as one of the hallmarks of postmodernist fiction.[13] But while McHale associates such uncertainty for the most part with clearly antirealist forms of narration, it is possible to claim, in the context of a risk-theory approach to narrative, that the destabilization of distinctions between the real and the nonreal can itself serve specific realist objectives. Making such distinctions is precisely the task that the characters in DeLillo's novel have to fulfill repeatedly in their assessments of risk or "unreliable menace," as the text calls it at one point (*WN*, 184). The novel's narrative mode, which exacts similar decision making from the readers, therefore mirrors in its narrative form the fundamental uncertainties that beset risk assessments in the "real world." Obviously, it is not necessary to assume that this use of satire is directed only at the portrayal of risk scenarios. Risk assessments are clearly not the only context in which DeLillo's protagonists have to make judgments about verisimilitude; the problem similarly arises in their encounters with mass media, advertisements, or scholarly arguments about culture. But decisions about risk do ultimately underlie many of these encounters, most obviously when media or advertising statements allude to real or imaginary hazards and miraculous remedies, or when discussions about popular culture turn on the way in which it portrays death. Because these topics recur so insistently, it is possible to argue that not so much in spite of as because of its use of satire, *White Noise* engages the problematics of risk in both its themes and narrative form. Many of the hyperboles and the simulations that have typically been interpreted as examples of postmodern inauthenticity become, from this perspective, manifestations of daily encounters with risks whose reality cannot be assessed with certainty.

Risk Theory

A brief overview of some approaches and ideas that have emerged in risk theory may help to substantiate my claim that the particular problems of realism in *White Noise* reflect some crucial issues in risk assessment. Most risk analysis has been carried out in sociology, anthropology, and psychology, though in the 1990s political scientists and economists have also become increasingly interested in the field. As a separate area of study in the social sciences, risk analysis dates back to the late 1960s and early 1970s. In 1969, a seminal article by the engineer Chauncey Starr analyzing social benefits and technological risks in relation to each other opened up the problem of risk assessment to systematic research, at a time when the public had become increasingly aware of and concerned about chemical, nuclear, and other environmental dangers. Since then, a range of theories has developed in the field.[14] In the context of literary analysis, two kinds of approaches to risk are particularly worth mentioning: theories about the underlying causes of technological risk and their impact on social structure, and investigations of risk perceptions.

The most famous, far-reaching, and speculative kind of risk theory was proposed by Beck in the mid-1980s. Beck links risk research to broader theorizations of social change: most importantly, to theories of modernization and globalization. Like sociologists Anthony Giddens and Scott Lash, he postulates that modern societies have entered a phase of "reflexive modernization" in which modernizing processes transform not traditional social structures but those created by earlier waves of modernization.[15] According to Beck, the hazards characteristic of this new era can be defined by two criteria: they are themselves the effects of modernizing processes and, thereby, they reflexively confront modern societies with the results of their own modernization. And some of these risks, such as global warming and the thinning of the ozone layer, are for the first time truly planetary in scope. Beck's most far-reaching claim is that risks such as these will lead to a new stage in the evolution of modernity. While social distinctions and conflicts at an earlier stage of the modern were centrally articulated around the production and distribution of wealth, Beck argues, "in advanced modernity, the social production of *wealth* is systematically associated with the social production of *risks*. Accordingly, the distribution problems and conflicts of the scarcity society are superseded by the problems and conflicts that originate in the production, definition and distribution of techno-scientifically generated risks."[16] Global risk, in other words, reaches across existing stratifications to create a new kind of social structure. Beck doesn't deny, of course, that at the moment, patterns of risk exposure frequently replicate structures of material inequality, but he argues that increasingly, the decisive risks will be those like Chernobyl, which affected vast areas of eastern, northern, and western Europe without regard for social difference. As I argued in the first section, it is possible to read *White Noise* as a fictional engagement with such risks that transcend conventional class distinctions.

Despite the enormous popularity that Beck's book gained in western Europe in the late 1980s and early 1990s, it also came under attack. Sociologists in particular have pointed out that little empirical evidence exists to support Beck's claim that social categorizations are indeed in the process of being rearticulated around issues of risk. But even some of his critics admit that the interest of Beck's argument may be polemical rather than descriptive: it is not really necessary to accept wholesale his theory of a fundamental social shift to see the force of his argument that risk is becoming one important area of sociocultural concern and conflict.[17]

A much more specific analysis about why risk has become so all-encompassing emerges from the work of the historian of technology

Thomas Hughes. What has transformed modern society, and American society in particular, Hughes argues, is not so much the invention of individual technological principles and devices—such as electricity, the telephone, or the automobile—as the creation of large-scale and extremely complex technoeconomic systems by means of which these devices are produced, distributed, and managed. For Hughes, the invention and implementation of these technological and organizational networks is the unique contribution of the United States to modern culture. The technological hardware is only one part of such networks, which also include transportation, communication, and information systems, as well as people and institutions with all their organizational, legal, social, and economic structures. In his perspective, these large-scale systems into which technologies are embedded have become so complex that they can no longer be easily understood or controlled, and therefore they give rise to risks whose origins and outcomes are extremely difficult to trace and manage.[18] As I will show later, this idea forms the narrative nucleus of Richard Powers's novel *Gain*.

In his analysis, Hughes cites the work of sociologist Charles Perrow, who proposed the notion of "system accidents" in the mid-1980s. Focusing more on the technological apparatus itself than the organizational networks around it, Perrow argues that the most serious risks derive from technological systems with such a degree of complexity that even experts cannot understand all the connections and feedback loops they contain, and, therefore, cannot predict some of their most dangerous failures. System accidents occur when several different and sometimes minor failures in independent but coupled subsystems interact in such a way as to produce failures in the system as a whole. This interaction produces risks that could not have been anticipated by an analysis of the system's normal functioning or of individual subsystem failures. Nuclear energy is such a complex and tightly coupled technology prone to system accidents, as Perrow demonstrates in a detailed analysis of the Three Mile Island accident. In his view, improved designs or better operator training will not lead to increased safety because the complexity of the technology itself will always defeat them. Technological systems that are prone to such accidents, he argues, pose the greatest and most unpredictable hazards for contemporary society.[19]

Beck, Hughes, and Perrow all analyze risk as it emerges in the context of complex social and technological systems. A different approach to risk, the one that has produced the greatest amount of research, focuses on how different social groups perceive particular risks and what reasons lead them to their assessments. Several theoretical schools constitute this part of the field.[20] In the psychometric approach, detailed empirical studies are carried out to determine how the public assesses a wide range of risks, and the researchers—many of them cognitive psychologists—then analyze the reasons for these assessments. The basic assumption in the psychometric approach is that these reasons are to be sought in individuals' cognitive behavior, and so they are explored with theories of heuristics and cognitive biases, that is, decision-making rules and selective information processing. A different approach, called cultural theory (not to be confused with the meaning of this phrase in the context of cultural studies), argues that individuals do not in fact make risk assessments on a case-by-case basis. As anthropologist Mary Douglas and sociologist Aaron Wildavsky in particular argued in the early 1980s, any social community is affected by a wide range of risks, but only some of these are selected for conscious awareness and given particular significance. This significance is best explained in terms of what it accomplishes for the values and ultimately the perpetuation of the social structure that defines it. On the basis of their association with certain types of social structures, the risk assessments of individuals can then be predicted in broad terms.[21] A third line of research has focused on technological controversies and on the interaction of stakeholders and their values in a particular technology.

One central issue informing research on risk across these paradigms is the difference between expert and lay perceptions. To give one notorious example, experts tend to rank the risk associated with nuclear power plants much lower than nonexperts, based on the limited number of actual accidents and deaths; nonexperts, regardless of the low statistics, assess them as much more hazardous than, say, coal mines or highways, which cause a much larger number of fatalities annually. Psychometric research in particular has focused on the variables that shape such perceptions. Some of the most important ones include the distinction between voluntary and involuntary risk (people tend to be much more tolerant of voluntarily selected risks than those imposed by others, as we already saw in *White Noise*), the scale and controllability of adverse effects, the presence or absence of a particular kind of "dread," and the level of public trust in the authorities that manage a particular risk.[22]

Closely associated with the difference between lay and expert assessments is the question of the objective or subjective nature of risk. In the 1970s, the prevailing assumption was that technical risk assessments by experts in science, statistics, and engineering represented the "objective" degree of risk; divergent risk perceptions by lay people were considered less objective, less rational, and in need of explanation as well as, ultimately, correction. In the course of the 1980s, this sharp distinction was increasingly questioned, and some parts of the field moved toward analyses of the social and cultural construction of risk. To begin with, it was pointed out that technical definitions of risk, which are mostly based on probability and magnitude of adverse effects, leave out crucial dimensions that a more comprehensive but perfectly rational assessment might want to take into account: for example, the unequal distribution of risks and benefits among different social and geographical groups or the emergence of indirect costs. Even judgments that are not based on these more broadly understood rational terms, however, might make sense when the social and cultural contexts are considered. In the mid-1980s, the concept of the "social amplification of risk" was proposed to describe the mediating processes and institutions that shape the social experience of risk and magnify or minimize it.[23] This concept has remained extremely important to the field today, and it points to precisely the problems of distinguishing realism from hyperbole that I mentioned in the discussion of *White Noise* earlier: in both analytical and literary contexts, the question is not only whose risk assessments are the most realistic but also what criteria should be used to gauge degrees of realism in the first place.

In a more radical perspective, though, it has been argued that even those elements of lay assessments that are not rationally founded cannot be used to mark an unequivocal boundary between objective and subjective judgments about risk. In this view, the assessments of experts are not exempt from bias, specific interests, and underlying value structures, and the concept of objective risk really makes no sense. Any debate about risk includes participants who have widely varying values and priorities, and their definitions of risk, as well as their assessments of what constitutes acceptable risk or of the size of a particular risk, will depend on these values; being an expert or nonexpert is only one variable in this priority structure. Any decision about risks is therefore at bottom political. This argument comes in several different versions, with some theorists willing to accept some distinction between different degrees of objectivity (if not between absolute objectivity and subjectivity), while others dismiss the notion of objectivity completely and associate their rejection with a more general critique of science as a privileged mode of knowledge.[24]

Needless to say, these controversies are far from mere academic quibbles. Risk assessment is a large, practical field in industry and government today, and sometimes comes loaded with political charges. In the area of risk communication—the study of how particular types of risks should be brought to the attention of the public—the assumption in the 1970s was that lay people's judgments needed to be aligned with those of experts. Much more sophisticated strategies of risk communication tend to be adopted today, but struggles over risk assessment often remain deeply embedded in conflicts over cultural values and the question of who has the right to make decisions over how technologies are implemented.

As even this extremely brief overview shows, risk theory deals not just with technological and other dangers in a narrow technical sense but defines its object of study within cultural contexts and social systems without which the notion of risk itself cannot be conceived. It is this constitution of risk from within specific sociocultural fields that establishes an interdisciplinary bridge to the concerns of literary critics. Cultural variables in risk analysis have so far been understood rather broadly, with relatively little attention to the impact that particular metaphors, plot patterns, or visual representations might have in the formation of risk judgments. The emergence of the oil-covered sea bird as an international symbol of environmental disaster or the impact of the Frankenstein story (in both its book and film versions) on current perceptions of genetic engineering, for example, call for close investigation.[25]

More generally, reasoning about risk, with its foregrounding of causal connections that are not immediately obvious and with its postulation of possible future sequences of events, calls for at least a rudimentary, and often quite elaborate, narrative articulation. Concepts of narrative analysis might therefore play an important role in examining the ways in which risk perceptions manifest themselves in both literary and nonliterary writings. Implicitly or explicitly, accounts of risk can invoke different genre models: the detective story, in the evaluation of clues and eyewitness accounts and in the discovery and exposure of the criminal; pastoral, in the portrayal of rural, unspoiled landscapes violated by the advent of technology; the gothic, in the evocation of hellish landscapes or grotesquely deformed bodies as a consequence of pollution; the bildungsroman, in the victim's gradually deepening realization of the danger to which he or she is exposed; tragedy, through the fateful occurrence of evil in spite of the participants' best intentions; or epic, in the attempt to grasp the planetary implications of some risks.[26] Along with the selection of such templates that make risk scenarios intelligible to the reader or viewer in a particular way, narrators have to make choices about which individuals or institutions are cast as protagonists or antagonists in technological controversies, about where and how to conclude their story, and about how to characterize their own relationship to the narrative material (for example, as eyewitness, victim, scientific expert, or journalist). Given such strategies, literary and cultural critics have a potentially important contribution to make to a finer-grained analysis of risk perceptions as they manifest themselves across a range of cultural artifacts.[27]

Inversely, risk analysis also has an important role to play in some parts of literary and cultural criticism. The question of what prompts individuals and groups to view certain technological and ecological risks as significant and to consider others as minor or nonexistent is itself a matter of crucial importance for an ecocritical perspective. Beyond that, the emergence of ecological and technological risk scenarios as a thematic component of various artistic practices warrants investigation for the pressures it brings to bear on existing aesthetic forms: Do writers and artists approach such risks mainly by way of established templates such as those I've mentioned, or do they modify them or invent new, experimental ones? How are particular representations of risk generated, reflected, worked through, or resisted by means of such formal choices? What might be their cultural and ideological implications? Through questions such as these, the analysis ultimately moves beyond the study of individual artifacts to the broader issue of how they participate in social and cultural processes of risk communication.

In an attempt to bring such an analysis to bear on a widely known novel, I have shown in the first section how *White Noise* examines the working of risk perceptions and communication at a mostly local level. The novel focuses on the confrontation between lay and expert approaches to risk (evident in the conversation I quoted at the beginning), voluntary and involuntary risk exposure, and the ways in which risk transforms individuals' experience of the public and domestic spheres. A novel that foregrounds somewhat different aspects of risk is Richard Powers's *Gain*, which elaborates on the theme of chemical exposure in terms that are comparable to DeLillo's and yet quite different in that they situate the problem much more explicitly in social and economic systems that span the globe.

Toxic Systems: *Gain*

Powers's *Gain* (1998) has two strands of plot that are narrated in alternating sections. The first outlines approximately 150 years in the development of a company that starts out as J. Clare & Sons, a family soap- and candle-making business in 1830s Boston. In the course of its long history of technological invention, shrewd business maneuvers, repeated near-failures, mergers, cutbacks, and expansions, this company evolves by the 1990s into Clare International, a multinational chemical and pharmaceutical corporation manufacturing everything from detergents, cosmetics, and drugs to pesticides, fertilizers, and synthetic construction materials. Clare's agricultural division is headquartered in the midwestern town of Lacewood, where it has for decades been the community's major employer and principal financial source. The other plot strand revolves around Laura Bodey, a middle-aged, divorced real-estate agent with two children who lives in Lacewood. During a routine medical examination, she is diagnosed with ovarian cancer, and the novel follows her through surgery and periods of chemotherapy to her final decline and death. In her last months, Bodey discovers not only that some of the chemicals Clare produces have been associated with cancer but also that a class action lawsuit is in progress against the company, which her divorced husband Don urges her to join. She does, after some resistance, and although the settlement money comes too late to benefit her, it is passed on to her children. A third narrative element is set apart from these two plots: descriptions and quotations of legal documents and, above all, advertising materials referring to the Clare corporation and its products, which often form an ironic counterpoint to the evolving story of Bodey's cancer.[28]

Gain has some obvious similarities with *White Noise* in its portrayal of technological risk. Both novels focus on chemical exposure; both describe it as befalling a dysfunctional but only too normal family in a midwestern small town.[29] In both cases, the choice of location and type of family signal risk scenarios affecting a social class that had formerly believed itself exempt from such environmental dangers. Most important, both novels attempt to capture the dual nature of chemical substances as killers and cures: the antithesis between poison and drug structures the juxtaposition of Nyodene D. and Dylar just as it does that of the herbicide that may have triggered Laura Bodey's cancer and the drugs she is given during chemotherapy. In both cases, the antithesis is an uneasy one, as the therapies fail and their side effects turn out to be potentially as serious as the symptoms they were designed to cure. But the play on toxins and drugs, on involuntary risk from chemical exposure and voluntary risk from substances that might bring benefit, is ultimately developed into a quite different conceptualization of risk in *Gain*.

White Noise puts considerable emphasis on the substances themselves, the way in which they enter human bodies and the time intervals and circumstances under which they take effect. This emphasis is not only obvious in the conversations Gladney has with doctors and technicians about his toxic gas exposure but also in the episode in which a neurochemist explains to him the sophisticated physical and chemical mechanisms of Dylar (*WN*, 187–89). Powers displays similar attention to detail in the description of Laura Bodey's chemotherapy, in which the names, quantities, ingestion times, and effects of all the medications are presented in excruciating detail. But the same is not true of the substance that might have caused Bodey's cancer, the herbicide she used in her gardening. The most obvious reason for this elision seems to be that there is no way of being sure. As Bodey discovers, once her awareness of environmental chemicals has been kindled, she is surrounded by them, to the point that it is impossible to get rid of them:

> No longer her home, this place they have given her to inhabit. She cannot hike from the living room to the kitchen without passing an exhibit. Floor by Germ-Guard. Windows by Cleer-Thru. Table by Colonial-Cote. The Bodey mansion, that B-ticket, one-star museum of trade. But where else can she live?
> She vows a consumer boycott, a full spring cleaning. But the

house is full of them. . . . They paper her cabinets. They perch on her microwave, camp out on her stove, hang from her shower head. Clare hiding under the sink, swarming in her medicine chest, lining the shelves in the basement, parked out in the garage, piled up in the shed.

Her vow is hopeless. Too many to purge them all. Every hour of her life depends on more corporations than she can count.[30]

This profusion of potentially dangerous products eerily echoes Heinrich's remark in *White Noise*: "'It's the things around you in your own house that'll get you sooner or later'" (*WN*, 175). One is tempted to pick out the herbicide from this line-up because it is the chemical that Bodey most obviously recognizes: when Don, in a whole list of Clare products suspected of being carcinogenic, mentions only the first two syllables of its name, "Atra-," Bodey immediately thinks of the garden she loves and agrees without further ado to join the lawsuit. In part, what is at work here is unquestionably the rhetoric of "disrupted pastoral" that Buell has diagnosed as one of the elements of discourse about toxic waste: the garden, Bodey's own plot of unspoiled nature, turns out to be what may be slowly killing her.[31] *May* be killing her: the novel never confirms that this is so, never even completes the name of the guilty product. This uncertainty is deliberate and points to a structure of causality quite different from the one that informs *White Noise*. If Jack Gladney declares somewhat melodramatically after his toxic exposure, "Death has entered. It is inside you" (*WN*, 141–42), no such concrete moment of poisoning can be identified in *Gain*. For Powers, the real poison lies not in any concrete substance but in the complex technoeconomic system that has evolved over more than a century to deliver chemical products to the individual.

It is, above all, the novel's narrative structure, with its stark juxtaposition of the rise of a company and the decline of an individual, that makes this point. From the outset, the inverted plot lines of these stories suggest that Clare is causally related to Bodey's illness, though the concrete circumstances only emerge later.[32] The causal link is reinforced through the play on words related to the body. The female protagonist's name, of course, is merely a misspelling of the word *body*, and her antagonist turns out to be an "incorporated" company:[33] "The law now declared the Clare Soap and Chemical Company one composite body: a single, whole, and statutorily enabled person. . . . an artificial being, invisible, intangible, and existing only in contemplation

of law" (*G*, 158). In the historical narrative, Powers spends considerable time describing the rise of the incorporated enterprise as a legal
concept in the late nineteenth century, which he characterizes as the
transfer of individual rights to the business company. Part of the point
in juxtaposing the two narrative strands, then, is to show how the corporate body and the individual body depend upon each other, and how
the corporate organism can become a lethal threat to the individual
one. More than any single substance and more even than the whole
array of products it delivers, it is the corporation as a social form that
kills Laura Bodey.

But the play on incorporated and embodied beings already reveals
that the relationship between the two narrative strands is not one of
pure antagonism. If the metaphor of the body connects them, so does
the metaphor of cancerous growth. Just as Bodey's cancer returns
and spreads after surgery and chemotherapy, so the Clare Company
keeps growing in spite of economic recessions, adverse legislation,
and internal crises that sometimes take it to the brink of failure.[34]
Through this continued expansion, the family business of the early
nineteenth century evolves into a multinational corporation by the end
of the twentieth. And even money that Clare disburses to its oppo-
nents seems inevitably destined to further corporate growth, as is
made clear by the settlement money that Bodey's children receive
from the class-action lawsuit after her death. Years later, Bodey's son
Tim starts working in the computer industry; he helps to develop software that predicts and even manipulates the behavior of certain protein sequences, producing a "chemical assembly plant at the level of
the human cell" that will be able, it is hoped, to cure cancer (*G*, 355).
In order to put this software to use, he and his friends decide that with
the help of his savings, they will incorporate. Indirectly and with considerable time delay, corporate money generates yet another corporate body. This new corporation may be able to cure the cancer the
old one caused, but in that very process it can only worsen the other
cancer that is incorporated business itself. The novel's ending, then,
is curiously optimistic and pessimistic at the same time.

Because he portrays the multinational corporation as a lethal risk
both in its products and by virtue of its structure, Powers has been
accused by some reviewers of mounting an "assault on corporate
America."[35] Others have pointed out a good deal of admiration and
optimism in his portrayal of capitalist enterprise.[36] These diverging

assessments are due to the fact that Powers, especially in the first half of the novel, considers risk in both its negative and positive dimensions: not only as danger or hazard but also as opportunity, as the voluntary acceptance of uncertainty or danger in the expectation of profit. One of the Clare founding fathers, for example, is described as "handl[ing] cotton and indigo and potash. But above all else, he dealt in risk. Profit equaled uncertainty times distance. The harder it was to haul a thing to where it humanly belonged, the more one made" (*G*, 10). There is indeed a good deal of admiration in Powers's descriptions of how the first few generations of Clares deal with economic risk and the frequent setbacks it imposes, and how they manage it with perseverance, ingenuity, and skill. But the breaking point seems to come with the rise of the incorporated enterprise, precisely because at that moment the company is allowed to continue making a profit without incurring all the risks it formerly had to confront. Powers places great emphasis on the concept of "limited liability" in this context: "If the Fifth and Fourteenth Amendments combined to extend due process to all individuals, and if the incorporated business had become a single person under the law, then the Clare Soap and Chemical Company now enjoyed all the legal protections afforded any individual by the spirit of the Constitution. And for the actions of that protected person, for its debts and indiscretions, no single shareholder could be held liable," he points out, and quotes the definition of a corporation from Bierce's *Devil's Dictionary*: "'An ingenious device for obtaining individual profit without individual responsibility'" (*G*, 159).[37] Business that faces risk and engages it creatively is described approvingly, while business that is shielded from risk becomes a hazard to those in its environment.

In *Gain*, then, the risk of chemical exposure is represented not so much in terms of the mysterious and dangerous substances that occupy center stage in *White Noise*; beyond such specific materials, it is a complex system of the kind described by Thomas Hughes that comes to embody risk in *Gain*. While DeLillo focuses on the hazardous substances whose origins and effects are difficult for average individuals to discover and understand, Powers shifts the emphasis to the complex technoeconomic systems that deliver such substances, and whose workings are even more impenetrable to the ordinary citizen. In fact, they are nearly impossible to control even by those who do understand them: toward the end, the novel gives a brief glimpse of

Franklin Kennibar, CEO of Clare International, reflecting on his own powerlessness in crucial decisions about the company. These systems beyond comprehension and control really are the overarching risk that *Gain* seeks to address, a risk of which household toxins are only the most minor, if still potentially lethal, manifestations.

Resistance to these complex systems is as futile in *Gain* as it is unimaginable in *White Noise*. Bodey's daughter and her friends publicly burn their Clare cosmetics in a televised protest against the company, but such temporary outbursts and the more protracted lawsuits against Clare in the end produce merely a shifting of the problem, with no solution.[38] With lower ratings on the Stock Exchange, Clare sells its Agricultural Division to Monsanto some time after Laura Bodey's death, and Monsanto two years later relocates the agricultural products plant to a *maquiladora*, precipitating Lacewood into economic ruin. Corporate deals and global expansion thereby cancel any possibility of resistance. Ironically enough, the character that comes closest to offering some hope for opposition is Bodey's former husband Don, whom she had divorced because, among other things, she could not stand his habit of seeing connections, conspiracies, and coverups everywhere. Don is the one who, as she herself notes, knows how to ask all the right questions about her cancer diagnosis and therapy, who studies the medical background, finds out about the Clare connection, and makes her join the lawsuit. Indefatigable in his search for accurate and comprehensive information, Don is the only one who achieves some measure of knowledge and success in the struggle with Clare.[39] But nothing he does approaches any serious challenge to the underlying system, and Powers's novel as a whole does not offer any prospects of change. Against the complex system of Clare's global body, the local bodies of individuals or small communities are powerless.

But while *Gain* portrays with astonishing conceptual sophistication individuals' inability to resist or even comprehend the worldwide networks that entangle them, its narrative structure does not in the end offer a persuasive formal correlative for this approach to the global. Indeed, Powers's narrative strategies suggest that whatever difficulties the characters may encounter in their attempts to grapple with the global corporate world, the readers can rely on the comprehensive map that the self-assured omniscient narrator unfolds before them. It is precisely the novel's split into two narrative strands that creates this schism: the historical narrative acquaints the reader with a wealth of detail regarding the development and functioning of multi-national corporations and their relation to risk scenarios, while such insight is not available to Laura Bodey and other characters, even though they may occasionally glimpse a fragment of this information. Mostly, the characters perceive the corporation through the kinds of language exemplified in the novel's third narrative component— snippets of advertising, corporate self-promotion, and legal documents gleaned from Clare's discursive archive. As noted earlier, these rhetorical samples often stand in ironic contrast to the actual evolution of Clare International, and even more so to its effects on the environment and public health as they are spelled out in the two narrative strands.

Powers here deploys a narrative technique that is derived from the modernist urban novels of John Dos Passos, James Joyce, and Alfred Döblin: the insertion of fragments of "authentic" discourse from a variety of modern institutions and media into a fictional story.[40] This transfer of a technique that originally served to illustrate the bewildering diversity and fragmentation of languages in the modernist metropolis to the portrayal of a multinational corporation is not unproblematic, since Powers ultimately aims to capture not heterogeneity at all but precisely the dangerous singularity of purpose that lurks behind the apparent diversity of consumer products. But whatever effect these high-modernist fragments might have is, at any rate, neutralized by their insertion into an omniscient narration that provides the reader with just the kind of overarching and authoritative information that is usually not available in *Manhattan Transfer*, *Ulysses*, or *Berlin Alexanderplatz*. The shock, surprise, and disorientation that such fragments cause in the high modernist novel are absorbed, in *Gain*, through a mode of narration that consistently restores context, control, and orientation to the reader; narrative collage is reabsorbed into orderly progression.

In the last third of the novel, Powers resorts to a somewhat different technique to portray the workings of Clare International. In some sections, he juxtaposes snapshots of individuals in some way involved with the company and its products across the globe; in one, he focuses on a specific consumer product, a disposable camera, and traces back the processes and materials that went into its making to their places of origin around the planet. This stylistically intriguing and innovative passage centers on the insight that "[p]lastic happens; that is all we need to know on earth. History heads steadily for a place where things need not be grasped to be used" (*G*, 347); it counteracts this reification of consumer objects by showing one of them gradually emerging out of a network of globally dispersed raw materials, production, and distribution processes:

> The camera jacket says: "Made In China With Film From Italy Or Germany." The film itself accretes from more places on the map than emulsion can cover. Silver halide, metal salts, dye couplers, bleach fixatives, ingredients gathered from Russia, Arizona, Brazil, and underwater seabeds, before being decanted in the former DDR. Camera in a pouch, the true multinational: trees from the Pacific Northwest and the southeastern coastal plain. Straw and recovered wood scrap from Canada. Synthetic adhesive from Korea. Bauxite from Australia, Jamaica, Guinea. Oil from the Gulf of Mexico or North Sea Brent Blend, turned to plastic in the Republic of China before being shipped to its mortal enemies on the Mainland for molding. Cinnabar from Spain. Nickel and titanium from South Africa. Flash elements stamped in Malaysia, electronics in Singapore. Design and color transfers drawn up in New York. Assembled and shipped from that address in California by a merchant fleet beyond description, completing the most heavily choreographed conference in existence. (*G*, 347–48)

From what follows, it is clear that this globally assembled object was once in the possession of Laura Bodey, who forgot it in a drawer next to one of her hospital beds. It is, in fact, a memento mori of sorts, following as it does the last scene in which the reader sees Bodey alive. But even if she were not yet dead by the time the narrator draws up the camera's map of global origins, it is clear that Bodey had no access to this kind of detailed information while the camera was in her possession. What presents itself to the character as a finished product that provides little information about itself—except, significantly, the manufacturer's warnings and disclaimers of liability—is portrayed for the reader as a shape that gradually emerges from the planetary dispersion of its raw materials. Interestingly, however, the human design, work, and organization that go into this emergence are downplayed in the passage above, whose lack of inflected verbs and passive constructions foreground its elision of agency: the object seems to be assembling itself before the reader's eyes. The critique implicit in this description clearly aims less at capitalism's exploitation of human beings than at its waste of global resources: "[T]he entire engineering magnificence was designed to be pitched. Labor, materials, assembly, shipping, sales markups and overheads, insurance, international tariffs—the whole prodigious creation costs less than ten dollars. The world sells to us at a loss, until we learn to afford it" (G, 348).

Tracing a trajectory from photosynthesis to photography—from the trees that are felled for the camera's cardboard packaging ("[a] thing that once lived for light" [G, 345]) to the pictures on its forgotten film—this section stands out by its conceptual sweep and its industrial lyricism. But considered as part of the overall narrative structure, it presents a problem similar to the alternation of the two narrative strands with their punctuation by fragments of corporate discourse or, for that matter, the occasional allegorization of Clare International as the protagonist of an unfolding bildungsroman.[41] All these strategies present to the reader a fictional world in which the individual is shaped by, dependent on, and intermittently threatened by networks of global capitalism but has few resources to recognize and comprehend, let alone resist, them. Yet the fundamental challenges to ordinary conceptions of individuality, privacy, and freedom that this vision articulates are not translated into any disturbance in the reading process. While the novel shows in detail how individuals and local communities cannot know or control the corporate forces that shape their existence, this panorama is drawn up by a narrator who knows the corporation in both its historical and its geographical extension down to the most minute details, and who delivers them in an idiom that never questions the reader's ability to grasp and connect these details. This narrative strategy is, in the end, far removed from DeLillo's, whose subtle deployment of satire defies the readers' sense of realism and reality in their encounter with a fictional world whose risk scenarios challenge the characters in a similar way. It is even more fundamentally opposed to the narrative techniques of Burroughs or Pynchon, as whose literary successor Powers has often been designated. But Burroughs, Pynchon, or Kathy Acker, all of whom similarly place their protagonists in worlds that are shaped by forces and institutions they are ill-equipped to understand or combat, persistently refuse to reassure their readers that they, after all, can grasp this world with the help of omniscient narrators and realist narration. On the contrary, these authors constantly challenge their readers to reflect on the kinds of cognitive strategies and language that might be able to map global connections, strategies at which their own novels can only hint. In Powers's *Gain*, by contrast, the self-assurance of the narrator's command of the global and his transparent (though complex) language remain in tension with the scenario of individual powerlessness vis-à-vis the global power networks that the novel portrays. In this respect, the novel's formal accomplishment lags behind its conceptual sophistication.

These differences notwithstanding, both Powers and DeLillo place their protagonists in environments fraught with multiple risks of the most varied kinds, and one of the central challenges for the characters is to gain awareness of these riskscapes and find ways of living and dying within them. In both novels, chemical toxins become the most crucial of these risks as agents that effectively blur the boundaries between body and environment, the domestic and the public spheres, and beneficial and harmful technologies. It is in the territory between these realms that the uncertainties of risk perception and risk assessment play themselves out. Aesthetically, *White Noise* remains the more interesting novel as it translates these uncertainties into the uneasy satire, the "unreliable menace" I analyzed earlier. But it is able to do so because it limits the conceptual horizon of risk perception to the individual and the local, while Powers precisely attempts to move beyond these limitations. Representing complex and global technoeconomic systems as a source of risk is one of the challenges that faces contemporary narrative, and no canonical form has yet emerged in response. It may well be that such a narrative architecture will have to rely on more experimental forms of storytelling, and perhaps even on the resources of new narrative media such as the multiple links of hypertext. What shape narrative innovation will take in the risk society is the uncertainty that literary critics face at the turn of the millennium.

Columbia University

Notes

I would like to thank the National Humanities Center, the John D. and Catherine T. MacArthur Foundation, and the American Council of Learned Societies for institutional and financial support during a fellowship year that allowed me to write most of this essay.
1   Lawrence Buell refers to risk-theoretical literature in "Toxic Discourse,"

Critical Inquiry 24 (spring 1998): 639–65, which is now the first chapter of his *Writing for an Endangered World: Literature, Culture and Environment in the U.S. and Beyond* (Cambridge: Harvard Univ. Press, 2001), 30–54.

2 See Mark Osteen's introduction to Don DeLillo, *White Noise: Text and Criticism*, ed. Mark Osteen (New York: Penguin, 1998), vii; this edition also contains materials documenting the novel's parallels with the Bhopal accident (353–62). Further references to *White Noise* will be to this edition and will be cited parenthetically in the text as *WN*.

3 See, for example, Michael Valdez Moses's Heideggerian interpretation of this scene in "Lust Removed from Nature," in *New Essays on "White Noise,"* ed. Frank Lentricchia (Cambridge, Eng.: Cambridge Univ. Press, 1991), 63–86.

4 For discussions of spectacle, simulation, and the role of media in shaping reality in *White Noise*, see John N. Duvall, "The (Super)Marketplace of Images: Television as Unmediated Mediation in DeLillo's *White Noise*," in *White Noise: Text and Criticism*, ed. Osteen, 432–55; Lentricchia, "Tales of the Electronic Tribe," in *New Essays on White Noise*, ed. Lentricchia, 87–113; N. H. Reeve and Richard Kerridge, "Toxic Events: Postmodernism and Don DeLillo's *White Noise*," *Cambridge Quarterly* 23.4 (1994): 303–23; Richard Kerridge, "Small Rooms and the Ecosystem: Environmentalism and Don DeLillo's *White Noise*," in *Writing the Environment: Ecocriticism and Literature*, ed. Richard Kerridge and Neil Sammells (London: Zed Books, 1998), 182–95. A different interpretation is proposed by Paul Maltby, who argues that a romantic sense of transcendence emerges in some crucial scenes of the novel, so that the postmodern scene of the simulacrum does ultimately lead to some experience of authenticity ("The Romantic Metaphysics of Don DeLillo," in *White Noise: Text and Criticism*, ed. Osteen, 498–516).

5 Interestingly, this remark occurs in a book review of Richard Powers's *Gain*, which I will discuss later (see A. O. Scott, "A Matter of Life and Death," *New York Review of Books*, 17 December 1998, 38–42). In *Gain*, unlike *White Noise*, Scott contends, chemical risk is not symbolic (41). But simply rephrasing "ambient dread" as "environmental dread" in Scott's claim would restore full materiality to the toxic event.

6 Buell, *Writing for an Endangered World*, 51.

7 The term *riskscape* is Susan Cutter's; quoted in Cynthia Deitering, "The Postnatural Novel: Toxic Consciousness in Fiction of the 1980s," in *The Ecocriticism Reader: Landmarks in Literary Ecology*, ed. Cheryll Glotfelty and Harold Fromm (Athens: Univ. of Georgia Press, 1996), 200.

8 See Ulrich Beck, *Risk Society: Towards a New Modernity*, trans. Mark Ritter (London: Sage, 1992); originally published as *Risikogesellschaft: Auf dem Weg in eine andere Moderne* (Frankfurt: Suhrkamp, 1986), which I will discuss presently in more detail. I've explored elsewhere the temporal perspective that arises from this focus on the risk society in *White*

Noise ("Die Zeitlichkeit des Risikos im amerikanischen Roman der Post-moderne," in *Zeit und Roman: Zeiterfahrung im historischen Wandel und ästhetischen Paradigmenwechsel vom achtzehnten Jahrhundert bis zur Post-moderne*, ed. Martin Middeke [Würzburg: Königshausen & Neumann, forthcoming]).

9   Buell, *Writing for an Endangered World*, 51.

10 Bianca Theisen, for example, accounts for DeLillo's narrative strategy by arguing that it is aimed at "the paradoxical enterprise . . . of dissolving plot by means of plot" ("White Noise," in *Im Bann der Zeichen: Die Angst vor Verantwortung in Literatur und Literaturwissenschaft*, ed. Markus Heil-mann and Thomas Wägenbaur [Würzburg: Königshausen & Neumann, 1998], 132). The translation to English is mine.

11 Beck, *Risikogesellschaft*, 96. It is tempting to relate Beck's concept of "second-hand non-experience" to Baudrillard's notion of the hyperreal, the copy without an original. But the context and import of the two con-cepts is ultimately different. Beck's argument is not so much about imi-tation as anticipation, and his aim is to explore the ways in which new types of risk overturn the modes of common-sense reasoning rather than to suggest the broader skepticism vis-à-vis the authenticity of contempo-rary culture that Baudrillard proposes.

12 Reeve and Kerridge argue similarly that "[f]or all the satirical pressure it applies to so many aspects of the contemporary world, *White Noise* rec-ognises that the positions from which any such overview can proceed are themselves continually at risk of undermining" ("Toxic Events," 305).

13 See Brian McHale, *Postmodernist Fiction* (New York: Methuen, 1987), 3–40.

14 See Chauncey Starr, "Social Benefit versus Technological Risk," *Science* 165 (19 September 1969): 1232–238. By tracing the field back to Starr, I follow the account presented in Ragnar E. Löfstedt and Lynn Frewer's introduction to their *The Earthscan Reader in Risk and Modern Society* (London: Earthscan, 1998), 3; Löfstedt and Frewer also outline a different account according to which the roots of risk theory can be traced back to the Chicago School of geography.

15 Ulrich Beck, Anthony Giddens, and Scott Lash, *Reflexive Modernization: Politics, Tradition, and Aesthetics in the Modern Social Order* (Cambridge, Eng.: Polity Press, 1994).

16 Beck, *Risikogesellschaft*, 25; the translation to English is mine.

17 For a well-articulated critique of this kind, see David Goldblatt, *Social Theory and the Environment* (Cambridge, Eng.: Polity Press, 1996), 154–87.

18 See Thomas P. Hughes, *American Genesis: A Century of Invention and Technological Enthusiasm, 1870–1970* (New York: Viking, 1989).

19 See Charles Perrow, *Normal Accidents: Living with High-Risk Technolo-gies*, 2d ed. (Princeton, N.J.: Princeton Univ. Press, 1999).

20 My summary of approaches to risk perception in this paragraph and the following is indebted to Löfstedt and Frewer's introduction to *The Earthscan Reader.*

21 See Mary Douglas and Aaron Wildavsky, *Risk and Culture: An Essay on the Selection of Technological and Environmental Dangers* (Berkeley and Los Angeles: Univ. of California Press, 1982); and Aaron Wildavsky and Karl Dake, "Theories of Risk Perception: Who Fears What and Why?" *Daedalus* 119 (fall 1990): 41–60. Steve Rayner gives an overview of cultural theory in risk analysis and offers a critique of the way in which Douglas and Wildavsky deploy it (see "Cultural Theory and Risk Analysis," in *Social Theories of Risk*, ed. Sheldon Krimsky and Dominic Golding [Westport, Conn.: Praeger, 1992], 83–115).

22 See Baruch Fischhoff, Sarah Lichtenstein, Paul Slovic, Stephen L. Derby, and Ralph L. Keeney, *Acceptable Risk* (Cambridge, Eng.: Cambridge Univ. Press, 1981), 61–133; Paul Slovic, "Perception of Risk," *Science* 236 (17 April 1987): 280–85; Baruch Fischhoff, Paul Slovic, and Sarah Lichtenstein, "Lay Foibles and Expert Fables in Judgments about Risks," in *Progress in Resource Management and Environmental Planning*, ed. Timothy O'Riordan and R. Kerry Turner, 4 vols. (Chichester, Eng.: John Wiley, 1981), 3:161–202.

23 See Roger E. Kasperson, et al., "The Social Amplification of Risk: A Conceptual Framework," *Risk Analysis* 8 (April 1988): 177–87; Roger E. Kasperson, "The Social Amplification of Risk: Progress in Developing an Integrative Framework," in *Social Theories of Risk*, ed. Krimsky and Golding, 153–78; James Flynn, Paul Slovic, and Howard Kunreuther, eds., *Risk, Media, and Stigma: Understanding Public Challenges to Modern Science and Technology* (London: Earthscan, 2001).

24 See Harry Otway, "Public Wisdom, Expert Fallibility: Toward a Contextual Theory of Risk," in *Social Theories of Risk*, ed. Krimsky and Golding, 215–28; and Brian Wynne, "Institutional Mythologies and Dual Societies in the Management of Risk," in *The Risk Analysis Controversy: An Institutional Perspective*, ed. Howard C. Kunreuther and Eryl V. Ley (Berlin: Springer, 1982), 127–43.

25 See Andrew Ross, *The Chicago Gangster Theory of Life: Nature's Debt to Society* (London: Verso, 1994), 159–201 (especially 166, 171–72); and Jon Turney, *Frankenstein's Footsteps: Science, Genetics, and Popular Culture* (New Haven: Yale Univ. Press, 1998).

26 In his discussion of the pastoral and the gothic in descriptions of toxicity, Buell has begun this kind of analysis (see *Writing for an Endangered World*, 36–38, 42–45). Leo Marx's *The Machine in the Garden: Technology and the Pastoral Ideal in America*, to which Buell alludes, is one of the most important sources for a study of how the pastoral genre in particular mediates the encounter of nature and technology (London: Oxford Univ. Press, 1964).

27 The question of whether risk theory itself is susceptible to an analysis in literary or rhetorical terms is much more complex and would require a detailed discussion of different types of risk theory that cannot be carried out here.

28 The juxtaposition of two storylines, which is also featured in Powers's other novels, has been widely commented upon by his reviewers (see Walter Kirn, "Commercial Fiction," review of *Gain*, *New York*, 15 June 1998, 103; Paul Quinn, "On the Tracks of the Rhino," review of *Gain*, *Times Literary Supplement*, 17 March 2000, 22; and Scott, "Matter of Life and Death," 40). For a perceptive discussion of how the relation between the two strands of plot in *Gain* differs from that in the earlier novels due to the absence of a mediating figure, see Charles B. Harris, "'The Stereo View': Politics and the Role of the Reader in *Gain*," *Review of Contemporary Fiction* 18 (fall 1998): 97–109, especially 98–99.

29 These two similarities are noted by Scott (who otherwise dismisses *White Noise* as a serious engagement with chemically induced illness) in "Matter of Life and Death," as well as by Michiko Kakutani ("Company Town's Prosperity and Pain," review of *Gain*, *New York Times*, 11 August 1998, E6).

30 Richard Powers, *Gain* (New York: Farrar, Straus & Giroux, 1998), 303–4; further references to *Gain* will be to this edition and will be cited parenthetically in the text as *G*.

31 Buell, *Writing for an Endangered World*, 36–38.

32 This inversion is discussed by Jeffrey Williams in his review of *Gain* ("The Issue of Corporations: Richard Powers' *Gain*," *Cultural Logic* 2.2 [1999], <*http://eserver.org/clogic/2–2/williamsrev.html*>, par. 9); and Bruce Bawer, "Bad Company," review of *Gain*, *New York Times Book Review*, 21 June 1998, 11.

33 This play on words is also discussed in Scott, "Matter of Life and Death," 38.

34 See Gail Caldwell, "On the Soapbox," review of *Gain*, *Boston Sunday Globe*, 7 June 1998, C4; Williams, "Issue of Corporations."

35 Caldwell, "On the Soapbox," C4; see also Kakutani, "Company Town's Prosperity," E6.

36 See Kirn, "Commercial Fiction," 103; and Williams, "Issue of Corporations."

37 Williams comments on this reversal in Powers's portrayal of business companies and his emphasis on "limited liability" in "Issue of Corporations."

38 Williams notes the absence of a "utopian prospect" and describes Powers's political program as "modest" but praises him for avoiding "rote political judgment" ("Issue of Corporations"). Buell also points to the "never-had-a-chance quixoticism of the resistance effort" in the novel (*Writing for an Endangered World*, 290 n. 5) but argues that corpo-

rate hegemony can at least be questioned through an examination of its impacts in the realm of the local and the individual body (56).

39   My interpretation of Don differs from Tom LeClair's, which claims that the novel rejects Don's "paranoid style" ("Powers of Invention," review of *Gain, Nation,* 27 July–3 August 1998, 35). That Don is cast as a much more positive figure than LeClair lets on is also indicated by the fact that Powers puts into his mouth one of the most crucial insights in the novel, namely, that human activities have subdued the earth to the point that it can bear no more (*G,* 353). See Powers's own comment on this scene in his interview with Jeffrey Williams: "This insight, on the part of a character who shouldn't have been able to reach it, is for me the emotional core of the book" ("The Last Generalist: An Interview with Richard Powers," *Cultural Logic* 2.2 [1999] <*http://eserver.org/clogic/2–2/williams.html*>).

40   The echoes of Dos Passos's and Joyce's techniques are mentioned briefly in Williams ("Issue of Corporations") and those of Dos Passos also in Buell (*Writing for an Endangered World,* 55).

41   Scott notes that Powers's "chronicle of Clare, Inc. . . . [is] less the company's history than its life story" ("A Matter of Life and Death," 38).

N. Katherine Hayles   Saving the Subject: Remediation in *House of Leaves*

Is it possible to save the subject now that it has been imploded by Jean Baudrillard, deconstructed by Jacques Derrida, and pronounced dead by Fredric Jameson, only to be revived as a schizophrenic? (Not to mention its re-creation as an infinitely malleable information pattern by biomedical practices like the Visible Human Project.) For writers who hope to make a living from their work, the problem with such high-tech and high-theory exercises is that the majority of mainstream, nonacademic readers continue to believe they possess coherent subjectivities; moreover, they like to read about characters represented as people like themselves, which the recent success of Jonathan Franzen's *The Corrections* demonstrates. In *House of Leaves*, Mark Danielewski has found a way to subvert and have his subject at the same time.

Camouflaged as a haunted-house tale, *House of Leaves* is a metaphysical inquiry worlds away from the likes of *The Amityville Horror*. It instantiates the crisis characteristic of postmodernism, in which representation is short-circuited by the realization that there is no reality independent of mediation. Rather than trying to penetrate cultural constructions to reach an original object of inquiry, *House of Leaves* uses the very multilayered inscriptions that create it as a physical artifact to imagine the subject as a palimpsest, emerging not behind but through the inscriptions that bring the book into being. Its putative subject is the film *The Navidson Record*, produced by the world-famous photographer Will Navidson after he, his partner Karen Green, and their two children, Chad and Daisy, occupy the House of Ashtree Lane in a move intended to strengthen their strained relationships and knit

American Literature, Volume 74, Number 4, December 2002. Copyright © 2002 by Duke University Press.

them closer as a family. Precisely the opposite happens when the House is revealed as a shifting labyrinth of enormous proportions, leading to the horrors recorded on the high-8 videos Will installed throughout the house to memorialize their move. From this video footage he made *The Navidson Record*, which then becomes the subject of an extensive commentary by the solitary Zampanò. When the old man is discovered dead in his apartment, the trunk containing his notes, scribblings, and speculations is inherited by the twenty-something Johnny Truant, who sets about ordering them into a commentary to which he supplies footnotes, which in *Pale Fire* fashion balloon into a competing but complementary narrative of their own. Zampanò's commentary, set in Times font, occupies the upper portion of the pages while Johnny's footnotes live below the line in Courier, but this initial ordering becomes increasingly complex as the book proceeds.

Equally complex is the ontological status of objects represented in the book and, ultimately, the status of the book itself. In his introduction, Johnny Truant reveals that the film *The Navidson Record*, about which he, Zampanò, and others write thousands of pages, may in fact be a hoax: "After all, as I fast discovered, Zampanò's entire project is about a film which doesn't even exist. You can look as I have, but no matter how long you search you will never find The Navidson Record in theaters or video stores. Furthermore, most of what's said by famous people has been made up. I tried contacting all of them. Those that took the time to respond told me they had never heard of Will Navidson let alone Zampanò."[1] Yet as the voluminous pages testify, the lack of a real world referent does not result in mere absence. Zampanò's account contains allusions, citations, and analyses of hundreds of interpretations of *The Navidson Record*, along with hundreds more ancillary texts. Johnny Truant's footnotes, parasitically attaching themselves to Zampanò's host commentary, are parasited in turn by footnotes written by the anonymous "Editors," upon which are hyperparasitically fastened the materials in the exhibits, appendix, and index (which like the index of Nabokov's *Pale Fire* turns out to be an encrypted pseudonarrative of its own).

To make matters worse (or better), this proliferation of words happens in the represented world on astonishingly diverse media that match in variety and strangeness the words' sources. The inscription technologies include film, video, photography, tattoos, typewriters, telegraphy, handwriting, and digital computers. The inscription surfaces are no less varied, as Johnny Truant observes about Zampanò's notes, which include writings on "old napkins, the tattered edges of an envelope, once even on the back of a postage stamp; everything and anything but empty; each fragment completely covered with the creep of years and years of ink pronouncements; layered, crossed out, amended; handwritten, typed; legible, illegible; impenetrable, lucid; torn, stained, scotch taped; some bits crisp and clean, others faded, burnt or folded and refolded so many times the creases have obliterated whole passages of god knows what—sense? truth? deceit?" (xvii). Despite his uncertainty (or perhaps because of it), Johnny Truant adds to these "snarls" by more obsessive writing on diverse surfaces, annotating, correcting, recovering, blotting out and amending Zampanò's words, filling out a journal, penning letters and poems, even scribbling on the walls of his studio apartment until all available inscription surfaces are written and overwritten with words and images.

None of the dynamics displayed in *House of Leaves* is entirely original, yet the bits and pieces add up to something specific, if not unique. What distinguishes *House of Leaves* is the way it uses familiar techniques to accomplish two goals. First, it extends the claims of the print book by showing what print can be in a digital age; second, it recuperates the vitality of the novel as a genre by recovering, *through the processes of remediation*, subjectivities coherent enough to become the foci of the sustained narration that remains the hallmark of the print novel. Remediation, the re-presentation of material that has already been represented in another medium, has a long and rich history, as Richard Grusin and Jay Bolter point out in their pioneering book on the subject.[2] But the cycling through media has been greatly expanded and accelerated by the advent of digital technologies. The computer has often been proclaimed the ultimate medium because it can incorporate every other medium within itself. As if learning about omnivorous appetite from the computer, *House of Leaves*, in a frenzy of remediation, attempts to eat all the other media. This binging, however, leaves traces on the text's body, resulting in a transformed physical and narrative corpus. In a sense, *House of Leaves* recuperates the traditions of the print book—particularly the novel as a literary form—but the price it pays is a metamorphosis so profound that it becomes a new kind of form and artifact. It is an open question whether this transformation represents the rebirth of the novel or the beginning of the novel's displacement by a hybrid discourse that as yet has no name.

These transformative processes are on display in an early scene between Will Navidson and Karen Green, related by Zampanò, who positions his readers as first-person viewers watching the film of *The Navidson Record* along with him. Since the film does not exist, his description, which inevitably interprets as well as remediates, creates the film as an object within the text and also as a putative object in the represented world. He describes how Navidson takes Karen's jewelry box out of a crate and removes the lid and inner tray to look inside, although "[u]nfortunately, whatever he sees inside is invisible to the camera" (10). Later when we learn that Karen keeps old love letters in her jewelry box, the moment retrospectively becomes fraught with an invasion of her privacy and Navidson's implicit jealousy. Then Karen comes in as Navidson is pulling a clump of her hair from her hairbrush. Watching him toss it into the wastebasket, she tries to snatch the hair, saying: "Just you watch, one day I'll go bald, then won't you be sorry you threw that away," whereupon Will grins and replies, "No." Zampanò's commentary focuses on "the multiple ways in which these few seconds demonstrate how much Will values Karen" (11). Despite the casual way Will handles her things, Zampanò's interpretation claims that Will has "in effect preserved her hair" and "called into question his own behavior" through the way he edits the images, thus contrasting his attitude at the time he edited the video with his apparent disregard for her privacy at the time that the high-8 camera caught his actions.

The layering here is already four-fold, moving from Will and Karen at the time of filming, through Will as he edits the film, to Zampanò's initial viewing of the film, and then to his re-creation of the scene for us, the putative viewers, who of course read words rather than see images and so add a fifth layer of mediation. The layering is further complicated when Zampanò introduces "Samuel T. Glade," a critic who points out the ambiguity of Will's "No," arguing that it could refer to "'watch,' 'bald,' or 'sorry' or all three" (11). As the meanings proliferate, Will's relationship with Karen becomes similarly multi-layered and complex, combining disregard with tenderness, jealousy with regret, playful resistance to her chiding with a deep wish to recover what he has thrown away. But these complexities all come from the multiple remediations of the supposedly original moment, recorded on a film that does not exist in a house that cannot be because it violates the fundamental laws of physics. Thus subjects (in this case, Will, Karen, and their relationship) are evacuated as originary objects of representation but reconstituted through multiple layers of remediation.

The pattern is repeated throughout the text. When relationships are not mediated by inscription technologies they decay toward alienation, and when they are mediated, they progress toward intimacy. Karen's distrust of Will grows as he becomes increasingly infatuated with exploring the House, and only when she makes a film about him, "A Brief History of Who I Love," can she see him with fresh eyes and rekindle her love. Here is Zampanò's interpretation of the process: "The diligence, discipline, and time-consuming research required to fashion this short—there are easily over a hundred edits—allowed Karen for the first time to see Navidson as something other than her own personal fears and projections" (368). Will undergoes a similar process when he makes "Tom's Story," his edited version of the videotape that records his brother Tom while Will forges ahead to explore the House. When Will returns to find that Tom has left his post, he bitterly complains: "'This is Tom. This is what Tom does best. He lets you down'" (277). Only in retrospect, after he edits the tape following Tom's death, does Will recapture their childhood closeness and recuperate a far more loving vision of Tom. Zampanò, calling the edited tape a "labor of love, a set piece sibling to Karen's short film on Navidson," stresses there is "nothing hasty about Tom's Story. Navidson has clearly put an enormous amount of work into these few minutes. Despite obvious technological limitations, the cuts are clean and sound beautifully balanced with the rhythm and order of every shot only serving to intensify even the most ordinary moment. . . . If Sorrow is *deep regret over someone loved*, there is nothing but regret here, as if Navidson with his great eye had for the first time seen what over the years he never should have missed" (274).

Although we can tease out a temporal sequence for the events represented in *The Navidson Record*, these actions are screened through a complex temporality of remediation. The mediation plot, if I may call it that, proceeds from the narration of the film as a representation of events; to its narration as an artifact, in which editing transforms meaning; to the narration of different critical views about the film; to Zampanò's narration as he often disagrees with and reinterprets these interpretations; and finally to Johnny's commentary on Zampanò's narration. Onto this already complex pastiche is layered a related but distinct temporality constituted by the different processes of inscription. This sequence begins with articles and books that Zampanò collects and reinscribes in his commentary, proceeds to Johnny's writing as he orders Zampanò's notes into a manuscript, and supposedly ends with the editors' emendations and publisher's interventions as they convert the manuscript to a print book. Onto the chronology of events and the order of telling are thus overlaid further temporal complexities introduced by recognizing that the narration is not an oral production but a palimpsest of inscriptions on diverse media. Consequently, the story's architecture is envisioned not as a sequential narrative so much as alternative paths within the same immense labyrinth of fictional space-time that is also, and simultaneously, a rat's nest of inscription surfaces. Moreover, these surfaces prove as resistant to logical ordering as the House is to coherent mapping. Locating itself within these labyrinthine spaces, the text enfolds together the objects represented and the media used to represent them.

At the same time, the text insists on its specificity as a print novel, showing a heightened self-awareness about its own materiality. This self-consciousness is evident if we compare the narrative strategies of *House of Leaves* with those of the turn-of-the-century novel as it began to move away from realism and into stream of consciousness. It is a critical truism that when Marlow sits on the deck of the *Nellie* and spins his tale in *Heart of Darkness*, his consciousness creates multiple layers within the narration. The account of Kurtz's death that he delivers to the Intended differs from his narration of that moment to the men on the ship, and both accounts can be supposed to differ, subtly or substantially, from the one he would relate to himself. But there is no recognition in the text of how these multiple oral narrations are transcribed into writing. However visible the mediations of consciousness (and unconsciousness), the technologies of inscription are invisible, their effects erased from the narrative world. Moreover, there is no consideration of how mastery of technique (or lack of it) might affect the inscriptions, whereas *House of Leaves* offers extended reflections on how Navidson's "great eye" affects the film Zampanò narrates.

In *Heart of Darkness* events are never seen apart from mediating consciousness; in *House of Leaves*, consciousness is never seen apart from mediating inscription devices. The latter text emphasizes that people within the represented world—Will Navidson and Karen Green on one level, Zampanò on another, and Johnny Truant on yet another—

exist only because they have been recorded. Moreover, these characters participate in further cycles of remediation as they use inscription technologies to explore past trauma, reenvision damaged relationships, and understand the relation of themselves and others to the inscriptions that bring them into being. The unreliable narrator, a literary invention foregrounding the role of consciousness in constructing reality, has here given way to the remediated narrator, a literary invention foregrounding a proliferation of inscription technologies that evacuate consciousness as the source of production and recover in its place a mediated subjectivity that cannot be conceived as an independent entity. The relevant frame is no longer consciousness alone but consciousness fused with technologies of inscription.

It is not difficult to hear in some of Zampanò's remarks the views of the author as he draws attention to this fusion. Zampanò's comments at the conclusion of the breathless narration in which the house eats Tom is a point where the action explodes and we are allowed for a moment to forget the layers of mediation separating us from the putative event. This momentary lapse into pseudorealistic narration ends as soon as the climactic sequence is over, when footnote 308 reminds us that "the chaotic bits of tape representing these events must be supplemented with Billy [Reston]'s narration" (346). Zampanò emphasizes that Navidson

> makes Reston the sequence's sole authority. This is odd, especially since Reston saw none of it. He is only recounting what Navidson told him himself. The general consensus has always been that the memory is simply too painful for Navidson to revisit. But there is another possibility: Navidson refuses to abandon the more perspicacious portion of his audience. By relying on Reston as the sole narrative voice, he subtly draws attention once again to the question of inadequacies in representation, no matter the medium, no matter how flawless. Here in particular, he mockingly emphasizes the fallen nature of any history by purposefully concocting an absurd number of generations. Consider: 1. Tom's broken hands→2. Navidson's perception of Tom's hurt→3. Navidson's description of Tom's hurt to Reston→4. Reston's re-telling of Navidson's description based on Navidson's recollection and perception of Tom's actual hurt. A pointed reminder that representation does not replace. It only offers distance and in rare cases perspective. (346)

The "pointed reminder" sharpens when we discover that the Last Interview is missing, so that we see the complex chain of mediation only through Zampanò's written remediation of it, remediated in turn by Johnny and the editors.

As if resisting its own dynamic, the narration has moments when it anguishes over the evacuation of the subject and substitution of proliferating mediations. The most dramatic centers on Navidson's relation to the photograph that won him a Pulitzer Prize, a representation of a starving Sudanese girl gnawing on a bare bone while a buzzard perches to one side.[3] Navidson's torment focuses not so much on the morality of representing the girl as on the priorities that made him take the photograph first and run for help second, a hopeless dash that failed to rescue her from death. Calling the image "Delial," he hoards the name to himself, thereby awakening Karen's jealousy when she hears him murmur the name in his sleep and he refuses to tell her who it is. She finally makes the connection while filming "A Brief History of Who I Love," when she discovers the name penciled on the back of the photograph. That the name refers to the photographic image is made clear in the tortured letter Will writes to Karen on the eve of returning to the House, confessing that it is "the name I gave to the girl in the photo that won me all the fame and gory [one of the significant typos Danielewski inserts], that's all she is Karen, just the photo" (391).[4] Although meant to reassure Karen that Delial is not her rival, Navidson's letter assigns the name to the image, not to the girl herself. A few lines later he tries to recover the girl—"Not the photo—the photo, that thing—but who she was," but he concludes this line of thought with the mediating phrase "you should have seen her," reimagining her as a picture he is taking now for Karen's benefit. When this thought is followed by "i miss miss miss," we can assume that his consciousness veers for a moment to the girl, but then it just as quickly slides back to the photograph—"but i didn't miss i got her along with the vulture in the background." The disgust that accompanies his return to remediation does nothing to mitigate its inevitability: "the real vulture was the guy with the camera preying on her for his fuck pulitzer prize" (392). Finally the issue is not whether mediation can be overcome but, rather, the price of sacrificing the evacuated subject to the demands of inscription technologies.

So intricate are the layers of mediation that seemingly unmediated moments are glaring in their incongruity once we notice them. Commenting upon how obsessed Navidson is with the house prior to his final exploration, Zampanò delivers the following account meant to show that Navidson has become deadened to stimuli that ordinarily would arouse intense emotions. The scene begins "back in October when Navidson first came across the tape of Wax kissing Karen," a sequence we have already read in another context. The point in Zampanò's retelling of the scene is that Navidson "hardly responded": "He viewed the scene twice, once at regular speed, the second time on fast forward, and then moved on to the rest of the footage without saying a word" (397). If we have not been entirely dazzled by the dizzying cycles of remediation, we might have our wits enough about us to ask, how can Zampanò possibly know how Navidson viewed this scene? There is no possibility that Zampanò was actually in the room, so he could know Navidson's reaction only if Navidson had recounted it in the missing Last Interview, about which nothing is said in the text, or had made a tape of himself editing the tape. But the tape of Navidson watching the tape would itself have been subject to editing, cuts, and other manipulations, so it could not function as a naive record but merely as another interpretation. Moreover, Zampanò's comments come not from his own viewing or reading but from his analysis of the Haven-Slocum Theory (HST), in whose view Navidson's lack of reaction becomes "highly climactic" precisely because it is an absence where there should have been a presence: "'The pain anyone else would have felt while viewing that screen kiss, in Navidson's case has been blunted by the grossly disproportionate trauma already caused by the house. In this regard it is in fact a highly climactic, if irregular moment, only because it is so disturbing to watch something so typically meaningful rendered so utterly inconsequential'" (397). The negative thrust of the convoluted argument may almost succeed in keeping us from noticing that there is no way the putative object of inquiry—Navidson watching the tape of the kiss—could have been observed by those who interpret it. This incongruity, a mediated version of what filmmakers call a continuity error, creates an absence at the center of the presence manufactured by the multiple layers of interpretation. The interpretation exists—several layers, in fact—but the real-world object is as elusive to conjure as the House of Ashtree Lane, an impossible object because its interior dimensions exceed its exterior measurements.

Mark Johnson and George Lakoff have written about the elemental schema that express themselves in "metaphors we live by," so pervasive and fundamental that they are often not even recognized as metaphors.[5] In the schema inside-outside and container-contained, for example, we assume, without thinking much about it, that the contained must be smaller than the container, if only by the thickness of the walls. Violating these preconscious assumptions, the impossible House nevertheless enters the space of representation, much like M. C. Escher's ascending-descending staircases (references to Escher's self-deconstructing spaces pepper the *House*'s footnotes). The House is undeniably present within the text, yet in crucial aspects it remains unrepresentable. The interior hallway that mysteriously creates a door in the living room where there was none before leads to spaces supposedly contained by the dimensions of an ordinary two-bedroom family house that are greater than the diameter of the earth and older than the solar system.

The absence at the center of this space is not merely nothing. It is so commanding and absolute that it paradoxically becomes an especially intense kind of presence, violent in its impossibility and impossible to ignore. Navidson, insisting that his documentary should be taken literally, is quoted by Zampanò as saying: "'And if one day you find yourself passing by that house, don't stop, don't slow down, just keep going. There's nothing there. Beware'" (4). Only if we read "nothing" as a substantive does this passage make sense, a negation converted into the looming threat of something, although it is impossible to say what unless it be negation itself, working to obliterate our everyday assumptions about reality.

One of the tropes for this threat is the beast that manifests itself through physical traces that always remain shy of verifiable presence. So we read about the mysterious claw marks of some enormous paw that Johnny finds alongside Zampanò's dead body; the deep growls that issue from the House, untraceable traces that may be the sound of the beast or perhaps just the House groaning in its endless rearrangements; the rending of the fluorescent markers with which the explorers try to map the House's interior, along with the destruction of their supplies; the rank odor that Johnny first encounters in Zampanò's apartment and that he identifies then with the smell of history; the ominous creatures that populate the margins of Chad and Daisy's classroom drawings, with the intense black square in the middle that grows larger in each painting; the black hand of darkness that swipes into the camera frame to consume Holloway's dead body. Representing both the interiority of psychological trauma and the exteriority of raging appetite, the beast, like the House itself, inhabits a borderland between the metaphoric and the literal, the imaginary and the real.

Nowhere is the dance between presence and absence more deftly executed than in the scene where Johnny goes into the storeroom at the tattoo shop to load a tray with ink. As the door swings shut behind him, he suddenly senses that something is going "extremely wrong" and thinks he sees the beast's eyes "full of blood." The narration from this point on is full of contradictions. He smells a stench, and we may believe it is the rank smell of the beast until Johnny confesses: "I've shit myself. Pissed myself too." Increasingly incoherent, he sees the "shape of a shape of a shape of a face dis(as)sembling right before my eyes" (71). He bolts from the storeroom through a door that is inexplicably open rather than shut and tumbles down the stairs as "[s]omething hisses and slashes out at the back of my neck." Although a client in the shop later calls Johnny's attention to the "long bloody scratch" on the back of his neck, other details he reported come undone in the continuing narration. He discovers, for example, that he has not soiled his pants after all. Moreover, the scratch that remains the only verifiable evidence of the encounter recalls the half-moon cuts his mother left on his neck when she tried to strangle him at age seven. Is the triply mediated "shape of a shape of a shape of a face" the face of the beast or of the mother who remains an incomprehensible object for Johnny in the intensity of her love, equaled only by the ferocity of her insanity and abuse?

The ambiguities already inscribed in the scene intensify when Johnny looks down at his body covered by the ink spilled in his mad dash down the stairs and sees it as an "omen." "I'm doused in black ink, my hands now completely covered, and [I] see the floor is black, and—have you anticipated this or should I be more explicit?—jet on jet; for a blinding instant I have watched my hand vanish, in fact all of me has vanished, one hell of a disappearing act too, the already foreseen dissolution of the self, lost without contrast, slipping into oblivion" (72). At this point the "foreseen" dissolution of his identity connects with the beast as a signifier of absence, a negation that spreads like an inkblot to encompass his subjectivity. But then the passage continues by recovering, through a doubly mediated reflection, the blotted-out subject: "until mid-gasp I catch sight of my reflection in the back of the tray, the ghost in the way; seems I'm not gone, not quite. My face has been splattered with purple, as have my arms, granting contrast, and thus defining me, marking me, and at least for the moment, preserving me" (72). The purple ink that brings back portions of his splattered face recalls the purple nail polish his mother wore the day her fingernails dug into his neck, marking him in a complex act of inscription that here merges with the purple and black ink to form an overdetermined double writing that operates simultaneously to negate and assert, obliterate and create, erase and mark.

Through innovative typography and other devices, *House of Leaves* foregrounds its materiality, which depends on physical properties, though not in a naive or unequivocal way, because the number of physical properties that can be brought into play is essentially infinite. Of all the attributes we might potentially notice about a book, a small number are selected by the semiotic content and mobilized as resources so that they become part of the book's signifying practices. Materiality thus *emerges* from the interplay between physical attributes and semiotic components.[6] As such, it cannot be specified in advance, for it will vary according to how a work mobilizes physical attributes to create meaning. Moreover, what these physical properties mean may change over the course of the narrative, their mutating significations functioning as a kind of materialist equivalent to character development. Something like a version of the hermeneutic circle is thus at work here. The verbal content gives meaning to physical properties, which inflect the verbal content at the same time. The verbal and nonverbal evolve together toward emergent meanings that change dynamically as the narrative progresses. When physical properties enter deeply into the text's signifying practices, as they do with *House of Leaves*, a mode of analysis attentive to the specificity of the medium is required to account for the full range of semiotic strategies the text employs. I have called this kind of inquiry media-specific analysis (MSA) and argued that the rich medial ecology of contemporary analogue and digital cultures makes MSA a necessity.[7] To develop this point as vividly as possible, I will enter the hermeneutic circle by considering first nonverbal marks, working out from there to their interplay with words and the resulting active construction of the book's materiality.

The two sites that will provide most of my examples are the typographically innovative chapter 9 and the action-oriented chapter 10, a convenient pair because, as opposites in many ways, they mobilize the book's physical properties for different kinds of work. Whereas chapter 9 has more words per page than any other chapter in the book, chapter 10 has fewer. The action in chapter 9 is subordinated to philosophical digressions, long lists of names that seem to be selected almost at random, and stories nested within stories vertiginous in their interconnections. By contrast, chapter 10 consists mostly of action sequences recounting Reston and Navidson's attempt to rescue the wounded Wax, and Jed's murder by the increasingly insane Holloway. Johnny Truant's footnotes in this chapter are remarkably sparse, allowing the focus to stay mostly with the action narrated by Zampanò. In the "Suggested Chapter Titles" included in the appendix, Zampanò names chapter 9 "The Labyrinth," orienting it toward a form deeply invested with metaphysical significance, whereas chapter 10 is called "The Rescue (Part I)," identifying it with the narrated action (540).

The most obvious physical attributes of chapter 9 are the diversity of fonts and the orientation of the type, set so that it goes in many directions, including upside down, sideways, and in reverse. The title "The Labyrinth" makes explicit what is already implicit in the typography: *House of Leaves* mirrors the House on Ashtree Lane, both of which are imaged as a labyrinth, a figure embossed in black-on-black on the cover. Like the House on Ashtree Lane, *House of Leaves* has a nothingness at its core so intense that it becomes an especially violent kind of presence, engaging in interplays that violate our assumption that the outside encompasses the inside and the container surrounds the contained. Zampanò, citing critic Penelope Reed Doob, quotes a passage in which she distinguishes between one who is trapped inside a labyrinth and so suffers confusion and one who can see the labyrinth from above and comprehend its plan. "Unfortunately," he continues in his own voice, "the dichotomy between those who participate inside and those who view from the outside breaks down when considering the house, simply because no one ever sees that labyrinth in its entirety. Therefore comprehension of its intricacies must always be derived from within" (114). Zampanò remarks that the same is true for the film *The Navidson Record*. Although he cannot say so from his position within the text, we might wonder if this immersion also holds true for us as we read *House of Leaves*, another labyrinth in which, Johnny warns, we will become so entangled that we will not be able to extricate ourselves. The labyrinth thus becomes a trope for incomplete knowledge as well as a site where paradoxical inversions become highly energized as absence flips into presence, the contained stretches far beyond its container, and outside becomes inside becomes outside.

The analogy between the labyrinthine physical form of chapter 9 and these inversions can be traced through footnote 144 (119). This extremely odd annotation perches near the top of the page inside a box outlined with a blue line, a significant hue because it is the color used for the word "House," which appears in blue throughout the text, including equivalent words in languages other than English (such as *casa* and *Haus*). The footnote is attached to a passage in which Zampanò remarks upon the "utter blankness" found within the House's mysterious interior: "Nothing there provides a reason to linger. In part because not one object, let alone fixture or other manner of finish work has ever been discovered there" (119). Despite Zampanò's comment that we should not linger, footnote 144 attempts to enumerate over the space of twenty-five pages everything that is *not* in the House, from hot-air registers and bathtubs to a Christmas tree. Since nothing is in the House, the list of what is absent, even if limited to accoutrements usually found in houses, is infinite. If we read the blue color as an evocation of the blue screen of a movie backdrop onto which anything can be projected, then the text is attempting to project into this space the linguistic signifiers for everything in the world, as if attempting to make up through verbal proliferation the absolute emptiness of the House as a physical space.

Moreover, the type is set so that when we turn the page over, the words inside the blue box are repeated from the other side—but in reverse, as if we were seeing them from the inside of a barbershop window decorated with text meant to be read from the outside. The box calls into question an assumption so commonplace that we are not normally aware of it: book pages are opaque, a property that defines one page as separate from another. Here the back of the page seems to open transparently onto the front, a notion that overruns the boundary between them and constructs the page as a leaky container rather than an unambiguous unit of print. Treating the page as a window can be seen as a way to compensate for the House's viewless interior. After denying us any transparency through which we can look into or out of the House, the text turns its own material substrate into a window that proposes to bring into view everything not in the house, an enterprise as paradoxical as it is quixotic.

Even after the words cease, the box in which they were inscribed continues to signify. It next appears bereft of words but filled with light blue color, as if it has once again become the blue screen of film production. The reverse of this page shows the box filled in with black ink, an image that suggests either nothingness or inscriptions so densely overwritten that they have obliterated themselves. The facing page shows only a blank space where the box has been, its defining blue border erased along with the text. Thus the fullness of an ink-black square is linked with nothingness, the blue screen of infinite malleability with the articulation of an infinite series, the opaque front of a page with a transparent back. The dynamic interplay between words, nonverbal marks, and physical properties of the page work together to construct the book's materiality so that it functions as a mirror to the mysterious House, reversing, reflecting, and inverting its characteristics even as it foregrounds its own role as a container for the fictional universe in which such an impossible object could exist.

These effects are specific to the print book; they could not operate in the same way in any other medium. In an interview with Larry McCaffrey and Sinda Gregory, Danielewski relates a fascinating story about the origins of *House of Leaves* that illuminates the privileged status the book claims for the print novel.[8] Danielewski's father was a midlevel filmmaker and a devoted student of the medium. He owned a projector and professional screen and would frequently bring films home for Mark and his sister to view, even when they were very young. After dinner the father would put on a film and expect the children to watch it with rapt attention. When it was over, the father would grill them, asking detailed questions about edits, scene construction, and other technical matters (a practice that no doubt sheds light on the theme of narcissistic parents that runs through *House of Leaves*).

A crisis in the relationship came when Mark was in his early twenties and his father was hospitalized for prostate cancer, possibly terminal. Distraught, Mark channeled his intense emotions into a short story, "Redwood," a coded narrative about his relationship with his father. He showed it to his father in the hospital, who understood it was about their relationship and responded by becoming enraged, taunting Mark by saying he should stop wasting his time writing and get a job at the post office. Mark was so devastated that he tore up the story and threw it into a dumpster. As far as he was concerned, that was the end of his writing career. A few days later, his sister invited him to dinner. After a lovely meal, she presented him with a manila folder. He opened it to discover she had retrieved the pieces of paper from the dumpster and painstakingly taped them back together. That rescued story became the kernel of *House of Leaves*.

The anecdote suggests that the book's remediation of film is, along with much else, the mark of a generational struggle, the son claiming the right to his own voice by encapsulating the father's medium within his. Moreover, although Danielewski has received several lucrative offers for movie options, he remains adamant that he will not allow the book to be made into a film.[9] Unlike artists and writers who choose to work in digital media, Danielewski, in his midthirties, is young enough to take computers for granted. The daring move for him is not to adopt them but to return to the print book and reinvigorate it by extending its claims in relation to a plethora of competing media. To designate texts that display this heightened sense of their materiality, I have coined the term *technotext*. Produced by inscription technologies, technotexts construct their materialities so as to foreground the inscription technologies that produce them.[10]

Richard Lanham has written about the complementary perspectives of *looking through* a page (when we are immersed in a fictional world and so are scarcely conscious of the page as a material object) and *looking at* the page, when innovative typography and other interventions encourage us to focus on the page's physical properties. When we struggle in *House of Leaves* to read the reverse type in the blue box, we are both concentrating on decoding text and aware of being positioned as if we are looking through the page to the other side. The blue box illustrates the more general phenomenon in *House of Leaves* of collapsing these two perspectives into one, so that *looking through* and *looking at* become the same action. Configured to create this double vision, the surface of the page is also arranged to accommodate multiple voices, signified in this chapter by different spatial orientations as the type runs in many directions. Even in chapters more decorous than this one, narrative multiplicity is indicated through spatial form. Rather than a spatially continuous narrative in which different voices speak in turn, as when dialogue is indicated by paragraph breaks in a realistic novel, *House of Leaves* creates spatially distinct narratives with multiple cross connections, as if multiple voices were speaking simultaneously. Instead of temporal sequence indicated by spatial continuity, *House of Leaves* uses spatial discontinuity to indicate temporal simultaneity.

This multiplicity is characteristic of hypertext, which Jane Yellowlees Douglas and others have defined as a rhetorical form having multiple reading paths, chunked text, and a linking mechanism connecting the chunks.[11] Many technotexts, including *House of Leaves*, also qualify as hypertexts. Remarking on the relation of his narrative to Zampanò's commentary, Johnny writes in chapter 8 ("SOS"): "There's just too much of it anyway, always running parallel . . . to the old man and his book, briefly appearing, maybe even intruding, then disappearing again" (106). He calls it "another type of signal," parodying it as "Here Come Dots," a phrase that applies as well to the dots that carry their own cryptic signals in this chapter. As Johnny's remark suggests, the linking mechanisms are diverse, consisting not only of footnotes on footnotes (on footnotes) but also positional cues, nonalphabetic marks such as the dots and alchemical symbols, and complex intertextual references as the narrative weaves from Zampanò's text remediated by Johnny to Johnny's text remediated by the editors.

Page position also serves as an important linking mechanism, especially in chapter 9, enabling the reader to follow one path (for example, the potentially infinite list in the blue-lined boxes on pages 119 through 144) or skip between paths. Alternative narrative strands include such supplementary material as footnote 182 extending over four pages and listing documentary filmmakers in no apparent order (139–42). Like the text in the blue box, footnote 182 is printed with the text appearing backward on the reverse page. Now the reverse text does not repeat the filmmakers' names but, rather, lists the names of their films. Rather than signifying a transparent window, the page functions here like a film screen, where in front sit the filmmakers (in the remediated form of names on a page), and behind the page are the titles signifying the represented world of their films. We read these titles as if we were positioned behind the screen, a typographic effect signaling an ontological distinction between us as readers in the real world (backstage of the action, as it were) and the filmmakers' names as marks within the represented world. The text of footnote 182 runs at 90 degrees to the blue box, suggesting an orthogonal relation between the page as window and the page as screen surface. Whereas the box lists everything that is not in the house, footnote 182 lists all the film-makers who presumably might have made a film like *The Navidson Record* but did not. One signifies the absence of objects, the other the absence of inscriptions that could represent these objects.

Chapter 10, in contrast to the densely worded pages of chapter 9, uses large expanses of white space to create visual patterns that mirror the narrative action. In a conversation with Danielewski, I suggested that the typography in this chapter is mimetic.[12] When the rope holding the gurney stretches as the stairway suddenly begins expanding, for example, the text also stretches, taking three pages to inscribe the word "snaps" (294–96). Other passages show the amount of text on the page decreasing as Navidson crawls into tighter and tighter passages, as if the body of the text were getting squeezed along with the photographer's body. While not denying these effects, Danielewski pointed out a subtler correspondence between reading speed and the emotional pacing of the narrative. Drawing an analogy with filmmaking techniques that correlate the intensity of the scene with how much the viewer's eye has to move across the screen, he suggested that the typography creates a similar correspondence between how much time it takes to read a page and the represented action.

His remark encouraged me to notice that in chapter 9, reading speed slows down enormously as the reader struggles with seemingly endless lists, separate narrative threads in different page positions, type that runs in many directions, and proliferating footnotes that amble on for pages. And what of the action? Chapter 9 is where Zampanò's narrative, with its inevitable interpretations and digressions, recounts Exploration #4, in which Holloway, Wax, and Jed explore the House's interior. As Holloway grows increasingly irrational, they separate and become adversaries. After the now insanely paranoid Holloway shoots Wax, presumably mistaking him for the beast, he begins to hunt his former comrades in earnest to wipe out the traces of his mistake. But the account of this action is often delayed, as when the narrative tells us that "even as Holloway Roberts, Jed Leeder, and Wax Hook make their way further down the staircase in **Exploration #4**, the purpose of that vast place still continues to elude them" (111), a remark that prefaces a seven-page digression before we return to this scene. The reader who understandably wants to turn pages quickly to find out what happens will be frustrated by philosophical meditations on how digital technology has eroded the sense of the real in photography, a crucial rewriting of the Minotaur myth by Zampanò in footnote "~~123~~" with overstrikes that continue in all the text associated with the Minotaur, and an account of a mutiny against Magellan carried out by Quesada with the help of his servant Molino.[13]

The effect of the multilayered digressions is to embed the action in such diverse information that either the reader foregoes the pleasurable suspense of the horror story or devours it and skips everything else. Just as the House can stretch to incredible dimensions and lure the explorers into long treks that culminate in dead ends, so the narrative entices us into following up on footnote 171, where Zampanò refers us to "*The Song of Quesada and Molino* by [XXXX]," to which is attached footnote 172 telling us the text in brackets is illegible (137), a tease repeated on a larger scale in Section E of the appendix, which contains only the title "The Song of Quesada and Molino" and footnote 433 by "Ed." telling us this document is missing (556).

The House can also mysteriously contract, transforming an impossibly long return into an easy stroll to the living room door. Analogously, the rescue recounted in chapter 10 proceeds with minimal digressions and often with only a few words on a page, allowing the reader to zip through this story of how Navy and Reston save the wounded Wax and lose Jed to Holloway's bullet. Whether excruciatingly slow or amazingly fast, the time it takes to read a page functions as a remediation of the narrative action in the life-world of the reader, linking real-time decoding with the intensity and pacing of the represented events in a correlation that itself is a remediation of eye-tracking in cinematic action. Here the materiality of the page is mobilized to create a cybernetic loop that runs from the page through the reader's body and back to the page, a process that links the temporality of reading with the emotional pacing of the narrative. As a consequence, the time of reading no longer takes place in an ontologically distinct realm separate from the narrative but itself is used as a resource for literary effects.

Another category of nonverbal marks that appears frequently in chapter 9 is the overstrike that marks all the passages concerned with the Minotaur, who would of course inhabit this labyrinthine chapter. The Minotaur is introduced in typically circuitous fashion by the theory that Zampanò summarizes from an article variously entitled "Birth Defects in Knossos" (which footnote 123 identifies as published

in the Sonny Won't Wait Flyer, Santa Cruz 1968) or "Violent Preju-
dice in Knossos" (identified by footnote 124 as appearing in the Sonny
Will Wait Flyer, Santa Cruz 1969, and followed by footnote 125 by
Johnny, which says he does not know why the two citations differ
[111–12]). In this monstrously double-headed article, Zampanò suggests that the Minotaur was actually the deformed son of King Minos,
who is ashamed of his offspring and hides him in the labyrinth; this
theory forms the basis for Taggert Chiclitz's play *The Minotaur* (perhaps a nod to the Bloody Chiclitz of Pynchonian fame). We know about
Zampanò's theory and Chiclitz's play only because Johnny includes
it despite the overstrikes, so we are constantly aware that the Minotaur text is under erasure. "Big deal," Johnny writes about his textual rescue, "except while personally preventing said eradication, I
discovered a particularly disturbing coincidence" (336). Although he
does not specify the coincidence, we can guess it is the discovery that
within the phrase "The Minotaur" is the anagram "O Im he Truant."
On a more general level, the coincidence may be the special affinity
this son of a crazy woman and doomed father feels for Zampanò's tale
of an abused son imprisoned by his father in a labyrinth, much as
Johnny becomes imprisoned in the textual labyrinth he inherits from
Zampanò (a correspondence hinted at in the Sonny Will/Won't Wait
flyers. Whose son is Sonny?).

In Chiclitz's play (as summarized by Zampanò), King Minos slowly
comes to love his deformed son and is devastated when the boy is
killed by a brutal Theseus (described by Chiclitz as a "drunken, virtually retarded, frat boy" [111]). The tale is remediated in Johnny's
dream, the first that he has been able to remember, when he experiences himself as a Minotaur wandering an enormous labyrinth, put
there "by an old man, a dead man," which would seem to refer to
Zampanò but also "by one who called me son though he was not my
father," the phrase Johnny uses to refer to his brutal foster father Raymond (404). In the dream, characters swirl and melt together. Johnny
encounters a "drunken frat boy" with arms scarred from hot oil, as are
Johnny's from the hot oil his mother dropped on him. The frat boy then
metamorphoses into a female figure, face glowing "with adoration and
warmth," who with infinite tenderness is trying to hack Johnny into
pieces (405). But then he remembers he is powerful: he can resist
and need not play the helpless victim. After the dream he sells the
hart-shaped locket he inherited from his mother, a remembrance with
which he had earlier said he would never part.

The locket connects his narrative to Holloway's mediated autobiography (narrated to a psychiatrist whose notes are appropriated by a critic whom Zampanò cites and criticizes). As an adult, Holloway is tormented by the memory of the girl, doe-like in her fragility, who jilted him when he was a teenager, linked in his mind with the doe he accidentally shot as a young man, earning the scorn of his father. Johnny, as if infected by Holloway through sharing the hart-doe image the way one drug addict infects another by sharing needles, buys two guns, one the same kind with which Holloway committed suicide, and keeps them under his bed as a last resort. "There's only one choice now," he muses: "[F]inish what Zampanò himself failed to finish. Reinter this thing into a binding tomb. Make it <u>only</u> a book, and if that doesn't help," the guns will (327). Zampanò, for his part, writes the following on a scrap of paper included in the appendix under "Bits": "Perhaps in the margins of darkness, I could create a son who is not missing; who lives beyond even my own imagination and invention; whose lusts, stupidities, and strengths carry him farther than even he or I can anticipate. . . . He will fulfill a promise I made years ago but failed to keep" (543). Johnny's determination to make the book stay decently under its covers, figured as a kind of death that will render the text safely inert, is subverted by the links to Johnny in Zampanò's narrative, an inversion of inside-outside that deconstructs the idea that this book can be bound so that its leaves will not spill out of their container.

What are we to make of Zampanò's suggestion that Johnny is the son who fulfills his promise? Logically, Johnny's commentary encapsulates Zampanò's notes, since it is Johnny who orders, edits, restores, and amends them. He can comment upon Zampanò, but not the other way around; in this sense, Johnny has ontological priority. As Kinbote observes in *Pale Fire*, "For better or worse, it is the commentator who has the last word."[14] But these commonsense rules no more hold in *House of Leaves* than the maxim that the inside of a house cannot be bigger than the outside. Musing on his commentary, Johnny senses a vertiginous inversion of inside and outside:

> More and more often, I've been overcome by the strangest feeling that I've gotten it all turned around, by which I mean to say— to state the not-so-obvious—without it *I* would perish. A moment comes when suddenly everything seems impossibly far and confused, my sense of self derealized & depersonalized, the disorientation so severe I actually believe—and let me tell you it is an

intensely strange instance of belief—that this terrible sense of relatedness to Zampanò's work implies something that just can't be,
namely that this thing has created me; not me unto it, but now it
unto me, where I am nothing more than the matter of some other
voice, intruding through the folds of what even now lies there agape,
possessing me with histories I should never recognize as my own;
inventing me, defining me, directing me until finally every association I can claim as my own . . . is relegated to nothing; forcing me to
face the most terrible suspicion of all, that all of this has just been
made up and what's worse, not made up by me or even for that matter Zampanò.

   Though by whom I have no idea. (326)

Johnny's intuition that he is "made up" by someone he cannot see
opens onto the higher ontological level of Danielewski, the creator
of this fictional world. These connections make clear that the book
refuses to lie quiescent in its "binding tomb." Just as the House
walls endlessly rearrange themselves, so the ontological distinctions
that separate Navidson from Zampanò, Zampanò from Johnny, Johnny
from Danielewski, and Danielewski from the reader keep shifting and
changing.

   The overstrike that marks all the Minotaur passages also functions
as a hypertext link; when it appears over text that is not obviously
about the Minotaur, it works to connect that text with the fabulous
beast. Marked similarly by overstrikes is the classical tale of Perilaus, fabricator of a life-sized brass bull designed as an instrument
of torture. Victims were shoved inside the bull, under which a fire
was lit; their screams as they burned were translated, via a series
of pipes cunningly built into the bull's head, into a sound that Zampanò in footnote 301 calls a "~~strange m[]sic~~" (337). The missing letter
in "music" reminds us that this tale is mediated through Zampanò's
notes as restored by Johnny. It functions as a hole or window in the
word, an absence that becomes a signifier of remediation. The connections with the Minotaur story are multiple, including the labyrinth as
an instrument of torture, the contrast between those trapped inside
the labyrinth and those who look on from the outside, and especially
the legend that Daedalus was imprisoned in the artifact he created.
Zampanò's closing sentence in footnote 301 makes the connection:
"~~Supposedly the tyrant Phalaris killed the inventor Perilaus by placing~~
~~him inside his own creation~~ [" (337).

The square bracket that ends this quotation is followed by a space of several lines, another signifier of absence. When its mirror twin finally closes the space, footnote 302 hangs off the closing bracket. In the footnote's content at the bottom of the page, Johnny says that he "[c]an't help thinking of old man z here and those pipes in his head working overtime; alchemist to his own secret anguish; lost in an art of suffering. Though what exactly was the fire that burned him?" (337). He offers an explanation as the footnote continues on the next page:

Zampanò is trapped but where may surprise you. He's trapped inside me, and what's more he's fading, I can hear him, just drifting off, consumed within, digested I suppose . . . his voice has gotten even fainter, still echoing in the chambers of my heart, sounding those eternal tones of grief, though no longer playing the pipes in my head.

I can see myself clearly. I am in a black room. My belly is brass and I am hollow. I am engulfed in flame and suddenly very afraid. (338)

The passage functions as a node in which several narrative threads come together. The image of Zampanò being digested recalls the House eating Holloway and Tom as well as the book eating all the other media; the fading echo of Zampanò's voice recalls the chapter on echoes, here linked with screams transformed into strange music, so that Johnny's story becomes a mediated conduction of Zampanò's cries. Experiencing himself incarnate in the bull makes Johnny an artifact created by Zampanò, yet in another sense he creates Zampanò by ordering and remediating his notes into a publishable manuscript. When figured as the bull's artificer, Zampanò becomes the source of Johnny's words instead of the narrator encapsulated by Johnny's commentary, an inversion flipped yet again when Zampanò is imprisoned inside his creation. The result of these vertiginous inversions is to destabilize the ontological priorities that would place Johnny in a superior position to Zampanò. By implication, it also destabilizes our ontological superiority, as readers in the real world, to Johnny and Zampanò as characters in a fiction.

An even more radical subversion is staged by the check mark that appears in the lower right corner of page 97. Before we arrive at this inscrutable sign, we read on page 72 in footnote 78 the advice from "Ed." to skip forward to Appendix II E, the letters Pelafina writes to Johnny. If we follow this advice, we come upon the letter in which

Pelafina, infected by growing paranoia, suspects the staff of interfering with her correspondence and asks Johnny to place a check mark in the lower right corner of his next letter if he has received her letter intact (609). Breaking the boundary of the page, the check mark crashes through the narratological structure that encapsulates Pelafina's letters within the higher ontological level of whomever arranges for the deceased woman's correspondence to be included in the manuscript (presumably Johnny) and the published book (presumably the editors).[15]

The implications of these subversions are extended by Pelafina's letter dated 5 April 1986, in which appears a semicoherent series of phrases encapsulated within dashes. If we use the simple coding algorithm Pelafina suggests to Johnny in an earlier missive of forming messages by taking the first letter of each word, we are able to decode the sentence "My dear Zampano who did you lose?" (615). The intimation that Pelafina can speak about Zampanò implies she may be the writer who creates both the old man's narrative and her son's commentary.[16] Combined with the check mark, this coded message suggests that apparently distinct ontological levels melt into one another. The subversion includes the reality that we as readers inhabit, for the page margins into which the check mark intrudes exist in a space contiguous with our world and *House of Leaves* as a book we can hold in our hands.

These paradoxical inversions prepare us for the unforgettable scene in which Navidson, deep in the bowels of the House and floating suspended in space, uses precious matches (which have their own history) to read the book *House of Leaves*. When he is down to his last match he lights the page, his eyes desperately racing to finish before the fire consumes it (465–67). The image of his reading the story that contains him presents us with a vivid warning that this book threatens always to break out of the cover that binds it. It is an artifact fashioned to consume the reader even as the reader consumes it. We cannot say we have not been warned. We have seen the writing devour Zampanò's life, render Johnny an obsessional wreck, and compel Navidson to reenter the House, though he knows he may die in the attempt. This is a technotext so energetic, labyrinthine, and impossible to command that we will not be able to leave it alone because it will not leave us alone. It grabs us, sucks out our center, and gives us back to ourselves through multiple remediations, transforming us in the process.

In these posthuman days, *House of Leaves* demonstrates that technologies do not simply inscribe preexisting thoughts. Rather, artifacts such as this book function as noisy channels of communication in which messages are transformed and enfolded together with inscription technologies as they are encoded and decoded, mediated and remediated. *House of Leaves* implicitly refutes the position Claude Shannon assigns to humans in his famous communication diagram, in which they are positioned outside the channel and labeled "sender" and "receiver."[17] As readers enmeshed in the book, we find ourselves, like Will Navidson, positioned *inside* the book we read, receiving messages but also constituted by the messages that percolate through the intersecting circulatory pathways of the book called *House of Leaves*.

The implication for studies of technology and literature is that the materiality of inscription thoroughly interpenetrates the represented world. Even when technology does not appear as a theme, it is woven into the fictional world through the processes that produce the literary work as a material artifact. *House of Leaves* provides a powerful example of why a fully adequate theory of semiotics must take into account the materiality of inscription technologies as well as a material understanding of the signifier. Technological effects can no more be separated from literary effects than characters can be separated from the writings that contain and are contained by them.[18] *House of Leaves* suggests that the appropriate model for subjectivity is a communication circuit rather than discrete individualism; for narration, remediation rather than representation; and for reading and writing, inscription technology fused with consciousness rather than a mind conveying its thoughts directly to the reader.

Focusing on materiality allows us to see the dynamic interactivity through which a literary work mobilizes its physical embodiment in conjunction with its verbal signifiers to construct meaning in ways that implicitly inscribe readers as well as characters. It gives us a way to think about the construction of subjectivity as something that happens outside as well as inside the text. The writing machines that physically create fictional subjects through inscriptions connect us as readers to the interfaces that transform us by reconfiguring our interactions with textual materiality. When *House of Leaves* fuses consciousness with inscription technologies, it emphasizes that our subjectivities do not preexist the writing that already defines us even before we learn to read.[19]

Moreover, through its emphasis on remediation, *House of Leaves* grounds subjectivity in a dynamic, ongoing material relation with the richly diverse medial ecology in which we are all immersed, including computers, television, and film, as well as print books. Participating in a medial ecology from which it could not isolate itself even if it wanted to, *House of Leaves* makes a strong claim to reposition (remediate) the reader in relation to the embodied materiality of the print novel. It implies that the physical attributes of the print book interact with the reader's embodied actions to construct the materialities of the bodies that read as well as those that are read. Inscribing consequential fictions, *House of Leaves* reaches through the inscriptions it writes and that write it to redefine what it means to write, to read, and to be human.

University of California, Los Angeles

Notes

1   Mark Z. Danielewski, *House of Leaves* (New York: Pantheon Books, 2000), xix–xx; further references to this source will be cited parenthetically in the text.
2   See Richard Grusin and Jay David Bolter, *Remediation: Understanding New Media* (Cambridge: MIT Press, 2000).
3   As Zampanò informs us, Navidson's photograph has a real-life source, Kevin Carter's Pulitzer Prize–winning photograph. Information on how Carter was able to get the photograph and his subsequent suicide can be found in Scott Macleod's "The Life and Death of Kevin Carter," *Time*, 12 September 1994, 70–73.
4   Johnny Truant's comment on the errors is significant: "I've come to believe errors, especially written ones, are often the only markers left by a solitary life: to sacrifice them is to lose the angles of personality, the riddle of a soul" (31).
5   George Lakoff and Mark Johnson, *Metaphors We Live By* (Chicago: Univ. of Chicago Press, 1983).
6   Johanna Drucker makes a similar point when she uses the visual qualities of digital media to insist on their materiality: "If 'form' is conceived in mathematical terms, it can be absorbed into an absolute unity of essence and representation, while if 'form' is conceived in terms of graphesis, then it resists this unity in part through the specificity imparted by material embodiment" ("Digital Ontologies: The Ideality of Form in/and Code Storage—or—Can Graphesis Challenge Mathesis?" *Electronic Art and Animation Catalogue*, SIGGRAPH 2000 [New York: Association of

Computing Machinery, 2000], 10–14, especially 14). Also relevant are Drucker's arguments in *The Visible Word: Experimental Typography and Modern Art, 1909–1923* (Chicago: Univ. of Chicago Press, 1994).

7   For more on media-specific analysis, see N. Katherine Hayles, "Flickering Connectivities in Shelley Jackson's *Patchwork Girl*: The Importance of Media-Specific Analysis," *Postmodern Culture*, January 2000, <*http://muse.jhu.edu/journals/pmc/toc/v010/10.2hayles.html*>.

8   I am grateful to Larry McCaffrey and Sinda Gregory for sharing with me their interview with Mark Danielewski.

9   Personal communication with Danielewski, November 2001.

10 This argument is developed in N. Katherine Hayles, *Writing Machines* (Cambridge: MIT Press, 2002).

11 See Jane Yellowlees Douglas, *The End of Books—or Books without End: Reading Interactive Narratives* (Ann Arbor: Univ. of Michigan Press, 2001).

12 Personal communication with Danielewski, September 2001.

13 Among the typographical features, "Exploration #4" appears in boldface. In the 2002 "red" edition, all the passages associated with the Minotaur and marked with overstrikes are also printed in red, a coloration desired by the author but omitted in the 2000 "blue" edition, presumably for financial reasons. In addition, the compass set in the middle of the labyrinth cover design has a red center in the "red" edition, a detail lacking in the "blue" edition. There is one further difference between the two editions: whereas "house" appears in blue in the blue edition, in the red edition it appears as light gray, as does the box on page 143.

14 Vladimir Nabokov, *Pale Fire* (New York: Vintage, 1962), 29.

15 Participants in my summer seminar for the National Endowment for the Humanities vigorously debated whether the check mark can be considered a hypertext link ("Literature in Transition: The Impact of Information Technologies," 2 July–6 August 2001, University of California, Los Angeles). If so, it links the interior world of the text to the readers outside the text by occupying a space that mediates between the book's content and its outside.

16 I am grateful to Erin Templeton for pointing out this encoding and its implications, a detail also mentioned at the *House of Leaves* Web site, www.houseofleaves.com.

17 Claude E. Shannon, introduction to Claude E. Shannon and Warren Weaver, *Mathematical Theory of Communication* (Urbana: Univ. of Illinois Press, 1963).

18 Friedrich Kittler takes literary criticism to task on this point, arguing that it remains "bounded by formal and hermeneutic models" because inscription technologies are seen only as the "more or less idiosyncratic preoccupations of authors, and never as textual evidence of a twentieth-century writing-down system" (*Literature, Media, Information Systems,*

trans. by Geoffrey Winthrop-Young and Michael Wurtz [Stanford, Calif.: Stanford Univ. Press], 20).

19   Friedrich Kittler argues that the introduction of phonetics transformed the experience of subjectivity by creating a reading technology that in effect associated reading with the interiorization of voice, particularly the mother's voice (*Discourse Networks, 1800/1900*, trans. by Michael Metteer [Stanford, Calif.: Stanford Univ. Press, 1992]).

**Jay
Clayton**
Convergence of the Two Cultures: A Geek's
Guide to Contemporary Literature

In *Geeks: How Two Lost Boys Rode the Internet out of
Idaho* (2000), Jon Katz introduces what some might consider a rare
creature: a teenage computer hacker who reads literature. Katz's nonfiction bestseller follows two working-class kids who achieve success
because of their technological savvy. They are members of an ever-
growing group, whose mastery of computers has suddenly made
them, in Katz's words, "culturally trendy."[1] They are "the new cultural elite, a pop-culture-loving, techno-centered Community of Social
Discontents" (*G*, xi). Jesse struggles to explain himself to the author
through months of conversations and e-mail exchanges. The break-
through occurs when Jesse thinks to ask Katz if he has ever read
David Copperfield. "That's how I feel about myself," Jesse says. "I can't
say it any better" (*G*, 81). The author of ten books of investigative
journalism, political commentary, memoirs, and detective fiction, Jon
Katz is an occasional college professor and a columnist for numerous
magazines—a writer whose journalistic passion about obscure social
outcasts has its own Dickensian quality. But it is the techie kid who
invokes Dickens. Katz is not surprised in the least: "A computer geek
who explains himself through Dickens is less remarkable a phenomenon than one might think. Geeks' passions often crisscross back and
forth between technology and more traditional forms of culture, with
unusual depths of interest in both" (*G*, 83).

Such crisscrossing is the hallmark of important sectors of American society at the turn of the millennium. From the young loners
Katz chronicles to their successful counterparts in Silicon Valley, from
role-playing gamers to the computer-special-effects wizards at movie

American Literature, Volume 74, Number 4, December 2002. Copyright © 2002 by Duke
University Press.

studios, from open-source mavericks to corporate Web designers, the freedom to range across diverse zones of interest and inquiry is a major source of creativity. To be passionate about technology, traditional culture, and pop culture all at once is less rare than many realize. "Journalists, educators, and pundits frequently fuss that kids like Jesse don't read or aren't well informed; in fact, they read enormous amounts of material online, and are astonishingly well informed about subjects they're interested in" (*G*, 41). If most of this cultural life takes place on-line,

> the single cultural exception [is] books. Perhaps as a legacy of his childhood, Jesse remained an obsessive reader. He liked digging through the bins of used bookstores to buy sci-fi and classic literature; he liked books, holding them and turning their pages. (*G*, 42)

As a result, this teenager "was almost shockingly bright" (*G*, 10) — his notion of culture mixed philosophy, films, literature, music, technology, and politics. For Jesse, and the computer pioneers who helped produce the Internet boom of the 1990s, the idea of separating technology from other domains of culture made little sense.

This essay will explore a group of writers who have also discerned that the relations among science, technology, and literature are shifting. They approach the two-culture split from the other side—the literary domain—but their sense of the interconnected nature of today's culture would appeal to many computer geeks. In the next section, I will introduce a new genre of contemporary literature that focuses on science and technology. Although not widely noted, a veritable explosion of such novels, short stories, poems, and plays has occurred in the last decade.[2] Indeed, the increase in fictional explorations of scientific issues is one of the most striking developments in American literature at the turn of the century. After sketching the outlines of this genre, I will turn to Neal Stephenson's *Cryptonomicon* (1999), a novel that participates in the trend but turns a skeptical eye on utopian accounts of what this change portends. Stephenson, like the best of the other writers surveyed here, does not imagine that combining literature with science will magically reunify culture, creating the kind of untroubled synthesis that Edward Wilson calls "consilience."[3] My essay concludes by indicating some of the ways in which one might conceptualize the reconfigured culture emerging in the twenty-first century.

■ ■ ■

In 1959 C. P. Snow famously lamented the trend in the twentieth century toward specialization, which opened a gulf between what he called the "two cultures," science and literature.[4] Snow framed his account with his own personal experience of attempting to pursue dual careers as a scientist and a novelist, but he intended his indictment to address more general conditions of modern existence. According to Snow, most "literary intellectuals" possess a "total incomprehension of science" and are "natural Luddites" (*TC*, 4, 11, 22), whereas most scientists are utterly ignorant of literary culture, often admitting only that they have "'*tried* a bit of Dickens,' rather as though Dickens were an extraordinarily esoteric, tangled and dubiously rewarding writer" (*TC*, 12). Dickens, it seems, poses a kind of litmus test for scientists. If you can get passionate about the Inimitable, then you have some chance of bridging the two-culture divide.

The split between literature and science was not the only consequence of modern specialization that Snow deplored. Equally important was the division that had emerged between pure and applied science. "Pure scientists and engineers," Snow writes, now seem to live in very different worlds and hence "often totally misunderstand each other" (*TC*, 31). Snow's polemic succeeds in dramatizing a critique of specialization that has been widely shared by sociologists, philosophers, and cultural critics throughout the century, even if none have highlighted the specific division between science and literature more memorably than Snow. Indeed, since Max Weber, most commentators have seen the increasing differentiation of the social sphere as one of the defining characteristics of modernity.[5] The growth in the number and autonomy of the professions, the compartmentalization of academic disciplines, and the division between "pure" areas of inquiry and applied research are crucial elements in the increasing rationalization of modern society that Weber describes.

Against this backdrop, I want to advance the thesis that the two cultures are once again converging. A change is taking place in the relationship between science, technology, popular culture, and the areas of literary and intellectual life called the humanities. Not since the early nineteenth century, before the full development of academic disciplines, has there been such synergy between technology and other forms of imaginative creativity.[6] Just as important is the way some engineers have begun to shape basic scientific discoveries, both in the computer field and in areas of biomedical research, particularly the Human Genome Project. The line between pure and applied research blurs frequently in these areas, as does the related distinction between academic and for-profit investigations. Even after the dot.com bubble burst, these technoscientific fields remain some of the most powerful engines driving the economy, and the cultural changes they herald are spreading throughout society. Silicon Valley and Redmond are harbingers of a reorientation that has also produced biomedical entrepreneurs such as Craig Venter, formerly of Celera Genomics, not to mention the venture capitalists and IPOs that funded their work.

This claim about the convergence of the two cultures will not be surprising to everyone. Stefan Collini anticipated my view in his informative introduction to the 1993 reissue of Snow's book (*TC*, vii–lxxi). Nicholas Negroponte, the director of MIT's Media Lab, also has argued that a "culture convergence" between "technology and the humanities, between science and art" is resulting from the "blend of technical and artistic" talents required by multimedia computer applications.[7] Daniel Dennett, philosopher and cognitive scientist, has emphasized how engineering is helping to break down traditional walls. Dennett maintains that the "sharp divide" Snow lamented is "threatened by the prospect that an engineering perspective will spread from biology up through the human sciences and arts."[8] He adduces Alan Turing, a pioneer of the computer who figures later in this essay, as an exemplar of an increasingly important intellectual style: Turing was "at one and the same time [an] awesome theorist . . . and deeply practical, epitomizing an intellectual style that has been playing a growing role in science since the Second World War."[9] J. David Bolter, a literary scholar who early recognized the cultural importance of computers, predicted that the computer "will provide the sturdiest bridge between the world of science and the traditional worlds of philosophy, history, and art. . . . It brings concepts of physics, mathematics, and logic into the humanist's world as no previous machine has done. Yet it can also serve to carry artistic and philosophical thinking into the scientific community."[10]

To say that the two cultures are converging is not to suggest that the United States will soon enjoy a seamless, integrated culture, in which literary intellectuals understand quantum theory and scientists in lab coats spend their free time reading John Ashbery and Rita Dove.

It would be foolish to forecast the creation of such a holistic culture anytime soon. But that is not the kind of convergence I am discussing. The convergence occurring today consists of people who live and work in an information economy forced to confront diverse kinds of knowledge from unrelated fields in their everyday occupations.[11] Dislocation is as much a part of this new order as integration. Downsizing and outsourcing follow in the train of this convergence as frequently as technological innovation and new digital forms of creativity. Living in an interconnected sector of the planet is having effects, for better and worse, on the way people think about problems, do research, and make decisions. The wired world is not just a mystification of the limited scope of the economic transformation of the 1990s; it is also a statement about material conditions, which affect the ways in which knowledge is produced and disseminated. Knowledge workers, including scientists and engineers as well as people with the interpretive skills and artistic backgrounds associated with the humanities, increasingly find themselves drawing on sources of expertise from both of the two cultures. There is no less emphasis on specialization today — simply a recognition of the importance of maintaining close contact with other specialties.[12]

Ripples from this change have spread throughout popular culture. Techies, hackers, and geeks have become prominent figures in our cultural imagination. Science fiction has moved from the margins to a central place in the entertainment industries, and computer workers learn how to think about the technological marvels they are constructing from the novels of William Gibson, Bruce Sterling, and Neal Stephenson. The hybrid female bodies that Donna Haraway theorizes in "A Cyborg Manifesto" are brought to the screen in the pumped-up physiques of Linda Hamilton in *Terminator II* (1989) and Sigourney Weaver in the later *Alien* films (1986–2001), then brought to the mall by health centers and personal fitness trainers.[13] Microsoft, AOL, and amazon.com have become as prominent in literature and popular culture as they are in the market, office, home, or, frequently, courtroom. MP3, Napster, and Morpheus, which are driven as much by youth culture as by technological innovation, threaten to transform the music industry, and perhaps ultimately, the entire conception of intellectual property. And computer geeks stalk contemporary folkways, whether as the frightening monsters blamed for the Columbine massacre or as the hip antiheroes in films and television shows.

From the literary side of the split, the most intriguing sign of convergence is the increase in imaginative writing about science. This trend is not restricted to American literature, but the development is most visible here, in the country that invests more money in scientific research than any other. Of special interest for my argument is a fascinating subset of this literature, a group of texts dedicated to discovering precedents for people who love both literary and scientific culture. In what amounts to a new subgenre, these works create imaginary ancestors for their contemporary characters, analogues from history for literary people (much like the authors, one supposes) who are captivated by science and technology. In contrast to the dominant ethos of literary culture in the twentieth century, which left no place in a humanist for a love of molecular biology, say, or for the mathematics of codes, these texts provide the missing heritage for their own kind of hybrid interests. They take up the challenge of constructing a lineage for the information age.

The characteristic feature of this subgenre is a two-generational plot, which alternates between a contemporary group of characters, generally scientists of some sort, and characters from an earlier generation. The origin of this newly popular twist on multiplot structure might lie in Thomas McMahon's first novel, *Principles of American Nuclear Chemistry* (1970), which parallels the life of an aimless, unsuccessful physicist in the 1960s with that of his father, who was a scientist on the team at Los Alamos that invented the atomic bomb. Much better known is Tom Stoppard's play *Arcadia* (1993), in which two sets of literary-scientific characters, separated by more than 150 years, enact symmetrical dramas in the drawing room of an English country house.[14] Another influential instance is Richard Powers's *The Gold Bug Variations* (1991), a novel that weaves together narratives from the 1950s and 1980s to establish a homology among computer code, the genetic code, the musical code in Bach's *Goldberg Variations*, and the poetic codes of literary language. George Bradley's lyric meditations on science in poems such as "E Pur Si Mouve," "I'm Sorry, Einstein," and "Very Large Array" combine characters and perspectives drawn from the present and the distant past.[15] Andrea Barrett's prize-winning short story collection, *Ship Fever* (1996), juxtaposes tales of contemporary scientific researchers with those of their eighteenth- and nineteenth-century predecessors. Carl Djerassi and Roald Hoffmann's play *Oxygen* (2001) alternates between the eighteenth and

twenty-first centuries in a debate over which scientist is most deserv-
ing of a "retro-Nobel" for the discovery of oxygen—Lavoisier, Priest-
ley, or Scheele.[16]

Other examples could be adduced, not least the novel I shall examine in the next section, Stephenson's massive and entertaining *Cryptonomicon*. Rather than extending this list, however, I propose to demonstrate how the literary status of these works generates insights
about today's culture convergence that might be less salient in other
accounts. My hypothesis is that a formal dimension of these literary
texts—their use of a two-plot structure—allows a dialectical element
to become visible in historical patterns that might otherwise seem
simply to mirror one another. If science and technology are the modern world's most visible tokens of the new, stories that feature scientific parallels from distant time periods provoke a strong sense of wonder. More important, they produce an idiosyncratic form of knowledge
about the present. The wonder stems from discovering that people
who lived in the past may have had ideas much like our own. The
special form of knowledge, however, comes from the realization that
the same only ever reappears as cultural difference. In the course of
paralleling scientific lives, these novels inevitably chronicle human
differences, alterations embodied not in laboratory equipment or scientific breakthroughs but in characters, choices, and actions. Here
literature's conventional (some would say old-fashioned) focus on the
uniqueness of individuals is put in the service of a dialectical project
that undermines common assumptions about the adequacy of historical Truth. Whereas traditional history of science traces continuity or
rupture, this body of literature gives emotional and cognitive force to
both similarity and difference. This fiction encodes time as humanly
meaningful by giving weight both to uncanny patterns of recurrence
and to the particularity of lived experience.

Today's two-culture works suggest that at least part of Snow's com-
plaint is no longer as relevant as it was fifty years ago—that writers
know nothing, and care less, about science. The other half of the problem, that scientists and engineers are alienated from the arts and
humanities, may be shifting as well, in ways that I sketched earlier
and shall return to in my conclusion. Now, however, I turn to a test
case for my hypothesis, a double-plot novel that portrays a breakdown of the barriers separating mathematics, engineering, music, and
literature.

■ ■ ■

Cryptonomicon is the ultimate geek novel. Its two sprawling but fast-paced stories parallel the activities of Lawrence Waterhouse, a code breaker for the Navy in World War II, with those of his grandson Randy Waterhouse, a computer programmer setting up an information technology business in the Philippines. The juxtaposition of their stories traces the birth of the digital computer back to a ragtag group of nonconformist code breakers in the 1940s. Stephenson accurately perceives that the interdisciplinary alliance forged by wartime conditions among humanists, scientists, engineers, the military, the intelligence services, and industry created the ideal circumstances for the conception of the computer. His novel suggests that a similar mixture of talents and interests lies behind the IT revolution today. This comparison establishes a genealogy for hacker culture, uncovering both the dangers and the opportunities that accompany its particular brand of innovation.

Stephenson's history postulates two periods of interdisciplinary ferment, separated by nearly fifty years of disciplinary isolationism. During World War II, Lawrence exploits an informal alliance among once discrete intellectual spheres. After the war, however, the long, inhospitable era of the Cold War perverts that alliance, and Lawrence responds by retreating to a university in Washington state, where he lives out the remainder of his life in obscurity. His grandson Randy, on the other hand, comes to age as the Cold War is ending. In the altered conditions of his world, Randy recognizes the impossibility of escaping from a global economy (in a university, a Philippine jungle, or anywhere else). He also recognizes the importance of hacking from within that system. The problem he faces is that the very alliance of interests that helps him and his geeky friends succeed also aids the so-called New World Order by bringing government and business interests into sync.[17] Although today's free-market ideology casts government regulation as the sworn enemy of commerce, the special conditions of the Internet revolution, according to Stephenson, are turning them into partners in the demand for technologies of control. To celebrate a freewheeling Internet culture but turn a blind eye to the way in which this same culture may inadvertently promote new forms of control will ultimately prove self-defeating. Randy, however, learns from the experience of his grandfather that neither utopianism about hacker freedoms nor paranoia about technological control is an adequate response to the moment in which he lives. He learns that one must augment one's techie skills with a keen sense of history and a critical perspective—one must develop, in short, "literary" values and techniques.

In its World War II sections *Cryptonomicon* dramatizes vividly the breakdown of disciplinary barriers that historians of science have attributed to the wartime emergency. As Julie Thompson Klein makes clear, "World War II was a major turning point." It fostered "problem-focused and mission-oriented research" and enabled a "rare level of collaborative effort" not only among the scientists and engineers employed by the Manhattan Project but also among linguists, historians, sociologists, anthropologists, and others working in newly formed area studies programs, which were "designed to produce knowledge about the contemporary foreign cultures of 'enemy peoples.'"[18] Although Klein does not focus on code breaking or computer science, these activities played just as great a role in promoting the kind of "interdisciplinary problem-focused research [that] gained prominence in World War II because it answered military needs."[19]

Stevenson's wartime chapters visit many of the historical scenes where fundamental breakthroughs in the development of computing took place. They also feature some of the actual historical players—most prominently Alan Turing, the British mathematician, who was one of the first people in the twentieth century to conceive of the computer. The fictional Lawrence Waterhouse encounters Turing at Princeton, where the mathematician did graduate work in 1936–37. After the war begins, Lawrence finds himself assigned to the code-breaking team at Pearl Harbor, where he learns cryptography from a fictionalized version of the eccentric Commander Joseph Rochefort. From there, Lawrence is transferred to the British code-breaking headquarters at Bletchley Park, where he reencounters Turing, who is now overseeing the decryption machines he helped invent: Bombe and Colossus. Before too long, Lawrence is part of a commando team, whose assignment is to plant disinformation in the field to prevent the Germans from learning that the Allies have broken the Nazi's Enigma codes. He also finds himself boarding a German submarine in an incident modeled on actual wartime events (the same events that inspired the movie *U–571*, released the year after *Cryptonomicon*). Ultimately Lawrence ends up back in the Pacific, where his commander—a fictional character named Colonel Earl Comstock—was, in peacetime, an executive of the Electric Till Corporation (ETC), a company sug-

gestive of IBM. In a comically outlandish episode, Lawrence invents a
fully operational digital computer, built on principles derived from his
musical training on pipe organs, the design for which Comstock steals
for his company. At the same time that this theft of intellectual property emphasizes the role a humanistic talent (music) might play in the
multimedia computers to come, it also lays the groundwork for ETC
to become a covert partner with the newly founded National Security
Agency (NSA), which has already recruited Comstock as an agent.

In the novel's 900–plus pages, Stephenson is able to do imaginative
justice to most aspects of the literary-scientific-engineering-military-
industrial-intelligence alliance forged by the exigencies of war. Each
wing of this alliance has a fictional character with his own elaborate
plot line devoted to it: both Lawrence and the real-life Turing were
pure mathematicians as well as unusually gifted electrical engineers;
civil engineering is explored in the story of a Japanese soldier Goto
Dengo; the story of Marine Sargent Bobby Shaftoe brings the military into the equation then evolves into a portrait of the role that
covert operations played in the development of cryptography from a
hobby for literary gentlemen to a full-blown scientific discipline; and
Comstock's machinations in the Pacific Theater provide an unpleasant
foretaste of the way in which the intelligence community would begin
to co-opt scientific research for the Cold War in the years to come.[20]

Alternating with the chapters set in World War II are chapters
that take place in the 1990s. These contemporary sections recount
the adventures of Randy Waterhouse, Lawrence's grandson, an overweight, romantically inept, former gamer and Unix system operator—
in short, a classic geek. Randy's life changes dramatically when he
joins with his friend Avi Halaby to form an IT company they call
the Epiphyte Corporation. Their efforts to get this start-up company
off the ground take them to the Philippines, where a series of carefully orchestrated coincidences—reminiscent of the coincidences that
structure Dickens's multiplot novels—bring Randy together with the
descendants of each of the main characters from the World War II
plot: Amy Shaftoe, the granddaughter of Sargent Bobby Shaftoe; Goto
Furundenendu, a civil engineer like his father; Paul Comstock, the law
officer opposed to freedom on the Net; and several peripheral characters, whose roles are too minute to discuss here but whose cameo
appearances are a frequent source of amusement.[21] These characters
inhabit a turbulent post–Cold War culture. The speculative energy and

unrestrained greed of the New World Order serve as a backdrop for the slowly emerging scheme of Randy and Avi. Their business plan turns out to have a surprising idealism at its core, a utopian motive that only gradually becomes apparent. To achieve their vision, they must negotiate a path among forces as intimidating in this contemporary setting as were the World War II enemies in their time: criminal consortiums from several countries, U.S. law enforcement agencies, a corrupt Filipino justice system, rival venture capitalists, high-powered legal challenges, and a native insurgency movement.

The stories set in each epoch revolve around what one might call hacker conspiracies, which contain both political and aesthetic dimensions. In the World War II period, Lawrence joins with Finnish, German, and American co-conspirators to steal a submarine full of looted Nazi gold in the waning days of the war. This band of intellectual nonconformists is motivated by impatience with the leaden thinking of the military bureaucracies and by their dawning realization that their discoveries will be co-opted by the postwar powers. Lawrence, a proto-geek, uses his eccentricities and pranks—what would today be recognized as typical hacker style and behavior—to hide the existence of his cabal from his superiors. Randy's conspiracy involves the secret construction of a data haven in an independent kingdom on a small island off the Philippines. A data haven is a secure hideaway where the absolute privacy of customers' electronic information can be guaranteed.[22] Although the U.S. government worries that such havens would be used for money laundering, gambling, child porn, and, after September 11, terrorism, hackers see total freedom of information as crucial to preserving individual liberties under globalization. In addition, the conspirators hope to establish an independent digital currency, backed by billions of dollars in wartime Japanese gold, which they have located in a hidden underground vault. This plan for a digital currency has as its ultimate aim freedom from all government control. Finally, Avi hopes to use the data haven to create an indestructible database filled with information to help oppressed peoples avoid future holocausts.

The novel consistently presents crypto as a "technology of freedom," to use Ithiel de Sola Pool's influential phrase.[23] One of the World War II conspirators speculates that "if you're smart enough to break hard codes, you're automatically going to be" opposed to oppression. Even though another character immediately scoffs at this notion as "naive," Lawrence endorses it as a "leap of faith" (*C*, 881), which is, at bottom, the idealistic faith at the heart of the entire book. The notion that crypto can protect freedom guides the actions of the protagonists in both time periods. Other things unite the two conspiracies: both involve illegal hoards of Axis gold, both require innovations in digital technology, and both demonstrate a subversive disregard for intellectual and political boundaries. Finally, there is the mysterious figure of Enoch Root—the only character to play a major role in both plots—who is a passionate believer in the importance of cryptography for freedom. But everyone in the two bands shares a basic antiauthoritarian spirit, a hackers' aesthetic, and a trust in the value of undisciplined free inquiry.

Although these two generations of computer hackers have much in common, Stephenson's genealogy of the information age turns out to be unexpectedly dialectical. The novel stages an internal conflict between a utopian impulse, which celebrates the freewheeling creativity of the interdisciplinary moment, and a kind of paranoia, which responds to the involvement of knowledge workers in larger structures of state power. The tug of each position counteracts the potentially overwhelming attraction of the other. If an easy utopianism, seen as much in the hackers' irreverent style as in their faith in technology, risks making them both self-satisfied and marginal to real structures of power, paranoia and a penchant for secrecy risk stifling the crisscrossing exchanges of ideas so crucial to their success. The dialectical conflict of these forces generates the historical movement of the novel, a history that should prevent readers from viewing the convergence of the two cultures through rose-colored glasses.

The two generations are separated by approximately fifty years, an entire generation of discovery and struggle, which happens also to be the exact period comprising the Cold War. This missing period haunts the stories of the generations on either side. Lawrence and Turing's wartime experiments were fueled by a liberating sense that anything was possible, that no disciplinary boundary or conventional assumption would be allowed to stand in the way of the scientific breakthroughs needed to defeat fascism. Yet the reader is never allowed to forget how the postwar military-industrial complex would exploit these same discoveries for the prosecution of its crusade against communism. Colonel Earl Comstock, who steals Lawrence's ideas for ETC, tries to persuade Lawrence to join the NSA, offering him the

chance to fight "our first cryptological skirmish with the Commu-
nists" (*C*, 897), and years afterward, Comstock is remembered as a
"Cold War policy guy—the brains behind the Vietnam War" (*C*, 127).
Thus the roots of Cold War paranoia were already present in the freewheeling interdisciplinary alliance behind Lawrence's discoveries.
This foreshadowing of a Cold War mindset is the negative moment, the
dialectical other, inside the intellectual ferment of the World War II
era. It inhabited even the most joyously anarchistic moments of the
earlier hacker conspiracy, for the success of their enterprises was conditioned on the wartime emergency, which brought together once distant spheres of society for a brief period of interdisciplinary creativity.

The Cold War also haunts the computer culture of the 1990s, when
anticommunist ideologues are supposedly a thing of the past. Paranoia and conspiracy theories abound among many of the hackers in
the novel, and although the hidden menace is not communism, the us-
against-them mindset is eerily similar. The extremist fringe of hacker
culture has been tainted by the violent mentality of the Cold War years
in which they grew up. In Stephenson's dialectical history, Cold War
paranoia did not simply go away with the fall of the Soviet Union.
Instead, it lived on, infecting not only repressive government agents
such as Paul Comstock but even the tactics of radical libertarians.

This haunting of each period by an intervening-but-absent time constitutes the core of the dialectic at work in the novel. The parallelism
between the two represented generations—in the absence of the kind
of linear causal chain that traditional history would use to explain their
connection—might be expected to produce an uncanny effect, as if the
past were inhabiting the present. But it doesn't. Instead, the amus-
ing double exposure, in which characters are duplicated in their children or grandchildren, is purely pleasurable, a narrative correlative of
the undisciplined high spirits that enable each generation's achievements. It is the missing period that produces a feeling of uneasiness.
The burden of the Cold War years becomes more haunting for being
unnarrated. And the uncanniness is transferred to the negative under-
currents in the stories on either side. The Cold War lends its oppres-
sive aura to the hackers' paranoia, while at the same time serving as
a warning against unthinking optimism.

A group of privacy freaks and encryption junkies known as the
Secret Admirers represent the negative potential among the contemporary hackers. None of the main characters in Randy's corporation

is a member of this group, but they all know members and tend to view their expertise as astounding and their political views as a little weird. The Secret Admirers share with their nemesis Earl Comstock the belief that a secret cabal called the Black Chamber, made up of the NSA, the IRS, the Secret Service, and their counterparts from other countries, is trying to run the world. The Secret Admirers hate the idea, whereas Comstock is completely behind it, but the world view is the same. As at the height of the Cold War, an identical belief structure governs the actions of adversaries on both sides. No doubt some of Stephenson's readers agree with the Secret Admirers, but Stephenson betrays his own sympathies when he has Randy say: "[T]he last thing he needs is to be hanging around with people who believe [their cause] is nothing more than a skirmish in a war to decide the fate of the Free World—a preliminary round of the Apocalypse" (*C*, 726). On the last pages of the novel, when Randy and Avi are about to recover the stolen wartime gold that will ensure the independence of their data haven, the Secret Admirers descend on their jungle camp in the Phillippines, making it almost impossible to work: "All of them apparently think they are present at some kind of radical societal watershed, as if global society has gotten so screwed up that the only thing to do is shut down and reboot it" (*C*, 908).

One might be tempted to conclude that there are two kinds of computer people in the novel, two kinds of geeks, if you will: the reasonable and the slightly cuckoo. But that would miss the point. The craziness is internal to geek culture, just as it is to mainstream culture. This self-destructive Manichaeism is a legacy of the Cold War era, which no one in the book evades entirely. The tendency to translate legitimate suspicion of control into paranoid fantasies is a displaced version of the McCarthy era mindset, and it taints the motives of everyone in the novel. Some characters are more consumed than others, but the tendency to think in us-against-them terms is the negative moment within the contemporary storyline, just as it was in the World War II plot. As in the earlier period of interdisciplinary freedom, a dialectical other inhabits the techno-libertarianism of present-day geeks.

Even Enoch Root has been infected. Enoch is presented as the wisest character in the book, but he has a blind spot, which implicates him in a disturbing racism. He believes that he is involved in an eternal war between Good and Evil. The fascists were the enemies once; now he is convinced that the Chinese have become the adversary.

His political paranoia is explicitly linked with his advocacy of science. Enoch is a mouthpiece for one of the fundamental tenets of hacker culture: "Science flourishes where art and free speech flourish" (*C*, 816). It is a doctrine that commands respect. But Enoch goes on to indict the Chinese tout court as the enemies of civilization: "If the Chinese are so civilized, how come they never invent anything?" (*C*, 815). He casts his defense of scientific freedom as America's new "Manifest Destiny" (*C*, 816). Enoch warns: "The next time the conflict is going to revolve around bio-, micro-, and nanotechnology. Who's going to win?" (*C*, 816).[24]

Despite Enoch's paranoia, Stephenson views him—and his like-minded brethren—with amused fondness. Stephenson has been part of this "Community of Social Discontents," to recall Katz's term, and he knows its habits intimately. One of the cute motifs in the book is his division of computer people into categories based on a typology derived from Tolkein's *Lord of the Rings*: "Dwarves (steady, productive, surly) and Elves (brilliant in a more ethereal way)," as well as Wizards, who are in charge of complex networks, and an occasional Gollum, who is a slinking, devious, obsessed type (*C*, 685). This typology comes into play during a confrontation between government agents intent on shutting down a computer owned by Epiphyte Corporation and an impromptu assemblage of hackers and antigovernment activists.

The scene is great fun. One cannot help rooting for the geeks, pitted against a vindictive lawyer (the Gollum), who has plagued Epiphyte throughout the novel, and an imposing array of law enforcement officers. Stephenson is rooting for the geeks too, but this does not prevent him from registering the threatening aspects of the encounter. There is a dark undercurrent running through the anti-establishment figures, lurking just below the fellowship and high fives, which reveals how some elements of geek culture have internalized the violent impulses of the very society they oppose. Many of the hackers who arrive uninvited on the scene bear an uncomfortable resemblance to extreme right-wing survivalists and home-grown terrorist groups: "Some of these guys are wearing long coats and some aren't," but "to a man, they are carrying long weapons out in plain sight. . . . Secret Admirers—who tend to be gun nuts—have taken to going around conspicuously armed" (*C*, 687). This confrontation, which develops into a near riot, ends when a group of Dwarves fries every computer chip within several blocks with a powerful "electromagnetic pulse" (C, 693), thus rendering useless the computer the Feds are trying to seize. The government forces have been thwarted, but only at the cost of having to imitate their tactics.

The novel ends with a more hopeful scenario, however. The victory of the contemporary protagonists suggests that an alliance might be possible between the alternative energies of geek culture and the productive potentialities of mainstream disciplines. This idealistic band of computer entrepreneurs triumphs because they shift nimbly between embracing the new global economy and remaining independent of government control, critical of the potential dangers of their own project, and aware of the historical burden their project carries into the future. They engage in what Alan Liu has called "ethical hacking" of the social and disciplinary spheres they inhabit.[25]

Like the World War II group who invented the computer, this band works both within and on the margins of the larger, global structures of the age—big science, big business, academia, law, government, and the military-industrial complex. Their ability to engage with these macroforces, rather than opt out of the entire system, is essential to their success. Without a willingness to deal with the actual conditions of global power, the high-minded idealism of their hacker ethos would be outclassed. As Randy comes to understand, there is no free haven, no place where one can escape completely from the entanglements of the world system. Instead, he must continue to work in the interstices of organizations far more powerful than he. He must remain a hacker, even if, at the end of the book, he has become a very wealthy hacker. His solace is that he has learned about others before him who have succeeded by employing the same measures.

■ ■ ■

Prophecy courts the ridicule of time, and those who dream of tomorrow often wake to laughter. Like Stephenson, I do not pretend to know what a convergence of the two cultures might bring, or even if current tendencies will continue. In lieu of prophecy, therefore, I shall conclude with some remarks about how one might conceptualize such a convergence, were it to proceed farther, and about what role literature might play in the resulting dispensation. I begin by suggesting that there exist three principal models for the end of the two-culture split: synthesis, hegemony, and alliance.

Let me start with the rosiest, and to my mind, least convincing vision. In *Consilience: The Unity of Knowledge* (1998), the biologist Edward Wilson proposes that a grand synthesis of all human understanding is within our grasp. The Enlightenment dream is about to be realized: "The greatest enterprise of the mind has always been and always will be the attempted linkage of the sciences and humanities. The ongoing fragmentation of knowledge and resulting chaos in philosophy are not reflections of the real world but artifacts of scholarship."[26] The basis for Wilson's optimism is his belief that science springs from the same impulse that lies at the heart of ethics, religion, literature, art, and all other humanities: "Perhaps science is a continuation on a new and better-tested ground to attain the same end."[27] Whether or not one shares Wilson's vision, it is easy to identify the literary genre in which he works. *Consilience* is an example of utopian writing, which has found a renewed market in recent years under the label nonfiction popular science. Not only evolutionary biologists like Wilson but also gurus of Internet culture, artificial intelligence, robotics, spiritual machines, collective intelligence, and self-organizing lifeforms have revitalized Utopia for the twenty-first century.

The writings of utopian futurists lack the critical skepticism that makes Stephenson's novel more than idle entertainment. Nor do they typically exhibit the self-reflexive irony of Stoppard's *Arcadia* or the multiple resonances of Powers's *The Gold Bug Variations*, to choose other examples from among works that present a complex view of science's place in culture. The utopianism in Wilson's late work is missing exactly what this new genre of literature aims to supply: a vision supple enough to affirm essential ideals without minimizing the countervailing pressures that may coexist within those ideals.

At the opposite end of the spectrum is the view that the two-culture split is no longer operative because science has achieved a virtual hegemony over all other forms of discourse. In this vision, literature and the other humanities have lost their claim to produce valid perspectives on the world and thus have become irrelevant to the real business of life. Science wins by default. The word *business* is not fortuitous in this analysis, because science's power is seen as stemming from its role in the global economy as much as from any superiority of its truth claims. This is the kind of convergence Alan Liu discusses in his sophisticated account of how the literary has been absorbed and "repurposed" by a culture now dominated by the needs of techno-science:

> Literature as traditionally understood no longer survives as an autonomous force. . . . Since the high point of its avowed self-possession (roughly from the eighteenth through the nineteenth centuries), literature has merged with mass-market, media, educational, political, and other institutions that reallocate, repackage, and otherwise "repurpose" its assets.[28]

There are only two roles left for humanists in this scenario: they may join the ranks of corporate knowledge workers (even if the corporation in question is a university), or they may attempt to subvert the global economy from within. In either case, prospects are bleak, as bleak as the literary genre that has responded to this future: dystopia. The literary tradition of dystopian thinking has proved hardier than its utopian forebear, and powerful science-fictions—from novels such as William Gibson and Bruce Sterling's *The Difference Engine* and Philip Kerr's *A Philosophical Investigation* to movies such as *Blade Runner* and *Gattaca*—level terrible charges against societies that permit science to get out of hand. These dystopian visions play an important role in contemporary culture, and I have written admiringly of each of them in other places. The argument of this essay, however, is that works that more fairly balance the claims of science and literature also cultivate talents and attitudes an equitable society needs.

The final model is the one I have examined here. Forging alliances among disciplines, in which tactical teams draw on diverse and shifting pools of expertise, seems like a desirable structure for convergence. In the business world, something similar has already arrived. Contemporary corporations, with their emphasis on "flexible specialization" and "project teams," have little respect for disciplinary boundaries. Emergencies appear to facilitate such alliances: World War II was one such emergency, the rapid transformation of American capitalism by IT is another, and the threat of terrorism might be a third. If this last turns out to be the case, then Stephenson's warning about the U.S. tendency toward political paranoia becomes even more timely. The trick is to find ways of turning effective responses to the present emergency, to echo Benjamin's phrase about Hitler's genocidal politics, into permanent critical strategies.[29] Is there a genre of writing that has attempted to imagine such strategies? Yes, and by now it should be obvious what that genre is: the literature about science discussed here.

Alliance building, however, is no panacea. There are as many dangers as opportunities presented by such a strategy. Evolving disciplinary norms, for example, have already undermined some long-standing safeguards of scientific research. The erosion of distinctions between pure and applied science, which has frequently drawn praise in this discussion, may also render conflict-of-interest questions more troubling. As most scientists know all too well, investigators in universities and the private sector are confronted with a bewildering range of choices about appropriate research ethics. There is little agreement on even the most basic issues involving informed consent, the rights of experimental subjects, and commercial exploitation of discoveries.[30] Some commentators actually blame this situation on the increasing influence of literary culture on scientific norms. Alan Sokal, Paul Gross, and Norman Levitt argue that the social constructionism and relativism found in postmodern theory have contributed to the breakdown in modern principles of scientific neutrality and objectivity.[31] Regardless of whether their worries are legitimate, the mere fact that some people are alarmed about the spread of humanistic methods into the social and natural sciences is a sign of difficulties to come. Sorting out such issues will require great critical care.[32]

Whatever lies in the future, it is evident that practices and values are shifting around the very divisions that Snow described: the two cultures. The lesson I draw from Stephenson and other novelists, poets, and playwrights who focus on science is that a critical engagement with technology, not withdrawal, is the best hope for what were once called humanist values. Celebrating nonconformity and disciplinary anarchism will not suffice for people who care about creating a just society. Negotiating between the advantages and the pitfalls of an undisciplined culture will require greater critical and historical perspective. And for that, what better guide than literature?

Vanderbilt University

Notes

I am grateful to Deak Nabers for extraordinarily intelligent comments on earlier drafts of this essay.
1   Jon Katz, *Geeks: How Two Lost Boys Rode the Internet out of Idaho* (New

York: Villard, 2000), xxx; further references to this source will be cited parenthetically in the text as *G*.

2 This trend is too large to explore in a single essay. Many of the texts that I do not have space to discuss here are treated in my forthcoming book, *Charles Dickens in Cyberspace: The Afterlife of the Nineteenth Century in Postmodern Culture* (New York: Oxford Univ. Press, 2003). The trend encompasses literature dealing with computer science: Rudy Rucker's *The Hacker and the Ants* (1994) and Richard Powers's *Galatea 2.2* (1995); virtual reality: Powers's *Plowing the Dark* (2000); physics: Lisa Grunwald's *The Theory of Everything* (1991), Louis B. Jones's *Particles and Luck* (1993), Anna McGrail's *Mrs. Einstein* (1998), Michael Frayn's *Copenhagen* (1998), and Rebecca Goldstein's *Properties of Light* (2000); oceanography: Susan M. Gaines's *Carbon Dreams* (2000); chemistry: Carl Djerassi's tetralogy of what he calls "science-in-fiction"; and genetics: Philip Kerr's *A Philosophical Investigation* (1992) and Simon Mawer's *Mendel's Dwarf* (1998).

3 Edward O. Wilson, *Consilience: The Unity of Knowledge* (New York: Knopf, 1998). This work is discussed in my final section.

4 C. P. Snow, *The Two Cultures* (1959; reprint, Cambridge, Eng.: Cambridge Univ. Press, 1993); further references to this source will be cited parenthetically in the text as *TC*.

5 Max Weber's analysis of the rationalization of society under modernity may be found in *The Protestant Ethic and the Spirit of Capitalism*, trans. Talcott Parsons (Gloucester, Mass.: P. Smith, 1988). Among Weber's many heirs, two who base their theories of modernity on the division of society into semiautonomous spheres are Jürgen Habermas (*Reason and the Rationalization of Society*, vol. 1 of *The Theory of Communicative Action*, trans. Thomas McCarthy [Boston: Beacon Press, 1984]); and Michael Walzer (*Spheres of Justice: A Defense of Pluralism and Equality* [New York: Basic Books, 1983]).

6 Scientific disciplines did not begin to assume their modern form until the second half of the nineteenth century. For accounts of the increasing disciplinary specialization of science after 1860, see Robert M. Young, *Darwin's Metaphor: Nature's Place in Victorian Culture* (Cambridge, Eng.: Cambridge Univ. Press, 1985), 126–63; Richard Yeo, *Defining Science: William Whewell, Natural Knowledge, and Public Debate in Early Victorian Britain* (Cambridge, Eng.: Cambridge Univ. Press, 1993), 32, 39; and Martin Fichman, "Biology and Politics: Defining the Boundaries," in *Victorian Science in Context*, ed. Bernard Lightman (Chicago: Univ. of Chicago Press, 1997), 94–118. For the impact of professionalization on the disciplines, see Magali Sarfatti Larson, *The Rise of Professionalism: A Sociological Analysis* (Berkeley and Los Angeles: Univ. of California Press, 1977); and Gerald Graff, *Professing Literature: An Institutional History* (Chicago: Univ. of Chicago Press, 1987).

7   Nicholas Negroponte, *Being Digital* (New York: Knopf, 1995), 81–83.
8   Daniel C. Dennett, *Darwin's Dangerous Idea: Evolution and the Meanings of Life* (New York: Simon and Schuster, 1995), 189.
9   Ibid., 207.
10 J. David Bolter, *Turing's Man: Western Culture in the Computer Age* (Chapel Hill: Univ. of North Carolina Press, 1984), xi.
11 In "The Future Literary: Literature and the Culture of Information," Alan Liu sees the "convergence between academic humanities research (the very term is symptomatic) and corporate, government, media, medical, and military knowledge" as a defining feature of the "juggernaut of post-industrial knowledge work" (*Time and the Literary*, ed. Karen Newman, Jay Clayton, and Marianne Hirsch [New York: Routledge, 2002], 67). See also Bill Readings, *The University in Ruins* (Cambridge: Harvard Univ. Press, 1996).
12 Compare with Collini, who writes: "In general terms, the most marked changes to the map of the disciplines in the last three decades have taken the apparently contradictory, or at least conflicting, forms of the sprouting of ever more specialised sub-disciplines and the growth of various forms of inter-disciplinary endeavour. But in one sense, these changes both tell in the same direction: in place of the old apparently confident empires, the map shows many more smaller states with networks of alliance and communication between them criss-crossing in complex and sometimes surprising ways" (introduction to *TC*, xliv). Collini emphasizes two concepts crucial to this discussion: interdisciplinary alliances and crisscrossing networks of communication.
13 See Donna J. Haraway, "A Cyborg Manifesto: Science, Technology and Socialist-Feminism in the Late Twentieth Century," in *Simians, Cyborgs, and Women: The Reinvention of Nature* (New York: Routledge, 1991), 149–81. Haraway was another early prophet of convergence, arguing that in a world where everyone is already integrated in the circuits of technology, scientist and nonscientist alike must take "responsibility for the social relations of science and technology," which "means refusing an anti-science metaphysics, a demonology of technology, and so embracing the skillful task of reconstructing the boundaries of daily life, in partial connection with others, in communication with all of our parts" (181).
14 A. S. Byatt's *Possession: A Romance* (1990) anticipates Stoppard's use of contemporary scholars as foils for a nineteenth-century plot. Although the Victorian characters are chiefly literary figures, like their twentieth-century counterparts, an important strand of the earlier characters' romance involves their interest in marine biology.
15 These poems appear in the following books, respectively: George Bradley, *Terms to Be Met* (New Haven: Yale Univ. Press, 1986), 37; *Of the Knowledge of Good and Evil* (New York: Knopf, 1991), 8; and *The Fire Fetched Down* (New York: Knopf, 1996), 43.

16   Novels that focus entirely on scientists from the past may be associated with this subgenre because they inevitably suggest an analogy with contemporary scientific developments. Gibson and Sterling's *The Difference Engine* (1991), Susan Sontag's *The Volcano Lover: A Romance* (1992), A. S. Byatt's *Angels and Insects* (1992), Victoria Glendinning's *Electricity* (1995), Roger McDonald's, *Mr. Darwin's Shooter* (1998), and Thomas Mallon's *Two Moons* (2000) fit this model, each in a distinctive way.

17   Here Stephenson's novel resonates with a book published in the same year by Lawrence Lessig, *Code and Other Laws of Cyberspace* (New York: Basic Books, 1999). Lessig argues that the needs of commerce for secure e-business transactions and for more reliable ways to identify consumers are exerting powerful pressures on the architecture of the Internet, which is increasingly making it possible for governments to control what goes on in cyberspace.

18   Julie Thompson Klein, *Crossing Boundaries: Knowledge, Disciplinarities, and Interdisciplinarities* (Charlottesville: Univ. Press of Virginia, 1996), 174–75.

19   Ibid., 208. For historians who stress the role of military-inspired interdisciplinary research in aiding Alan Turing, Norbert Wiener, John von Neumann, and others to develop the computer, see Peter Galison, "The Ontology of the Enemy: Norbert Wiener and the Cybernetic Vision," *Critical Inquiry* 21 (autumn 1994): 228–64; Andrew Hodges, *Alan Turing: The Enigma* (New York: Simon and Schuster, 1983); and Simon Singh, *The Code Book: The Evolution of Secrecy from Mary Queen of Scots to Quantum Cryptography* (New York: Doubleday, 1999).

20   Stephenson's delight in playing with names is positively Dickensian. The character Bobby Shaftoe goes to sea and returns to marry a woman he has left behind, just as in the nursery rhyme "Pretty Bobby Shaftoe." Goto is a pun on the computer programing term *GOTO*. Enoch Root puns on another computer term, a system's root directory. But the name of Earl Comstock presents a more complex case. The surname *Comstock* inevitably calls to mind the zealous nineteenth-century crusader for public morality. The character's full name is identical to that of a real-life technology aide to Senator Ted Stevens, who in 1998, the year before the publication of *Cryptonomicon*, was a prominent spokesperson on behalf of the Senator's efforts to regulate the Internet, a cause that Stephenson passionately opposes. The joke continues into the contemporary generation depicted in the novel, where one of the chief villains of the 1990s plot is the fictional Earl Comstock's son, Paul Comstock, who is cast as the attorney general of the United States and who is said to be engaged in a personal crusade to criminalize advanced encryption techniques on the Net, a continuing subject of debate today. Stephenson, needless to say, also opposes any effort to restrict crypto techniques. While composing *Cryptonomicon*, he published a manifesto on-line advocating strong cryp-

tography and open-source codes (see *<http://www.cryptonomicon.com/ beginning.html>* [5 December 2000]). This essay has since been published as a book (*In the Beginning . . . Was the Command Line* [New York: Avon Books, 1999]).

21 In the interests of full disclosure, I should say a word about one of these minor characters because he is a parody of academics like me. Early in the novel, Randy encounters an obnoxious Yale professor who is a self-professed authority on the misnamed "Information Superhighway." This professor, Dr. G. E. B. Kivistik, defends a stereotypical version of post-modern dogmas about the relativity of values and the indeterminacy of language. Stephenson's parody of academic jargon is not very astute; in comparison with someone like David Lodge, who exposes this kind of academic posturing brilliantly, Stephenson has a tin ear. But Randy does get the better of Kivistik in a debate about the Internet by pointing out that he ought to know something about technical matters before he pontificates about the Net in the media. Nothing much more is heard about Professor Kivistik. Late in the novel, however, a baby is born to a woman in the World War II plot, who has been romantically involved with three of the main characters in that time period. Since this woman does not know which of the men is her child's father, she names him after all three: "Günter Enoch Bobby Kivistik." As in other such intersections between the two plot lines, nothing overt is said about the baby's connection with the Yale professor, now in his fifties, whom Randy had encountered more than 700 pages earlier (see Neal Stephenson, *Cryptonomicon* [New York: Avon Books, 1999] 81, 851); further references to this source will be cited parenthetically in the text as *C*.

22 The concept of a data haven is being put to the test by the newly founded HavenCo, which has joined forces with the cash-strapped royalty of Sealand, a country established on an abandoned World War II British gun tower six miles off England in the North Sea. Sealand became an independent country in 1967, as a result of a lawsuit brought by a self-described "former English major," now "Prince Roy" of Sealand (see http://www.sealandgov.com/history.html). HavenCo, which shares many of the ambitions of Stephenson's fictional Epiphyte Corporation, invokes Stephenson's precedent on its own Web site. If one browses to the Web site http://www.eruditorum.org/, which is a name of a secret society in the novel dedicated to privacy and good crypto, one finds the message: "welcome to the societas eruditorum. This is not a datahaven. HavenCo is," with a link to HavenCo's actual home page (*<http://www.havenco.com/>* [16 December 2000]). The existence of this corporation confirms, at least in one instance, the oft-repeated rumor that Stephenson's novels serve as the business plans for many computer companies.

23 Ithiel de Sola Pool, *Technologies of Freedom* (Cambridge: Harvard Univ. Press, 1983).

24 In an extended philosophical debate with Randy, Enoch reveals that he believes that history has been nothing but an everlasting battle between Athena and Ares (*C*, 801–8). Ares, the god of war, is evil because of his destructive predilections; Athena is good because, in Enoch's system, she is not only the goddess of wisdom but also of technology. She is the patron saint of hackers, and as such, is associated with other trickster gods: the Sumerian Enki, the Norse Loki, and the Native American Coyote. To readers of Stephenson's other novels, this invocation of mythology is a familiar feature. Enki, as a hacker-trickster, is a major motif in *Snow Crash* (New York: Bantam Books, 1992). I confess that I find this aspect of *Snow Crash* ridiculous: it smacks of adolescent pseudoprofundity, particularly in its sexist fixation on rape and its association with a similar racism. It is hard to assess Stephenson's investment in his various New Age versions of ancient mythology. In *Snow Crash*, these philosophical flights seem to be an integral part of the overall theme. In *Cryptonomicon*, they are confined to just a few passages and are subjected to critique by skeptical characters such as Randy. Stephenson has promised a prequel to this novel, set in the seventeenth century. There are hints that Enoch's *Societas Eruditorum* goes back to that earlier century and so may figure in the projected novel. If so, my hope is that Stephenson continues the critical perspective on this kind of fuzzy mythology, which he has begun here.

25 Liu writes in "The Future Literary": "My highest ambition for cultural criticism and the creative arts, in short, is that they can in tandem become 'ethical hackers' of knowledge work. . . . Many intellectuals and artists will become so like the icy 'New Class' of knowledge workers that there will be no difference; they will be subsumed wholly within their New Economy roles as symbolic analysts, consultants, and designers. But some, in league with everyday hackers in the technical, managerial, professional, and clerical mainstream of knowledge work itself, may break through the ice" (68).

26 Wilson, *Consilience*, 8.

27 Ibid., 7.

28 Liu, "The Future Literary," 62.

29 Walter Benjamin, *Illuminations* (New York: Schocken, 1969), 257.

30 At a conference at the National Institutes of Health on 16 August 2000, the newly appointed head of the Office for Human Research Protections, Dr. Greg Koski, called the current system for regulating conflicts of interest in science an "Edsel" and declared that "the system may have gotten entirely out of control"; quoted in Philip J. Hilts, "Medical-Research Official Cites Ethics Woes," *New York Times*, 17 August 2000, A25.

31 See Alan Sokal, "Transgressing the Boundaries: Toward a Transformative Hermeneutics of Quantum Gravity," *Social Text* 46–47 (spring-summer 1996): 217–52, and "A Physicist Experiments with Cultural

Studies," *Lingua Franca* 6 (May–June 1996): 62–64; Paul Gross and Norman Levitt, *Higher Superstition: The Academic Left and Its Quarrels with Science* (Baltimore: Johns Hopkins Univ. Press, 1994).

32 For an example of the kind of careful work required, see John Guillory's penetrating examination of the disciplinary stakes raised by the Sokal affair in "The Sokal Affair and the History of Criticism," *Critical Inquiry* 28 (winter 2002): 470–508.

Martha
Nell
Smith

Computing: What's American Literary Study Got to Do with IT?

Two encounters, five years apart, inspired the question in my essay's title. The first one occurred in spring 1995, when the *Dickinson Electronic Archives* was launched. A long-term fellowship from the Institute for Advanced Technology in the Humanities (IATH) at the University of Virginia had enabled the Dickinson Editing Collective to develop this hypermedia archive of the manuscripts of Emily Dickinson. By 1995, my colleagues in the University of Maryland English department had begun to hear that not only was I developing this scholarly Web site, and possibly a CD-ROM, but that I also planned to devote much of my intellectual energy to a critical digital edition of Emily Dickinson's correspondence.[1] The most senior Americanist in the department, who had chaired the committee that hired me, stopped me in the hall. "What is it I hear you are up to?" he inquired. As I began to tell him about my work in digital studies, my excitement grew, but so did the furrows in his brow. He lowered his voice and, sotto voce, implored: "This is the English department, not computer science or mathematics. You will never be promoted to full professor doing this kind of work."

Five years later, I was a full professor and director of the Maryland Institute for Technology in the Humanities (MITH), funded by a Challenge Grant from the National Endowment for the Humanities. In late winter 2000, two highly regarded humanities computing scholars were about to visit the University of Maryland as guests of MITH. For their joint presentation, they had no title. Flyers had to be produced, announcements made. When I called each of the speakers, they both told me to use whatever title I thought best. As I sat in my office,

American Literature, Volume 74, Number 4, December 2002. Copyright © 2002 by Duke University Press.

staring at my computer screen, I thought about what they were likely to say as well as how my colleagues throughout the English department and the College of Arts and Humanities generally responded to digital studies, new media productions, cyberculture studies, and the complex markup schemes of computing devised specifically for literary texts, all of which had come to shape the routines of my scholarly life during the last half decade of the twentieth century.

My office at the time had a glass wall overlooking the Reserves Room in the main research library. At that moment, Reserves was packed, each student working separately in an individual study carrel. I mused upon my colleagues' response to humanities computing as I peered down into a quiet room full of scholars working separately in the traditions of the individual talent. In response to my excitement about this brave new world of electronic text encoding, digital imaging, digital sound reproduction, and transmission of all of these via the World Wide Web, DVD, or CD-ROM, colleagues would often insist that digital studies has no relevance to their own areas of literary critical inquiry. And I would continually puzzle over this resistance from scholars working in Americanist traditions that include such key critical studies as Leo Marx's recently reprinted *The Machine in the Garden*, still a classic after 35 years.[2] As I pondered these matters, Tina Turner was in some way serving as muse, for although her voice was not blasting from my cool new computer speakers, the title for our visitors' comments suddenly came to me: "Computing: What've the Humanities Got to Do with IT?" I knew immediately that I had seized upon the proper technological tool—which is of course what titles are—to convey a sense of what the audience could expect to hear. That title bears repeating now and is, in fact, perhaps even more relevant, for in our swiftly changing world of ever larger (gigabyte-size) pentium chips, larger RAM requirements (4- instead of 3-digit megabytes) for personal computers unimagined five years ago, sleek 20-inch or larger flat screen monitors, OS 10 MAC operating systems that have married UNIX, and Windows XP operating systems as well as new on-line resources (books, scholarly journals, major literary research archives, virtual museums), hard-headed evaluation of computational strategies and their relationships to our low-tech world of crumbling printed pages is more relevant and important than ever.[3]

My examples here will focus on American literature—and most

often on the *Dickinson Electronic Archives*, MITH, or IATH, because these are the digital productions I know best. But my observations apply as well to other major Americanist projects, such as *Making of America*, a cross-institutional collaboration; *Documenting the American South*; and *Uncle Tom's Cabin and American Culture*.[4] In fact, they apply to all fields of literary study, as well as to humanities study in general, and thus my critical reflections begin with observations about the phrase that describes the discipline now inextricably conjoined in my working life with that of American poetry and literature: humanities computing.

To some, this phrase might border on the oxymoronic. The *OED* defines computing as "the action of calculating or counting," especially with a computer, specifically an "automatic electronic device for performing mathematical or logical operations." Such defining terms call to mind not poetry, novels, or plays—the stuff of literary history—but logarithms, algorithms, arithmetic, processes, or sets of rules. Whatever philosophical rigor imbues our critical inquiry, no literary theorist I have heard argues that her work computes, performs the hard logic bound by sets of rules, or processes via algebraic equation. By contrast, we find the humanities defined as "learning or literature concerned with human culture" in all its messiness and imprecision. Humanists—professors of literature, art, history, music, theater—think of ourselves not as tribes of information technologists but as knowledge producers.

Yet increasingly scholars are interested in challenging what are in fact relatively new disciplinary distinctions. Defining *humanities*, the American-originated *Webster's Tenth* includes in its list of "the branches of learning regarded as having primarily a cultural character" both literature and the calculating, computing fields of equations, exemplifying the cultural branches of knowledge as "usu. including languages, literature, history, mathematics, and philosophy." And in defining myself as a humanities computing specialist, I join a group of scholars who have been arguing for the profound advantages of employing computer resources in our literary work for the past generation or more, even before the advent of the World Wide Web in the early 1990s. In 1949, for example, Father Roberto Busa initiated the first electronic text project in the humanities, *Index Thomisticus*, a concordance to the works of Thomas Aquinas. At this point, extending many of the arguments made by these proponents of humanities computing, I believe that digital resources are more than advantages for our work—they are necessities.

The necessities are demanded by several developments, but I will content myself with mentioning two: the budget and funding crisis in the book and paper-bound journal publishing industries, which are the technologies by which we judge whether someone should be rewarded with a career in postsecondary humanities—with, in other words, promotion and tenure in a college or university; and the crisis in humanities education—the diminishing roles of professors, lecturers, graduate students, and other humanities workers in the rapidly evolving, increasingly corporatized university. I do not mean to suggest that publishing on the Internet can simply replace book publication or stop the drift of higher education toward profit-driven enterprises. But it can certainly provide us with a means to think about how to overhaul a system whose priorities are, in some cases, questionable and in others—such as the traditions for awarding tenure—untenable. And in the process, digital publishing technologies offer not only potentially wider audiences than those of the Gutenberg galaxy but also creative new directions and more visibility for our work. Humanities computing offers several technologies that already serve humanities education and scholarship well and will do an exponentially better job as more humanists consciously exploit them.

Designating the resources under discussion here as technology may surprise some readers. What I label technologies are the means by which we accomplish various ends—the tools and devices on which our critical suppositions rely. In what follows, I will focus on four areas in which I believe the humanities will significantly benefit from the tools afforded by the new technologies, areas in which we may turn our "crises" to productive ends.

Primary Materials: Democratizing the Technology of Access

Democratizing access to primary materials involves a more capacious range of objects to study and treasure and a much wider audience of readers able to examine these previously unavailable resources. In the digital environment, both terms of access—numbers of objects and numbers of audience members—are facilitated on an unprecedented scale. By access in the first instance I refer to BE–O objects—artifacts that have customarily been viewed By Experts–Only. Making available images that were previously locked away in library and museum archives for exclusive view by a very few is probably the technological boon with which scholars and readers are most familiar, for such access really is quite a big (and well advertised) affair. That which primary materials get to be seen and who gets to see them are both changing at such a breathtaking pace informs the more demotic ethic characterizing new paradigms of scholarly editing in the digital realm. No longer is the image of a Dickinson or a Whitman manuscript available only to the eye of the specialist, who gets to view the original artifact or its photostat replica, while only its verbal description (represented in editions usually made by the access-privileged specialists) is available to the general reader.

On-line, the common reader can now view images and painstakingly encoded (thus deeply searchable) transcriptions of Dickinson's poetic and epistolary manuscripts; of Whitman's drafts for "Song of Myself" and "Calamus," as well as all printed editions of *Leaves of Grass*;[5] and of hundreds of nineteenth-century American novels. These technologies make more visible the quantity and variety of work that has gone into the making of American literary history. Such access to primary and out-of-print materials was unimaginable only a decade ago. In fact, most scholarly editorial projects are still produced as if this kind of access is not possible; thus, detailed notes, rather than digitized photographs with detailed notes, are the conventional surrogates for the objects under study.

An outstanding example of a contemporary variorum employing high standards but nevertheless relying on detailed description and print translation to serve as surrogate for the manuscript text is R. W. Franklin's *The Poems of Emily Dickinson* (1998). Expected to set the standard for Dickinson study, this edition depends almost entirely on description and print translation to help readers visualize Dickinson's poetry. Representing her lyric poems, in all their various versions, Franklin contextualizes them with the twin assumptions that Dickinson's highest writing goals incorporated the conventions of poems she saw published in the print medium and that she thus held to conventional genre distinctions between prose and poetry. In Franklin's introduction are eight exemplary halftone photographs to demonstrate how he regards Dickinson's compositional practices and what he considers the key characteristics of her writing habits. With only eight images to represent writing across 1,789 poems (by Franklin's count), many with multiple drafts or copies (thus the number of documents represented by the eight images easily exceeds 3,000), assessments of Franklin's generalizations depend on highly selective, subjective criteria. From the examples and the print translations, the new variorum's readers are asked to imagine the record of Dickinson's literary work, which is practically all in manuscript. Franklin is especially concerned with transporting lyrics from the messiness of Dickinson's written work, so he separates text that has been or can be identified as a line or stanza of a poem from writing that may be poetic but has not been deemed poetic enough to count as a constitutive part of a lyric. In doing so, Franklin's judgments and subsequent representations, or print translations of Dickinson's poetry, are usually formed according to codes of hearing and metrical conventions, not codes of seeing.[6]

Franklin's position is certainly reasonable. After all, Dickinson's writings indicate her acute consciousness of and work within and outside nineteenth-century conventions of poetry, which were driven by aurally oriented metrical designs, such as iambic tetrameter, and *abab* rhyme schemes. However reasonable, such a position is nonetheless presumptive, as are all editorial projects in determining what scholarly and general readers alike get to or do not get to see of Dickinson's writing practices. Thus, access to data that, in turn, is used to render critical judgments is mediated, the presumption being that there is a consensus around the meanings of the data to be found in Dickinson's manuscripts (how lines are arranged horizontally and vertically; where lines are physically broken; what marks of punctuation go up, down, or are curved in unconventional ways; and what her lower-, upper-, and middle-case letters might signify), especially in regard to their trajectory toward publication of her work.

The presumed consensus is that the ideal Dickinson envisioned for her poems was a printed corporealization. In other words, Dickinson critics have characteristically imagined her poems as print objects, assuming that any variable in the handwriting that does not cohere with the regularizations of print is due to her personal writing utensils and that such accidents need not be conveyed to readers. As it is transmitted into print, manuscript data is accordingly mediated. The *Dickinson Electronic Archives* has not solved the problem of data mediation, but the technology allows us to involve readers differently in the experience of Dickinson's manuscripts, especially in regard to their trajectory toward publication. The reader can actually trace for herself each document's journey from Dickinson's desk to a correspondent or to a manuscript book or to a sheet left unbound, then to an editor, to print, to the image on one's computer screen. With this focus on process, images of extant manuscripts are offered for readers' perusal, and readers can then test assertions that Dickinson's poetic embodiments clearly evolved, that for her, the "iconic page, or the image of the poem, moved from the printed to the handwritten object."[7] By contrast, centering editorial judgments on the printed poem results in offering print translations for readers' perusal and appraisal. Thus, decisions about the meanings of Dickinson's holographic marks and choreographies (angled marks, line breaks, letter cases, arrangements on the page, and juxtaposition of genres) are, as my examples show, necessarily made for readers of print editions.

What are the costs, then, to us as critics, interpreters, and theorists if what is being argued about cannot be seen by the readers who must judge the validity of the arguments? In the case of Emily Dickinson, and more than a half century of authorized, purportedly definitive productions of her texts, debates about the erasure of aspects of her graphocentric corpora have been launched in books and journals, and audiences have been asked to formulate opinions without access to evidence and without sufficient reflection on the ways in which knowledge and texts are produced and reproduced for our field. On what, then, would we base evaluations of her textual play and literary experimentation that depend only or primarily on those analytical descriptions? Extending that question to American literature in general, on what do we base our histories of authorship, textual play, and literary experimentation?

To see and then judge the examples provided thus far, readers of this essay might find it irritating to have to turn to the computer, sign on, and log in to determine whether what I have written about Dickinson's manuscripts is accurate; they might then argue that this new unwieldiness in navigating among media is one of the problems with digital studies. If that is the case, then I ask that readers simply trust my descriptions of the contrasts between Johnson's and Franklin's typographical choreographies and that of Dickinson's own hand, and also trust that the editors' hands make ontological commitments for texts being definitely prose or poetry that Dickinson's manuscripts do not necessarily make. My request asks no more faith from the reader than Franklin, Johnson, and Ellen Louise Hart and I ask for any of our print editions of Dickinson's handwritten works. Just as I ask you to trust my analytical description if you do not want to take the time to examine the images in the *Dickinson Electronic Archives*, so each of the Dickinson editors asks readers to trust the accuracy of his or her analytical description of manuscripts housed in libraries where you cannot see them. Such faith in editorial accuracy underwrites any print edition. Without examining the images of the handwritten texts produced so differently by Johnson, Shurr, Franklin, and Hart and I, readers cannot evaluate, for example, whether Hart's assertions about "Morning / might come" are acute insights or overreaching arguments.

The physical grammars of "Morning / might come" show that, like many other poets, Dickinson began to mingle and choreograph the elements of prose and poetry to produce what Susan Dickinson called "letter-poems." Hart notes that this letter-poem's first segment concludes with the extraordinary logic that "doubt measures the strength of commitment that faith demands and is itself the form in which faith continues," that Dickinson in turn marks this leap in faith with a "leap in the [letter-]poem, which appears physically as a break between" segments. The letter-poem "pairs opposites that are actually complements, morning and night, faith and doubt, eternity and memory, finally leading to the poem's central pair, 'Sue' and 'Emily.'"[8] The print translations of this Dickinson missive produced by Johnson, Shurr, Franklin, and Hart and I are all hieratic. Inscribed in our transcriptions are choices about genre (and thus textual identity) that are forced upon the reader by the editor(s). Like all makers of print editions, each of these Dickinson editors beseeches readers to have faith. Thus, any notion of a definitive print edition is not only hieratic; it is faith-based.

A medium that reproduces images as well as print translations of Dickinson's holographic and handmade literary works creates opportunities for far more members of her audience to take into account elements of writing practices not seen in print. Many more pairs of eyes have the opportunity to join in informed debate about Dickinson's manuscripts than has been previously possible. Humanities computing and the group work it requires can engender a critical ethos that is decidedly more demotic. It makes clear to readers what editors have long known: editing is interpretation, critical storytelling, writing.[9] Editing actually produces a narrative, a story or set of stories, about texts. Humanities computing allows "readers" both to witness the process and to participate in it. Thus I see the *Dickinson Electronic Archives* as an extension of the kind of project that Ellen Louise Hart and I undertook in *Open Me Carefully: Emily Dickinson's Intimate Letters to Susan Huntington Dickinson*. In that work, we sought to represent the context of Dickinson's writing literally as part of that process. That Dickinson "published" herself in her 99 or more correspondences, and that the bulk of the writing she shared with her contemporaries went to a single audience, Susan Dickinson, actually requires that we think differently about genre when we read Dickinson. The electronic archives allow us to make that case—to show how process is inextricably a part of product, how her manuscripts show that she was not bound by the print-determined distinctions between poetry and prose. And best of all, the technology allows the readers to draw different conclusions based on their own first-hand experiences not only of the materials but also of the editorial process; something closer to a critical, rather than a priestly, method can therefore drive definitions of and critical debates over what constitutes a Dickinson poem, a letter, a letter-poem. A decade ago such widespread access to her manuscript work and the consequent ability for the scholarly community to take in a much wider range of readerly opinion was unimaginable.

Although my example is from Dickinson studies, the technology has the potential to intervene positively in the canon debates, again providing access to material deemed not financially expedient to publish. Those involved in recovery projects have long been aware of how the publishing industry skews literary history. A "minor" woman writer as prolific as Catharine Sedgwick, for example, is known primarily by only one work (*Hope Leslie*) while every long-canonized novel that James Fenimore Cooper published is available in an affordable paperback. Via electronic publications, such as *Early American Fiction* at Virginia's Electronic Text Center, a much broader scope of texts written by "minor" writers can be made available than the one the print industry has been able to bear; can foster critical inquiry into a much wider range of African American, Asian American, Native American, and other "minority" writers and texts; and can offer thereby a much richer sense of literary history.[10]

Technology of Multimedia Study Objects, Digital Surrogates, and Born-Digital Artifacts

If technology has given us new access to original manuscripts, the new media have also introduced new means and standards of organizing and structuring information. Initiatives calling for quality in encoding standards (such as Text Encoding Initiative, or TEI) will require even the most scrupulous editors to be more responsible and accountable, as the details of editorial processes and practices become more widely visible. Moreover, because critical editions can be revised without incurring the expense of reprinting, the editorial process will be increasingly dynamic and collaborative. These changes will encourage editors to exploit theories and practices of structured information for creative ends.

Additionally, on-line editors must make decisions about how to translate textual material into, and preserve it in, digital form (in what are known as markup languages). Crucial components of any multimedia display, markup languages make a tremendous difference in determining what kind of electronic tool is at a researcher's disposal. Markup languages can significantly enhance search and retrieval capacities, thereby transforming the way scholars conduct research.

For example, indexing and cataloging are tools for completing successful research that many take for granted. The Library of Congress catalog numbers point precisely to the spot in the stacks where a book should be. Yet book indexes are not so precise, for they point to the page and not the exact line that might be sought. Web searches are even less precise. Every researcher familiar with the Web knows its powerful ability to ferret out resources not so easily obtainable from conventional library finding aids, but Google and other Web-based search engines will return thousands of hits for every item sought. As with book indexes pointing to pages and not specific lines, search engines, depending on HTML markup, point to a URL on which information can be obtained but not to the exact place on the Web-based document. By contrast, SGML and XML markup provide for unparalleled textual search, navigation, and retrieval facilities. When documents are marked up with one of these languages, especially using the protocols of TEI, search results point directly to the place in the text one wishes to find. Via the XML/TEI–encoded markup, a researcher can quickly arrive at the exact location of the information desired and does not have to depend on searching by name or title or place alone. In fact, because retrieving word strings is possible, the markup allows searches that no index could ever provide. The constraints of HTML tagging limit searches to exact matches solely on the displayed page, unless one has access to a search engine that can search an entire site. For example, a search for the letter *I* would yield all instances of *I* on a single page. By contrast, texts encoded with XML/TEI can distinguish between *I* used as a pronoun and *I* used as the heading of a chapter. Through an XML-aware search engine, multiple pages can be easily searched, as can more subtle variations on words, phrases, or themes, facilitating uniform retrieval of contemporary and archaic language, nicknames, or even euphemisms. Thus an XML-encoded text or series of texts would not only retrieve a search term such as *greed*, but also an archaic synonym like *avarice*, as well as any other more remote references throughout a text, regardless of the number of pages involved.[11] Annotations in such a digital publication are likewise marked up and can be searched in ways no book provides or can be made to provide. Thus, one advantage of digital surrogates for texts is the publication of highly structured information that will expand and deepen information retrieval with precision and scope heretofore impossible. A vast new potential for scholarship emerges as these new search tools not only enable but actually encourage us to unbind ourselves from exclusive reliance on the familiar subject-author-title catalogs.

Digital surrogates are not only textual; electronic publication incorporates audio, video, and high-quality imaging that books simply cannot reproduce. These diverse elements in publication provide innovative forms of annotation that can powerfully demonstrate the relevance of scholarly work in ways that the variorum, the compendium, and even the reader's edition have not, even as these audio, visual, and image-based elements offer new avenues for critical inquiry. Incorporating multimedia, critics have the opportunity to develop interpretive approaches that account not only for the role of spatial and temporal dimensions but also for technical features such as text encoding; hypertext design; Web design; and sound, image, and video delivery in the production of works' meanings. One of MITH's closest collaborations at the University of Maryland is with the David C. Driskell Center for the Study of the African Diaspora. MITH's work with the Driskell Center and with David Driskell, widely considered the nation's leading authority on African American art, focuses on exploiting new media resources so that the scholarship and art displayed through MITH and the Driskell Center reach as wide and diverse an audience as possible. *Hughes@100*, a Web-streamed poetry slam celebrating Langston Hughes's legacy, is one product of this collaboration.[12] These digital resources aim to be *of* the medium and not simply *on* the medium in order to incorporate as many ways of communicating complex ideas and relationships as can be imagined.

An important resource being developed along these lines is *Dark Passage: A Chronology of the TransAtlantic Slave Trade*, which relies on the Web designer tool Flash.[13] Able to create frame-by-frame animations that stream and include sound, Flash offers content creators ways to choreograph expressions of their ideas, critical observations, propositions, and theories that import auditory and visual performances impossible to render through words. When a user chooses a date from the slavery time line—1481, for example—the information that the Portugese built "Elmina, the first of scores of infamous slave castles dotting the west African coast," is not simply conveyed linguistically but is augmented by African song and an image of the castle. Thus the form of critical expression can be radically altered, possibly to profound effect.

The advantages of this technology are evident in a project such as *Titanic Operas, First Folio: A Poets' Corner of Responses to Dickinson's Legacy*, which features digitized readings by twentieth-century women poets.[14] Listeners can hear and see poets like Gwendolyn Brooks, Maxine Kumin, Adrienne Rich, and Toi Derricotte reading not only Dickinson's but also their own poems as they honor the centennial of the New England poet's death by reflecting on her legacy in American poetry, specifically for women poets. This technology not only marks a return to emphasis on the aural, which for centuries was the poet's tradition, but also adds the dynamically visual to the experience of poetry. Dickinson herself surely had in mind the power of sensory input when she wrote: "[A] Pen has so many inflections and a Voice but one,"[15] for tone binds linguistic elements into meanings, removing ambiguities produced when tone is not evident. If these transmissions are more conscriptive, is that necessarily problematic? Why should scholarly commentary, even on the literary, be sentenced to grammatical units and textual logic only? Whether it be the memory of slavery or a Dickinson poem, texts do not live simply on the printed page. The new media challenge us to consider what can be gained by amplifying our critical commentary into more media and how our critical-theoretical tools can be shaped to exploit multimedia most effectively.

New Models of Work: The Technology of Collaboration

For the humanist tribe, at least in the Western world of the academy, the primary work model has been the singular author-scholar sitting at her desk, like the students I observed in the Reserves Room, laboring independently. Even after decades of critical understanding informed by insights about the corporate nature of the author and the author function, humanities scholars remain invested in individualistic notions of genius and authorship, which are in turn inscribed in the academy's promotion and reward systems. In contrast to our colleagues in the sciences, who value coauthorship, collaborative humanities work is often, perhaps even usually, seen as inferior to that produced alone. By its very nature, humanities computing demands new models of work, specifically those that exploit the technology of collaboration, for humanities computing projects cannot be realized without project managers, text encoders, scanners, visionaries, and others with a variety of responsibilities to produce effective multimedia projects. Although these models demand different kinds of formulas for evaluating and rewarding individual contributions and thus additional work for referees and for tenure and promotion committees, the necessity that work in humanities computing be self-consciously collaborative is all to the good (not least because recognizing collaborative contributions disrupts our conventional reward systems, which are increasingly recognized as outmoded and themselves insufficiently evaluated).

While collaboration is not easy, learning to work in teams, in laboratories for humanistic scholarship, is worth the investment by humanities scholars in all fields. The challenges of collaboration only begin with issues of who gets credit and reward; there are also issues of who does the most work, and whether the measure is quantity or level of difficulty; of who is going to collaborate with whom, and when; of how to define collaborative groups, who in part define themselves through exclusionary criteria or practices; of how status is achieved through collaboration, because some kinds bring higher acclaim than others.

Still, retraining ourselves to work effectively in teams revitalizes our scholarly praxes, for through these teams, mentoring proceeds not simply downward vertically from professor and senior researcher to student and junior researcher but also laterally from researcher to researcher and student to student, as well as vertically and up from student to senior researcher. Building these teams, these virtual research laboratories for humanities scholarship, will undoubtedly change the way humanists work and greatly enhance one of American literature's most important "commons"—ways of understanding cultural and social developments that have influenced formations of ideology and values.[16] While anyone engaged in collaborative work knows its difficulties, a change in emphasis from the solitary to the collective good promises to alter critical ethos and, as scholars like David Damrosch suggest, may well offer new and productive models for scholarship.[17]

Collaboration not only increases the opportunities for critical exchange but also challenges individualistic contests over whose story of reading is the official, the authentic, the authorized one. The technologies that I have been describing implicitly encourage collaboration. The dynamic interplay of the audience, the original writer who inscribes the marks, and the editors communicating these marks to posterity is thereby more likely to open what Emily Dickinson would call "doors and windows of possibility."[18] In turn, these myriad perspectives can enable a much more sustained reflection on the production and transmission of our critical findings, on the mechanisms of authorization, and on the criteria for authenticity. These assessments can then begin to penetrate critical mystiques in ways likely to expand rather than restrict knowledge, and to focus attention more on the knowledge itself than on the individual responsible for bringing it to the fore. Access to such knowledge can in turn foster a variety of new coeditorial collaborations among authors, editors, and readers, for digital surrogates make definitive analytical descriptions neither possible nor desirable.

While print editions are containers for static objects, by definition unchangeable, the world of digital surrogates practically demands new models for editorial praxes in which editors and readers work together, models encouraged by the fact that in a world with access to photographic copies of texts and images, no one has to bear the burden of forging the perfect linguistic description of the artifact.

After all, digital surrogates featuring high-quality full-color images of Dickinson's manuscripts render a more ample sense of their textual conditions, including the conditions for the writing scene in which they were produced. Informed more fully about the textual conditions, readers can collaborate with the postulating editor in ways not possible when decisions have already been made to exclude or include data and seal the result into print.

To think of this model as a collaboration is already to make a case for how new technologies might change the idea of critical practice in the humanities. While that model may still be hard to recognize when we are talking about individual readers, it is more visible when we turn to the editorial practices already at play in the electronic archives. Hart, Lara Vetter, Marta Werner (the other general editors of the *Dickinson Electronic Archives*) agree neither with one another nor with me on every point to be made about Dickinson's handwritten work, but we do not need complete consensus in order to produce digital editions together. None of our opinions needs to override, supersede, act as more definitive than that of the others; rather, the various viewpoints, analytical interpretations, and disagreements can all be displayed and in fact become part of the critical work of the dynamic editions. After all, disagreements about the constitution and ontologies of Dickinson's texts (from determining their genre to what counts as a poetic line and what punctuation her marks represent) are legion, and the various constituencies can be represented in a digital edition in ways that are nearly impossible in print.

Linda Hutcheon's observations in a recent essay in *PMLA* about the more general state of the spirit of critical inquiry warrant repeating:

> Academic conferences—even the MLA convention—are often sites of combat and one-upmanship, where a clever and articulate speaker can savage a fellow scholar with razor-sharp wit and be lauded (and applauded) for it. We are a profession that values critical thinking—as we should—but we're also a profession that increasingly defines that quality as the wolfish belittling and even demolishing of opposing positions.[19]

By contrast, when editors work together to make as much about a text visible to as wide an audience as possible, rather than to silence opposing views or to establish one definitive text over all others, intellectual connections are more likely to be found than lost. A brief example from the editorial practices of the *Dickinson Electronic Archives* shows the importance of forging intellectual connections and of having as many pairs of eyes as possible looking at primary evidence. My example also demonstrates how vital are "recent moves to reframe objectivity from the epistemic stance necessary to achieve a definitive body of knowledge to a contingent accomplishment of dynamic processes of knowing and acting" for enriching our intellectual commons.[20]

Editing *Writings by Susan Dickinson* began in the most conventional way, with a solitary editor (me) transcribing documents in the Houghton Library at Harvard University and the John Hay Library at Brown University. Susan Dickinson's handwriting is even more difficult to read than Emily Dickinson's, and no one had transcribed her corpus before, so I began developing a key to her alphabet, recording how various letters were shaped during different times of her life and noting variances between her private draft hand and her performance script for her readers. I transcribed a series of her poems housed at the Houghton and was very excited after determining that one began, "I'm waiting but the cow's not back [*sic*]." That might seem an odd first line for a poem, but I knew that one of Susan Dickinson's most beloved original art works was John F. Kensett's *Sunset with Cows* (1856), first discussed by Barton Levi St. Armand. Later in a short biography for *An Emily Dickinson Encyclopedia*, I interpreted Susan's draft lyric as a poetic response to that painting.[21] Reviews of that short biography especially praised me for making the connection and remarking on such an important textual "fact." Had editing of *Writings by Susan Dickinson* remained a conventional enterprise, the error of what I had deemed and what others had received as fact might have remained inscribed in literary history for years. However, in 1999, Lara Vetter, Laura Lauth, and I began to work on an on-line critical edition of *Writings by Susan Dickinson*, and that made all the difference.

As coeditors working within conventional frameworks, Vetter and Lauth might have relied on my multiply checked transcriptions and photocopies of the originals and worked to coauthor critical notes from analytical description and lower-grade facsimile reproduction. Perhaps we would have found the money for one of them to travel to the Houghton to check my transcriptions yet again, but that trip would probably not have taken place. Many assistants on "definitive" editions never see the primary sources that the head editor sees, especially if they are graduate students working with a faculty advisor. Concomitantly, many head editors view a primary document once or a very few times and then rely on their notes and perhaps photocopies. Yet to produce an on-line edition, we digitized high-quality color slides taken of the originals so that we could render surrogate images of Susan Dickinson's papers as part of the production. In doing so, we realized that our fact checking would supersede even the most punctilious fact checking used for print transcriptions. Working in concert with one another, we began to improve our respective keys to Susan Dickinson's alphabet, and Vetter and Lauth fastidiously began to check my transcriptions by repeatedly viewing the high-quality, luminous images of the originals. In February 2000, a little over a year into the process, I received an e-mail from Vetter, with the subject line "Houston, we have a problem."

The "problem" was that Vetter and Lauth had identified an error in my work. Vetter's e-mail read: "MN, you're not going to believe this. . . . but. . . . It's not 'I'm waiting but the cows not back' but rather 'I'm waiting but she comes not back.' Laura and I have been working on the dawn and cow poems all afternoon, and we're sure about this. Laura pointed out that it is on the verso of part of SD's notes for a volume of ED, so we might read it now as an homage to Emily. I always wondered how a cow could have outstretched hands. . . ."[22] (see fig. 1). Had we not been working in concert with one another, and had we not had the high quality reproductions of Susan Dickinson's manuscripts to revisit and thereby perpetually reevaluate our keys to her alphabet, my misreading might have been congealed in the technology of a critical print translation and what is very probably a poetic homage to Emily Dickinson would have lain lost in the annals of literary history.

Instead of viewing the "objective knowledge" proffered by a critical edition "as a single, asituated, master perspective that bases its claims to objectivity in the closure of controversy," objective knowledge in the production of a dynamic critical edition on-line can more easily be seen as "multiple, located, partial perspectives that find their objective character through ongoing processes of debate" and through the processes of comparing and evaluating those different angles of seeing. As my example from editing the *Writings by Susan Dickinson* makes plain, objectivity therefore depends on parallactic perspectives. The locus of objectivity is not "an established body of knowledge . . . produced or owned by anyone" but "knowledges in dynamic production,

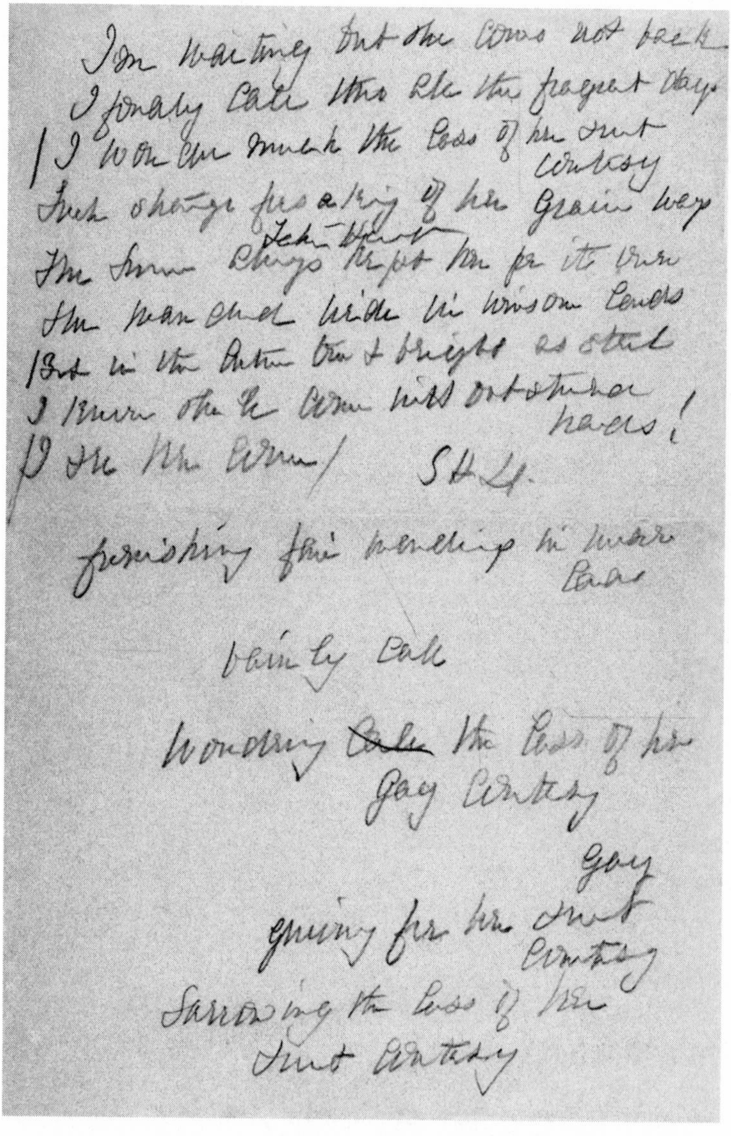

Fig. 1. Susan Dickinson, manuscript of "I'm waiting but she comes not back" (H bMS Am 1118.95, Box 9); reproduced by permission of the Houghton Library, Harvard University (see < *http://jefferson.village.virginia.edu/dickinson/susan/zcow.html*>).

reproduction and transformation, for which we are all responsible."
By contrast, the combative models cited by Hutcheon do not acknowledge how "layered and intertwined" are the "relations of human practice and technical artifact"[23] and how the warring model obstructs rather than facilitates intellectual connections, treating editorial and critical works as "finished . . . achievements" rather than as ongoing research activities and part of a "process of accretion" of editorial technique and knowledge, part of midrash, as it were.[24]

Technology of Self-Consciousness

As it promotes a collaborative model of scholarship, new technology also demands that we rethink the basic premises of research and its rewards. Self-consciousness is a technology with which humanists are familiar: highly self-conscious literary works are usually highly valued. But I am interested in the ways that this technology unsettles us and in ways that this unsettling can be effectively exploited. Thus I will flatly begin with the proposition that the technology of self-consciousness required by computer encoding of texts produces a healthy self-consciousness about what Bruno Latour and Steve Woolgar describe in *Laboratory Life* as "black-boxing"—which occurs when one "renders items of knowledge distinct from the circumstances of their creation."[25] In black-boxing, critical opinion becomes fact; more often than not, amnesia sets in after that factual instantiation, and having been effectively black-boxed, "fact" becomes "truth."

My earlier examples show how refusing to take certain data into account black-boxes packets of information so that some analyses are put out of reach while others become practically foregone conclusions. Black-boxing occurs in methodologies that rely on the solitary, revered scholar, the priest, to pronounce what exists (as in the text of a poem) and pass it along to users rather than self-consciously insist on methodologies that rely on many different sets of eyes to observe, record, and analyze data, then agree on what has been seen. Of course, literary scholars have aspired to open their editorial and critical work to such scrutiny long before we had these new media, but as I have been arguing, the new media make it much more effective. A science of human behavior is like "a science of chaos," about which N. Katherine Hayles observes:

[The phrase] may seem to be a contradiction in terms. In the scientific sense, however, chaos means something different than it does in common usage. At the center of chaos theory is the discovery that hidden within the unpredictability of chaotic systems are deep structures of order. "Chaos," in this usage, denotes not true randomness but the orderly disorder characteristic of these systems. The science of chaos seeks to understand behavior so complex that it defeats the usual methods of formalizing a system through mathematics. Hence the science of chaos has also been called the science of complexity—or more precisely the sciences of complexity. . . .[26]

Maintaining relentless self-consciousness about how critical "facts" have been produced, about how items of knowledge are part of the circumstances of their creation, is crucial for responsibly providing the provisionality that characterizes the best kind of science of chaos. This acute self-consciousness about the foundational materials taken for granted, but on which we base our critical conclusions, is likewise vital for providing democratizing access to materials while maintaining intellectual rigor. More than a decade ago, before Franklin had produced the variorum, before Hart and I made *Open Me Carefully*, and before I was aware that there could be anything called an electronic archive, I noted that "neither the reproductions of texts nor critical interpretations can be innocent of or superior to politics, since both require negotiations among authors, editors, publishers, and readers. Dickinson interpretation will be powerfully enhanced by cultivating constant awareness of the 'official' repatternings of the variorum, the three-volume letters, and the separate publication of the 'Master' documents."[27] My work on the electronic archive has only reinforced these words for me (as it has provided me with tools to make such considerations possible beyond my earlier dreams), and the words apply to the reception of all editions, including any in which I have had a hand.

So how might all these technologies and their potential begin to address crises in publishing and in humanities education? They implicitly argue for new publishing models and for reconfiguring humanities education. New models of publishing are already evolving, in which universities and libraries formulate paradigms of funding and exchange that are not driven by profit margin models. Readers' willingness to spend time with Susan Dickinson's work is undoubtedly encouraged by the fact that those resources are freely available. There is no charge for viewing them, for printing out transcriptions of them, for incorporating them into scholarly work. In developing models outside the profit-driven box, university presses and libraries also need to play key roles in restoring copyright laws to their original goals, which Siva Vaidhyanathan describes as "encourag[ing] the investment of time and money in works that might not otherwise find adequate reward in a completely free market." Copyright was intended to promote learning and distribute knowledge for the common good. "When properly balanced," Vaidhyanathan contends,

> copyright allows users to enjoy the benefits of cultural proliferation at relatively low cost through a limited state-granted monopoly. Libraries help that process by letting the wealthy subsidize information for the poor. And a thin, leaky copyright system allows people to comment on copyrighted works, make copies for teaching and research, and record their favorite programs for later viewing. Eventually, a copyright runs out, and the work enters the "public domain" for all of us to enjoy at an even lower cost. But when constructed recklessly [to protect the publisher and not the free flow of information,] copyright can once again be an instrument of censorship.[28]

I do not have the formula for these new publishing models, but I am persuaded that protecting the flow of information should trump protecting profit in academic publishing. Economic sustainability for such models needs to be achieved outside the reward system of the free market. The newness of this technology—its uncharted domain—offers us the opportunity to examine, refine, and reform our current procedures.

Besides these new models of publishing, new models of scholarly and pedagogical praxes are needed. What would it mean for critical inquiry if we really incorporated a wider range of user and multimedia responses into our critical review processes, for example?[29] What if we changed the ways in which we train our students, really incorporating group work throughout our humanities mentoring system? Rather than rewarding work done primarily in a solitary carrel using a single pair of eyes to then report results, serious work on collaborative projects requiring many pairs of eyes to look at and achieve consensus (or generative dissensus) on what is seen could be rewarded and its value recognized. In humanities computing, one cannot work otherwise. Indeed, humanities computing will continue to change the way humanities scholarship is practiced, expanding objects of study and lines of critical inquiry, thereby making more expansive, responsible critical histories. As these evolutions occur, we need to be relentless in the scrutiny of our tribe's practices. The new media, and the new critical technologies they produce, require that we scrutinize anew how our items of knowledge come into being, who makes them, and for what purposes.

Maryland Institute for Technology in the Humanities

Notes

1   See Martha Nell Smith, Ellen Louise Hart, Lara Vetter, and Marta Werner, eds., *Dickinson Electronic Archives*, Institute for Advanced Technology in the Humanities (IATH), University of Virginia (1995) <*http://jefferson.village.virginia.edu/dickinson/*>. Further references to this source will be cited parenthetically as *DEA*.
2   See Leo Marx, *The Machine in the Garden: Technology and the Pastoral Ideal in America* (1964; reprint, Oxford, Eng.: Oxford Univ. Press, 2000).
3   These hardware and software specifications will probably be outdated by the time *American Literature*'s readers see this essay.
4   See *Making of America*, University of Michigan and Cornell University, <*http://moa.umdl.umich.edu/*> (spring 2002); and <*http://moa.cit.cornell.edu/moa/*> (spring 2002); *Documenting the American South*, University of North Carolina, <*http://docsouth.unc.edu/*> (spring 2002); Stephen Railton, ed., *Uncle Tom's Cabin and American Culture*, 1998, <*http://jefferson.village.virginia.edu/utc/*>.
5   See Ed Folsom and Ken Price, eds., *The Walt Whitman Archive*, 1996, <*http://jefferson.village.virginia.edu/whitman/*>.
6   Sometimes when Franklin's decisions are driven by the work of a previous editor, writing on the same manuscript pages characterized by the same rhythmical and rhyming schemes is dismembered into prose and poetry as if textual geographies are clearly distinct, though they are not, as in the case with "Show me eternity, and I will show you memory" (see R. W. Franklin, ed., *The Poems of Emily Dickinson* [Cambridge: Belknap Press of Harvard Univ. Press, 1998], poem 1658; and William H. Shurr, ed., with Anna Dunlap and Emily Grey Shurr, *New Poems of Emily Dickinson* [Chapel Hill: Univ. of North Carolina Press, 1993], 10; see also Ellen Louise Hart and Martha Nell Smith, *Open Me Carefully: Emily Dickinson's Intimate Letters to Susan Huntington Dickinson* [Ashfield, Mass.: Paris Press, 1998], text #246). Further references to *Open Me Carefully* will be cited parenthetically as OMC. Shurr edited

using only print translation (Thomas Johnson's edition, *The Letters of Emily Dickinson*). He marked lines from a single document as poetic and others as prose because Johnson had made some appear stanza-like and others not in his print layout (although all the elements look alike in the manuscript). Although Franklin had access to the manuscript, he followed Shurr and Johnson's lead and allowed the print translation to hold sway. At other times, he discounted print translation and decided that lines that have clear schemes such as iambic tetrameter do not count as poems, though a previous editor had seen them as such. The line "Who loves you most and loves you best" (*New Poems*, ed. Shurr, 95), declared a quatrain by Shurr, is declared prose by Franklin, and in exception to his rule, codes of seeing trump codes of hearing, perhaps because the lyric seems rather inconsequential—of the "low" domestic, and not the stuff of poetry (Franklin, *Poems*, Appendix 13; A–13–3). To view images of these manuscripts, see "Morning / might come . . . Show / me Eternity (<*http://jefferson.village.virginia.edu/dickinson/letter/hb90. html*>), in "The Letter-Poem, a Dickinson Genre," *DEA*; and ". . . Who loves you most" (<*http://jefferson.village.virginia.edu/dickinson/working/ zhl9d.html*>) in "Correspondence with Susan Dickinson," *Emily Dickinson's Correspondences, DEA*.

7   Martha Nell Smith, "Corporealizations of Dickinson and Interpretive Machines," in *The Iconic Page in Manuscript, Print, and Digital Culture*, ed. George Bornstein and Theresa Lynn Tinkle (Ann Arbor: Univ. of Michigan Press, 1998), 195.

8   Ellen Louise Hart, "The Encoding of Homoerotic Desire: Emily Dickinson's Letters and Poems to Susan Dickinson, 1850–1886," *Tulsa Studies in Women's Literature* 9 (fall 1990): 264.

9   See Martha Nell Smith, *Rowing in Eden: Rereading Emily Dickinson* (Austin: Univ. of Texas Press, 1992), 1, 18–19, 31, 44, 57.

10   See *Early American Fiction*, Electronic Text Center, University of Virginia, <*http://etext.lib.virginia.edu/eaf/*> (spring 2002).

11   I am indebted to Susan Schreibman, Assistant Director of MITH, for assistance with this description of heightened searchability with XML/ TEI encoding. The example given here is part of her contribution to MITH grant and conference proposals; see "MITH's Mean, Lean Versioning Machine," *ALLC/ACH 2002 Conference: New Directions in Humanities Computing*, <*http://www.uni-tuebingen.de/cgi-bin/abs/abs? propid=93*>.

12   See *Hughes@100*, produced by MITH and the David C. Driskell Center, 9 February 2002. Digital video clips available: <*http:// www.mith2.umd.edu/hughes*> (spring 2002).

13   See *Dark Passage: A Chronology of the TransAtlantic Slave Trade*, produced by MITH for the Driskell Center, Flash design by Thomas Stanley, <*http://www.driskellcenter.umd.edu/slavery*> (spring 2002).

14 See Martha Nell Smith, with Laura Lauth, eds., *Titanic Operas, Folio One: A Poets' Corner of Responses to Dickinson's Legacy*, 1998, <*http://jefferson. village.virginia.edu/dickinson/titanic*>.

15 Emily Dickinson, Letter 470, *The Letters of Emily Dickinson*, ed. Thomas H. Johnson, 3 vols. (Cambridge, Mass.: Belknap Press of Harvard Univ. Press, 1958).

16 Lawrence Lessig's review of the original intent of copyright to protect the intellectual commonwealth is worth reflecting upon when considering how to foster the most effective collaborations: "If there were no copyright laws, unscrupulous publishers would simply copy popular works and sell them at a low price, paying no royalties to the author. But just as importantly, the framers and later jurists concluded that creativity depends on the use, criticism, supplementation, and consideration of previous works. Therefore, they argued, authors should enjoy this monopoly just long enough to provide an incentive to create more, but the work should live afterward in the 'public domain,' as common property of the reading public" ("Copyright and American Culture," *The Future of Ideas: The Fate of the Commons in a Connected World* [New York: Random House, 2000], 21). Thus copyright was not conceived as simply property right, as a matter of who owns intellectual material; rather, any temporary individual monopoly was seen as an incentive for subsequent creation by others, for generating new ideas and works. In recent years, the emphasis has veered toward protecting individual claims rather than fostering the collective good.

17 See David Damrosch, "The Mirror and the Window: Reflections on Anthology Construction," *Pedagogy* 1.1 (2001): 207–14; see also Damrosch, in collaboration with Vic d'Ohr Addams, Martha Doddvic, and Dov Midrash, *Meetings of the Mind* (Princeton, N.J.: Princeton Univ. Press, 2000).

18 Dickinson, poem 466, *Poems of Emily Dickinson*, ed. Franklin.

19 Linda Hutcheon, "Presidential Voices 2000: She Do the President in Different Voices," *PMLA* 116 (May 2001): 524–25.

20 Lucy Suchman, "Located Accountabilities in Technology Production," Published by the Department of Sociology, Lancaster University; <*http://www.comp.lancs.ac.uk/sociology/soc039ls.html*> (fall 2001).

21 Barton Levi St. Armand discusses Austin Dickinson's art collection and mentions the works purchased or especially prized by Susan Dickinson. Her name is penciled on the back of *Sunset with Cows* (see *Emily Dickinson and Her Culture: The Soul's Society* [Cambridge, Eng.: Cambridge Univ. Press, 1984], 251, 260, 282). See also my biographical sketch, "Dickinson, Susan Huntington Gilbert (1830–1913)," in *An Emily Dickinson Encyclopedia*, ed. Jane Eberwein (Westport, Conn.: Greenwood, 1998), 78–82.

22 Lara Vetter, general editor, *Dickinson Electronic Archives*, e-mail to the

author, 23 February 2000. I should also point out here that one problem was my knowing too much; that is, my awareness of Susan Dickinson's special affinity for the painting made me unable to read the words I had painstakingly transcribed differently once I interpreted the poem as an artistic response to work in another medium.

23 Suchman, "Located Accountabilities."

24 Thomas S. Kuhn, *The Structure of Scientific Revolutions*, 2d ed., enlarged (Chicago: Univ. of Chicago Press, 1970), 1–3.

25 Bruno Latour and Steve Woolgar, *Laboratory Life: The Construction of Scientific Facts*, 2d ed. (1979; Princeton, N.J.: Princeton Univ. Press, 1986), 259 n.

26 N. Katherine Hayles, introduction to *Chaos and Order: Complex Dynamics in Literature and Science*, ed. Hayles (Chicago: Univ. of Chicago Press, 1991), 1. Hayles extends some of her early observations and analyzes many of the challenges and opportunities in the digital age in *How We Became Posthuman: Virtual Bodies in Cybernetics, Literature, and Informatics* (Chicago: Univ. of Chicago Press, 1999).

27 Martha Nell Smith, *Rowing in Eden: Rereading Emily Dickinson* (Austin: Univ. of Texas Press, 1992), 94.

28 Siva Vaidhyanathan, *Copyrights and Copywrongs: The Rise of Intellectual Property and How It Threatens Creativity* (New York: New York Univ. Press, 2001), 8, 184.

29 The humanities professions would surely benefit from establishing an e-print archive such as those based on activities supported by the U.S. National Science Foundation, Cornell University, and the Los Alamos National Laboratory. Papers are posted on these Web sites for open critical review before they are published in peer-reviewed journals, which counts as a kind of publication, and also broadens the vetting process (see *e-Print Archive*, U.S. National Science Foundation with Cornell University, <*http://arXiv.org/*> [spring 2002]; and *e-Print Archive mirror*, Los Alamos National Laboratory, <*http://xxx.lanl.gov/*> [spring 2002]).

Robyn Wiegman   Intimate Publics: Race, Property, and Personhood

On 24 April 1998, Donna Fasano, a white woman, and Deborah Perry-Rogers, a black woman, underwent in vitro fertilization at a fertility clinic in midtown Manhattan.[1] Six weeks later they both learned of the mistake made that day: while each woman received her own fertilized eggs, Donna was given Deborah's eggs as well. Only Donna became pregnant, and in December 1998, she gave birth to two boys, one of whom, DNA tests showed, was not genetically hers. As the media declared, Donna Fasano had delivered "twins," "one white, one black," but the status of her motherhood was challenged as Deborah and her husband Robert filed for custody of their genetic child.[2] In March 1999, the couples reached an agreement: The Fasanos would give "Joseph" to the Rogerses if the twins would be raised as brothers. "We're giving him up because we love him," Donna Fasano explained to reporters.[3] In May 1999, one day after Mother's Day, as the *Washington Post* duly noted, the Fasanos relinquished the child to the Rogerses, who renamed him Akiel.[4]

The pact between the couples was short-lived, however, and in June 1999 they went to court. The Fasanos claimed that the Rogerses had broken the custody agreement by refusing to allow Akiel to spend a weekend at their home; the Rogerses cited a failure of trust between the couples, based in part on an incident that occurred during a scheduled visit. According to Deborah Perry-Rogers, Donna Fasano had referred to herself as Akiel's mother, encouraging him to "Come to Mommy" and comforting him that his "mommy is here."[5] David Cohen, the Fasano attorney, explained the white couple's perspective: "The Fasanos don't see [Joseph] as someone else's black baby; they

American Literature, Volume 74, Number 4, December 2002. Copyright © 2002 by Duke University Press.

see him as their baby."[6] Or in Donna Fasano's words: "He has two mothers. I am his mother and Mrs. Rogers definitely is his genetic mother."[7] Rudolph Silas, attorney for the Rogerses, countered: "The child can only have one mother, and on that we're very adamant."[8] By the end of summer, the court moved to settle the dispute once and for all by declaring Deborah Perry-Rogers the biological (and hence legal) mother.

While earlier court cases involving reproductive technologies raised similar issues about the authoritative status of genetics versus gestation, the Fasano-Rogers case is importantly unique in the history of assisted conception in the United States: It features the first woman, Donna Fasano, to be defined as both genetic mother (to the white child) and gestational surrogate (to the black child) in the same live birth.[9] In addition, there is Deborah Perry-Rogers, an infertile black woman, whose very infertility is culturally illegible in a dominant imaginary overwritten by notions of hyperreproductive and socially vampiristic black maternity.[10] How she secures her claim to natural maternity is a story of twin contracts: with the fertility clinic that offered technological assistance for genetic reproduction and with the state that sanctioned and naturalized, via the patriarchal marriage contract, her (hetero)sexual activity and the procreative property it might beget. At work in both of these contract relations is the property logic of liberal personhood, by which I mean the formation of social subjects within a modern state that recognizes and confers personhood on the basis of contractual relations—on the ability to enter into and stand as a responsible agent in a contract obligation to both the state (as citizen) and to other citizens (as transactors of labor and property ownership on one hand and as recognized heteronormative married subjects on the other). These domains of contract obligation—of citizen, spouse, and laborer-owner—have operated historically as powerful technologies for the production and excision of proper national subjects, mediating the relationship between the seemingly private world of personal affect, intimacy, and reproduction and the public realm of social exchange, itself evinced by the birth certificate, the voting card, the draft card, and the marriage license. From within the dynamics of liberal personhood, then, the Rogerses win their claim as natural parents, an infrequent event in the racialized discourse of reproduction in the United States.

My contribution to this special issue operates as a series of critical meditations on the cultural problematics raised by the Rogers-Fasano story. My goal is to make legible the messiness of affect, personhood, property, and kinship that thinking about race in the context of reproductive technology forces us, analytically speaking, to confront. Early on, my deliberations will stray from the Fasanos and Rogerses as I look at the precedent-setting case of *Anna J. v. Mark C.*, in which genetics and gestation were first defined in a hierarchical relation to one another and in such a way that the black gestational mother lost her claim on the white-Filipino child she bore for a wealthy interracial couple. This case is interesting to me for two primary reasons. First, the scholarly archive, like the media discourse on the case, has insisted on categorizing the contested child as white, which raises a whole series of questions about the ways in which we can and cannot understand the new reproductive technologies within the racial discourse of property and reproduction set into play by slavery. Second, by considering the critical consequences of the racial dualism of black-white mobilized to discuss *Anna J. v. Mark C.*, I read the story of white paternity differently, not as the repetition of the desire for racial homogeneity but, rather, as a desire for multiracial kinship—a desire that also animates the Fasanos who regard both of the twins as theirs. To track these stories in ways that pay attention to the generic terms of white paternity's sentimental romance with multiraciality, I turn to the national imaginary of popular culture (specifically the 1993 film *Made in America*) to think about how discourses of multiracial kinship function as a social pedagogy to redefine the affective dimensions of normative white masculinity at the beginning of the twenty-first century. This redefinition is critical to understanding how the present contestations around notions of race and kinship speak in relation to multiple histories and processes of racialization and bear an intimacy with the privileges and subjugations of gender, sexuality, and class.

In making an argument about how multiracial kinship functions to remake white masculinity, I am extending deliberations begun elsewhere on the power of "liberal whiteness" to reconfigure the substance and scope of white subjectivity in the popular imaginary in the postsegregationist era.[11] In doing so, I hope to be able to define how the absence of interracial sexuality in the Rogers-Fasano case is critically important to the presence of white multiracial desire, and hence to explore how the new reproductive technologies can quite literally provide the technological assistance for narrating kinship relations that do not require interracial sex as their originating, pro-creative moment. This distinction between multiraciality (itself the precondition of multiculturalism) and interraciality allows for a hege-monic move toward a kind of panethnicity that hopes to sacrifice little in the way of white masculine power by bearing none of the horror that founding U.S. culture on the actual act of interracial generative (hetero)sex would imply.[12]

How, then, does the story of Donna Fasano and Deborah Perry-Rogers speak in, through, and even against the histories of both racial-ized maternity and paternity in the United States? What claim, if any, does Donna Fasano have on the "child" she bore whose genetic material—the fertilized egg—was not her own? By what strategy or cultural logic can the babies be said to be "brothers"? If the Rogerses are Akiel's "parents," as the courts have affirmed, what assumption bans them from kinship with their child's white "twin"? What critical understanding, in short, begins to map the complexity of this "family" tree?

As my use of quotation marks makes clear, new reproductive tech-nologies bring with them a crisis of signification, pressuring the natu-ralized assumptions that have enabled the most common of kinship terms—family, mother, father, brother—to operate as if they require no critical attention to their social constitution.[13] Indeed, in their reconfiguration of U.S. culture's language for and critical conception of the embodied relationship between heterosexual acts and human reproduction, new reproductive technologies raise knowledge ques-tions about the meaning and origins of both persons and life.[14] While I believe it is too sweeping a statement to say that new reproductive technologies represent an epistemic shift in cultural understandings of kinship (in part because the United States cannot be understood as epistemically coherent), they have certainly become a cultural site for the negotiation of contradictions raised by the racial-national dis-course of "blood tie" and a scientific world view that has been radically reconfigured in the late twentieth century by the gene as the informa-tional sign, in Sarah Franklin's words, "of life."[15]

But how, one might ask, can I plan to make so much of what begins, in the story of the Rogerses and Fasanos, as a clinical mistake? This is, after all, kinship by accident, not design; as such, my critical analysis bears none of the assurances of a humanist project that tracks indi-vidual or collective intention. Hence, my interest in the category of liberal personhood as the domain of a certain kind of abstraction works to divorce my analysis from the calculus of lived experience, which various methodological approaches would seek to make palpably real. As such, what conclusions can be drawn about the very frames of reference—liberal personhood, the national imaginary, multiracial desire, interracial sex, the subject and the state—that I will use to call my arguments into being? These questions raise the methodological and disciplinary stakes of my analysis and draw attention to some of the enduring problems of any cultural criticism that makes no overt methodological claim to knowledge. By foregrounding this essay's methodological failure to make an evidentiary link between law and culture—or to center human experience—I want to stage the increasing tensions between rhetorical approaches and methodological ones, tensions that underlie contemporary disciplinary organizations of knowledge and that pose important challenges for interdisciplinary critique itself. At the same time, my un-methodological linkage of disparate discursive sites, subjects, and formations offers its own demonstration of the ways in which race is today performed within a highly mobile and radically inconsistent discourse of embodied nature. In this mobile inconsistency, the "mistake" as the origin of my critical deliberation on race, nature, and kinship emerges as a productive interruption in those processes of normalization that otherwise function to settle the incoherencies and failures of the white supremacist racial project in the United States. To read the "mistake" is thus an attempt to understand the inability of the grammar of race to find its normative production in a stabilized nature.

Maternity

When the court gave Deborah Perry-Rogers legal maternity, it departed from an unstable but nonetheless standard legal stance in the United States, where, in every state except California, the gestational mother holds legal status.[16] This standard, like nearly all court rulings that deal with the social intricacies of new reproductive technologies, has been applied inconsistently, often betraying the class, race, and heterosexual assumptions about "proper" maternity and "good" family that coalesce in the naturalization of the white patriarchal nuclear family as the state's normative ideal. In a much discussed case, *Anna J. v. Mark C.* (1991), for instance, Anna Johnson, an

African American woman, challenged her surrogacy contract with the Calverts, a white and Filipina American couple, in order to seek legal custody of the child she bore.[17] Johnson, herself a single mother, was found to have no legal claim on the child, in part because she was not its genetic mother. For feminists analyzing the case, the construction of Anna Johnson's body as a surrogate in the most mechanical sense has served as a profound indictment of the gendered and racial politics of the new reproductive technologies, which operate to privilege, on one hand, the contractual relationship that defines genetic material and new persons as property and to reinforce, on the other hand, a cultural imaginary in which black women can give birth only to black children. As Deborah Grayson notes, the very idea that Anna Johnson might be the child's "natural mother," as the court referenced her surrogacy challenge, meant "that the court would have to make [the child] black."[18] On appeal, a higher court denied Johnson's petition by relying on the Calverts' *intention* to raise a child genetically theirs.[19]

As the first instance in the United States in which a surrogate who was not genetically related to the child fought for legal custody, the case reveals the legal distinction that reproductive technologies in the 1990s began to yield: that biology as the epistemological foundation for the naturalness of human reproduction could be hierarchicalized, with gestation and genetics vying for priority in determinations of legal maternity. Since 1991, surrogacy has witnessed a taxonomic division into traditional and nontraditional forms. *Traditional* references a contractual situation in which a surrogate performs, through artificial insemination, the role of both gestational and genetic motherhood. *Nontraditional*—what Sarah Franklin calls "total surrogacy"—identifies the less frequent situation in which the gestational and genetic roles are not embodied in a single individual.[20] In the total surrogacy relations of both *Anna J. v. Mark C.* and the Rogers-Fasano cases, it is the distinction between genetics and gestation that operates to define custody. As such, these cases form symbolic bookends for a decade popularly overwritten by advances and scandals in the world of technological reproduction. From the planet's first sextuplets to Dolly, the cloned sheep, to the final DNA detection of Thomas Jefferson's enslaved children, we have witnessed the growing incoherence of reproduction as a natural embodied process and a profound reconfiguration of the way property and personhood commingle in the commodification of bodily life. But the racialization of this commodification, much like the commodification of race, is difficult to read in any kind of comprehensive scope. Therefore, I want to look more closely at *Anna J. v. Mark C.* in order, first, to chart the path of nineteenth-century slavery and its property logics of kin as, configuring and undergoing reconfiguration, it moves through this case of contract-based conception, and second, to identify how reproductive technologies operate within the postsegregationist cultural imaginary, providing the means for reimagining white paternity in the context of multiculturalism.

I begin, then, with what both the media and scholars have found insignificant about the *Anna J. v. Mark C.* case: that the child Johnson bore was—to use the commonsense language of race—racially mixed. Dorothy Roberts, for instance, interprets the case as a concerted effort on the part of the U.S. courts to guarantee white racial reproduction. "By relying on the genetic tie to determine legal parenthood," she writes, "the courts in the Johnson case ensured that a Black woman would not be the natural mother of a white child" (*KBB*, 281). While Roberts notes that Crispina Calvert was not white, "the press," she emphasizes, "paid far more attention to Anna Johnson's race than to that of Crispina Calvert. It also portrayed the baby as white." Grayson similarly reiterates the media presentation of the case when she defines Crispina Calvert as an "honorary white" by pointing to the cultural stereotype of Asian Americans as the "model minority."[21] In this consolidation of a triangle of race into a dualism between black and white, Grayson and Roberts both struggle to establish *Anna J. v. Mark C.* within the property logics of race and (non)personhood that governed nineteenth-century slave culture. Writes Grayson, "The continuing legacy of miscegenation laws that used . . . the 'one drop rule' to maintain distinctions and separations among groups of people place a high value on white skin—white blood—because those who can have it are strictly limited and monitored. . . . To say that Johnson could be a mother to baby Christopher would be to indicate a willingness on the part of the courts and the public to relinquish or, at minimum, to blur racial-familial boundaries."[22] And states Roberts: "The vision of Black women's wombs in the service of white men conjures up images from slavery. . . . In fact, Anna Johnson's lawyer likened the arrangement Johnson made with the Calverts to a 'slave contract'" (*KBB*, 282).

In constructing the notion of a "slave contract," Johnson's lawyer was no doubt hoping to mobilize the history of enforced kinship and state control over black women's reproduction as a discursive tool in arguing against the wealth and marital status that conferred privilege to the Calverts. But to the extent that critics reiterate the analogy between slavery and surrogacy, they fail to distinguish between these two forms of human property relations, overlooking at least two crucial issues: first, that being married to a white man does not make Crispina Calvert white nor does it make her children unambiguously white; and second, that Anna Johnson is not a slave woman; she has access to the liberal rights of personhood that enabled her to enter into the contractual relation with the Calverts in the first place. While such contractual rights do not enable Johnson to enter either the court or the media on par with Mark Calvert, it is important to articulate the specificities of racialization through which Johnson is disempowered here. As Saidiya Hartman discusses, the transformation from slavery to contractual personhood that took place in the Reconstruction era (and that has been furthered with the demise of official segregation as a national policy) did not "liberate the former slave from his or her bonds but rather sought to replace the whip with the compulsory contract . . . [L]iberal notions of responsibility modeled on contractual obligation, calculated reciprocity, and most important, indebtedness . . . played a central role in the creation of the servile, blameworthy, and guilty individual."[23] From this perspective, it is Johnson's status as an indebted liberal subject that explicates the mode of racial subjection operating here where her responsibility to the social world that recognizes her as worthy of universal inclusion makes her guilty of the failure of honoring the contract, a failure made manifest in the media discourse that represents her as a former welfare cheat.

None of this is to say that the history of slavery has no significant bearing on *Anna J. v. Mark C.*; far from it. But its bearing is less analogical than discursive: the case transmutes the ideology of the racialized system it fails to fully reenact through the descriptions of Johnson as a default queen, the one who risks social chaos by discarding her responsibility to fulfill the obligations of the social, borne through contract. This is, then, a historical trace of the transformations that black maternity in the United States has been forced to yield: where, first, reproduction in the slave economy writes black women as naturally hyperproductive (and thereby increases productivity in fulfillment of the property logic of accumulation), and where, second, freedom engenders a palpable fear about monstrous reproductivity in the context of a cultural discourse about native black social irresponsibility.[24] Anna Johnson's value, we might say, arises from her obligation to contractual personhood and its twentieth-century reformulations of racialized servitude. Thus, while the media representation of *Anna J. v. Mark C.* ignored Crispina Calvert's racial specificity in order to privilege the white father's paternity over both the genetic and gestational mothers, the subsequent reinstallation of such an analytic in feminist discussions of the case disables our ability to render historically palpable racialization as a multiply scripted cultural and historical process on one hand and the status of contract as a means of securing the liberal entitlements of personhood on the other. It also critically negates the significance of the marital contract between Mark and Crispina Calvert that, while offering a state sanction to interracial sexuality, places their sex fully within the law as a disciplinary practice for normative heterosexuality and monogamous reproduction. The Calverts' desire for a child that "looks just like us" repeats, ideologically, the fantasy of merger that the romance narrative of heterosexuality repeatedly effects, naturalizing the equation between the founding of culture and the act of heteroprocreative sex.[25] But significantly, that naturalization is not materially realized in this case, as reproductive technology begets a multiracial child who is decidedly not the consequence of interracial sex. This is a point I will return to presently.

The analytic adopted by Grayson and Roberts is not unfamiliar to those reading the feminist archive on reproductive technology, as it works to counter the patriarchal political economy of surrogacy (which, as in the Baby M case, gave priority to the contractual father) with a moral or political clarity about the material labor of the gestating body.[26] While giving birth to a child that the law refuses to name as legally one's own does repeat the theft of the body that slavery enacted, reproductive technologies in assisted conception produce the contract as a form of social mediation that differentially commodifies the relation between bodies and life. In this new economy of the body, the contract serves to secure the ideology of liberal personhood as that which, precisely, differentiates the past from the future. It is this differentiation that functions to place liberal personhood within the progress narrative of modernity, transforming the violence of "bodily theft" under slavery into the seemingly benign social relations of autonomy and choice that the contract is made to speak. This does not mean that for Anna Johnson the contract was not coercive; but it does differentiate among forms of coercion that enable us to examine and anatomize the racializing apparatus of the state after slavery's official dissolution and that underwrite, as we shall see, the deployment of various naturalizing discourses of race in the context of reproductive technology today.

More to the point, the contract logic of liberal personhood is central to understanding the racial complications of the Rogers-Fasano case, where genetics replace gestation as the foundational language of property-as-life, and maternal affect is rerouted in the language of the law from the discourse of the body to the property life of the gene. For the Rogerses, this is the dream of liberal personhood from its other side where the contract obligation borne by the fertility clinic and its manipulation of bodily material enables the nonreproductive black woman to succeed in attaining legal maternity. The theft of the body that characterized slavery—in which maternal affect was unrecognizable as either human or real—and that wrote the gestating black body out of maternity is replaced by capital's authority to mediate two mistakes: nature's "mistake" of infertility and the clinic's mistake of improper property implantation. In paying for a service that promises to give nature-as-reproduction "back" to the province of the body, the Rogerses can guarantee their right to liberal personhood through the contract. In this way, Deborah Perry-Rogers comes to own the labor of another woman's gestation, as the property logic of personhood extends itself to the level of the gene.

And what of Donna Fasano, a white woman who gave birth to a black child she hoped to legally claim as her own? As the beneficiary of the mistake, she inherits property that is not, legally speaking, her own, and hence she is, as a white subject in the United States, emblematically "pregnant with history"—a history of improper property acquisition. This is nothing new, to be sure, as the social construction of whiteness in both the nineteenth and twentieth centuries has borne an intimate relation to property of all kinds: corporeal, private, and public—and such intimacy has been repeatedly conditioned on both social and personal disavowals of property theft.[27] From this perspective, Donna Fasano's attempt to privatize her own reproduction, to make her body speak the authority of gestation—of labor and belonging—was both a form of defense against her symbolic historical positioning and a kind of historical repetition of the property logic of race.

But it was also not simply a repetition, in the sense that her desire to authorize white maternity of a black child, to have her body recognized as the agency of black life, placed her in the realm of what I call multiracial desire, a desire enabled by and in this case quite contingent upon the fertility clinic's "mistake." Through the mistake, multiracial kinship, *for the white subject*, was disarticulated from the material lineage of coercion and cultural disavowal that has governed, quite literally, interracial sex and reproduction in the United States. Donna Fasano could embrace the idea of her maternity, in short, without encountering the specter of her own participation in sexual miscegenation. As epistemology, then, the mistake makes legible for us a compelling distinction, wrought by reproductive technologies and the cultural imaginaries they inaugurate, between interracial sex and multiracial desire, allowing us to understand on one hand the historical complexity of the maternal affect that Donna Fasano asked the court to recognize and, on the other hand, the sheer force that the gene as propertied personhood now culturally encodes.

The distinction between interracial and multiracial runs along a number of critical axes and in the next section of this essay I want to demonstrate how it performs itself in contemporary U.S. life by thinking about and through popular culture. But first I want to meditate further on the complexity of cross-racial feeling, which underlies the Fasano's claim to Joseph and their insistence that the boys be raised as brothers. I return to the disturbing language of race and belonging used by their lawyer: They "don't see [Joseph] as someone else's black baby; they see him as their baby." On the face of it, this statement suggests a kind of radical deracialization of the child Donna Fasano bore, such that the baby is marked black only at the scene of his potential genetic ownership by Deborah and Robert Rogers; in the structure of the Fasano family, he appears then as simply "their baby." But is this the only possible reading? After all, the Fasanos have to make their claim to the child through the discourse of gestation, which means that they must privilege relationality over property and hence kinship through the body over racial categorization as a naturalized mode of familial belonging. As such, seeing Joseph as their baby—not as someone else's black baby—is not in any simple way a negation of racial difference but a means to subvert the gene's ability to naturalize race as property, which functions here to undermine the Fasano's ability to claim cross-racial kinship. To see him as "their baby" is not, then, a definitive refusal to see the child as black; rather, it is a refusal to index his blackness as that which would naturally locate his belonging elsewhere.

In this complex structure, Joseph's blackness—as a pure description of his category of social person—is that which gives him back to the property logic of the gene and hence that which annuls the affective economy of gestation and birth within which the Fasanos make their claim to parenthood (an economy overdetermined, as I will discuss, by the gender structure of patriarchal marriage and its legislation of reproduction via the contract by the state). In the televisual coverage of the case (both *20/20* and *Dateline* ran segments), the Fasanos talk about the social challenge of raising a black child in a white family. Images of the family in their home show that they assembled a collection of toys for the boys that included figures in both black and white. In this way, the Fasanos claim Joseph as "their baby" not to deny racial difference but to incorporate that difference into the language of family, as evinced by their emphasis on the boys as both "twins" and "brothers." Most crucially, this brotherhood is grounded in the idea (and ideal) that the boys shared the same environment and life force from conception to birth. It is this simultaneously social and familial bond, bred in and itself naturalized by the womb, that makes possible a kinship formation that translates the clinic's "mistake" into cross-racial feeling. For the Rogerses, of course, the imposition of kinship with a white couple has both a structural and historical horror, and in interviews they repeatedly refused the idea that the boys could be brothers. For them, brotherhood required a relation of genetic kinship with a shared parent; hence the boys were twins because of their life in the uterus but they were not and could not be brothers. The war established here between conceptions of race that naturalize it in two ways—as genetic and propertied and as familial and affective—is an important feature of the contemporary terrain of reproductive technologies and the cultural imaginaries they beget. Most crucially for my argument, this war in which race is naturalized by the body in openly contested ways is central to the affective and political articulation of white multiracial desire, as I hope to explain.

Paternity

If feminist histories of racialized maternity are brought into critical reconsideration by the issues that lead up to and involve the Rogerses and Fasanos, it is not yet clear how the distinctions I have been forging between the property logics of slavery and those of liberal personhood, on one hand, and between concepts of interracial and multiracial, on the other, shape paternity, which has historically vied with gestation as the lingua franca of natural reproduction. In the case of *Anna J. v. Mark C.*, as elsewhere in the world of racialized technological reproduction, white paternity goes up directly against black gestational maternity and wins the day, as the contribution of genetic material and the contract take priority in a contest bound to commerce and property. This is the case, under different conditions of racialization, for Robert and Deborah Rogers, whose contract with the fertility clinic underwrites their final legal claim to Akiel. But what of Richard Fasano's claim to Joseph's paternity? The Fasanos, as I have discussed, "don't see [Joseph] as someone else's black baby; they see him as their baby." And this is the case even though the couple learned six weeks into the pregnancy that Donna was carrying a fetus that was not genetically hers. The pedagogic power of gestation and birth to make visible what conception itself has been socially written to mean—as normatively and romantically the life merger between husband and wife—functions here in the absence of the couple's ability to retrospectively construct an originary procreative moment of mutually embodied experience. The marital contract is thus the only vehicle for Richard Fasano to enter into this story as a legal player, and it is precisely that contract that renders his paternity coextensive (at the very least) with Donna's gestational claim.

For Richard Fasano, then, paternity is indicated in the "old-fashioned" way, based on the marital contract that legitimates his right to the reproductive consequences of his wife's womb, regardless of his actual status as genetic father. What strikes me as particularly important here is the ideological work that the detachment of sex from birth performs in the cultural imaginary of race. Richard Fasano can imagine himself Joseph's father without encountering any of the historically defined horror of miscegenation, as his wife's birthing of a black child bears none of the affect of extramarital interracial sex. For a white man to claim the obligation of kinship to the black child his wife bore is more than a far cry from the kinship structures engendered by slavery that consecrated, through the hierarchical arrangements of property and (non)personhood, the cultural disavowal of violently extracted interracial reproduction. This claim to kinship is, it seems to me, a symbolic rearticulation of white paternity, avowing the formerly disavowed and reconfiguring the romance narrative of implicitly homogeneous heterosexuality into a sentimental form that nurtures cross-racial feeling, made safe by the eradication of sex itself.

This last point is the one I want to pursue in this section by looking at how the development of a multiracial national imaginary in the post–Civil Rights era has worked to reconfigure the popular discourse on race and sexuality, forging what I think of as an increasingly sentimentalized white masculinity that rewrites its centrality to the nation by embracing new modes of cross-racial feeling. These modes stand in stark contrast to public discourses of separation, segregation, and violence that have marked earlier dominant forms of white supremacy in which white masculinity was culturally legible as racial affect through its legal, psychic, and epistemological disavowal of interracial sex. It is my contention here that by refusing such forms of white supremacy that sought, violently, to preserve the unpreservable (racial purity), the new sentimental white masculinity participates in the project of liberal whiteness by incorporating—as a standard of inclusion and political expansion—multiracial desire as its dominant cultural affect. To make this claim in the context of new reproductive technologies and the cases this paper examines entails, at the very least, interpreting Richard Fasano's paternity claim to a black child in its historical transformation of white masculinity's grammar of racial affect, emphasizing as I have above, the force of the heterosexual contract and its propertied relation to the labor of the wife's gestating body as a vehicle for the production of cross-racial feeling. It means also understanding how, in the Calvert-Johnson case, Mark Calvert's whiteness was not deployed to ensure its unambiguous racial reproduction but to claim a mixed-race child. In these forms of what I want to think of as progressive multiracialism, we can understand how the cultural imaginary in which white masculinity today takes shape has undergone its own pedagogical reconstruction.[28] That this multiculturalism is often set against blackness, as in the Calvert case, or deployed to renaturalize race into a corporeal logic is one of the crueler aspects of liberal whiteness: Its dream of panethnicity is materially bolstered by the persistent status of white patriarchal authority as the arbitrator of ethnic hierarchies on one hand and as the standard of responsible contractual citizenship on the other.

Nowhere in the popular imaginary have these issues been more cogently portrayed than in the 1993 film *Made in America*. This film was no box office hit, to be sure, but it represents one of the first attempts to explore in popular cinema the new reproductive technologies as an arena for cultural rearticulations of race, kinship, and national belonging. Starring Whoopi Goldberg as Sarah Matthews and Ted Danson as Hal Jackson (and writing their very public affair of the early nineties into cinematic history), the film is, narratively speaking, a paternity plot. It opens in biology class where Sarah's daughter Zora (Nia Long) and her friend Tea Cake (Will Smith) complete an assignment to determine their personal blood type. What Zora learns sends her on a quest that culminates in a twin discovery: that artificial insemination was her conception's sexless primal scene and that her biological father, Hal Jackson, is white. What strikes me as particularly important about this film is the ideological work that reproductive technology performs in the cultural imaginary of race, engineering a liberal fantasy about the origin and existence of multiracial families that detaches reproduction from interracial sex.

Made in America accomplishes precisely this detachment of interracial sex from the reproduction of multiracial families and persons that I take to be a central symbolic reconfiguration of white masculinity in the contemporary era.[29] It does this through the initial narrative focus on artificial insemination as the origin point of cross-racial alliance, thereby crafting the multiracial family as possible without the procreative enactment of literal interracial sex. And yet even this disembodied reproduction is not in the end ideologically safe enough. So anxious, in fact, is the film about the specter of interracial sexual reproduction that its final discovery must reverse its inaugurating one: Hal is not Zora's biological father after all. The fertility clinic's records, it turns out, were woefully scrambled when it sent its handwritten documents "overseas" for translation to computer. This last small detail seems hardly worth repeating, except that it provides an ideologically salient displacement: the origin of confused racial origins is external to the nation—it happened "overseas." By its end, the plot thus refuses the technological compromise it seemed initially willing to accept, settling instead on the ideologically normative representation of reproduction as a monoracial domain. With this move, *Made in America* makes sure that both racial *and* national categories maintain their biogenetic distinction; Hal has not fathered a black woman's daughter; Zora is not a white man's child; the fertility clinic's records have been miscegenated by unseen forces "overseas." If interracial union, then, is disavowed through the focus on artificial insemination and artificial insemination as a vehicle for biracial reproduction is ultimately rendered impossible, how precisely does the film manage to produce a multiracial family as the cultural destination for a distinctly new American kinship relation?

It does so by offering the proposition that white acceptance of the idea of interracial kinship is itself a healing pedagogical power, for both individuals and the nation. When Hal consents emotionally to the possibility of his paternity to a black child, he is transformed from a neoliberal-racist bachelor who lives in a white mansion on a hill to a member of a black family, indeed its new father-husband figure.[30] The construction of the scene that marks his affective conversion is crucial to understanding the national discourse that reverberates throughout *Made in America* (the title, displayed in the opening credits in red-white-and-blue script, certainly makes no effort to conceal its national dedication). Sitting alone drinking beer and watching television, Hal becomes emotionally transfixed by the triumphant final scene of *The Little Princess* in which Shirley Temple, that icon of white American girlhood, is reunited with her soldier father and the two embrace. In a wistful identification with this father-daughter reunion, set against the backdrop of melodramatic nationalism, Hal sentimentally accepts Zora as his daughter. The pedagogy of this moment of white liberalism is life transforming; embracing the idea of his parentage of a black woman's child, Hal quits a whole range of bad habits, including his emotionally empty attachment to his girlfriend. The film thus mobilizes the idea of multiracial kinship as a pedagogical lesson in soulful living, thereby rescuing the white man from the very dangerousness that he has come to inflict on himself (through drinking, smoking, reckless driving, and emotional detachment). This lesson is so successful that Hal becomes dejected when he learns that Zora is not his biological daughter. But since the pedagogical lesson requires finally only the acceptance of the idea of white paternity of a black child and not its literalization, Hal's sense of loss is recuperated in the final scene as Zora calls him "my father." Through these plot maneuvers, *Made in America* transforms the specter of interracial procreative sexuality into nonprogenitive multiracialism, as the multiracial family form emerges, distinctly, through something other than sexed means.

To a certain extent, one could argue that this last fact demonstrates the film's own understanding of the anthropological distinction between social and biological parenting, as the narrative works to denaturalize the cultural insistence that genetic relatedness founds the affective economy that generates the social ties of kin. The film's ideology of family pivots, after all, on the idea that acknowledging the possibility of fathering a biracial child provides the proper feeling to maintain the psychological link otherwise thought to be initiated by blood. But while the escape from kinship's biological grounding is ideologically enticing—and while the clarity about human interrelations as after-effects of kinship formations is intellectually exciting— even the social constructionist reading lacks the power to fully rehabilitate the film's invested desire in sentimental feeling as itself a natural domain for the multiracial family's national belonging. For in the translation of Hal's paternity from a biological to a symbolically patriotic claim that arises from sentimental feeling, the film does not relinquish the discourse of nature but simply relocates it; in the process, it manages to leave intact the fantasy of distinct bioracial lines. To be sure, *Made in America* does not bar interracial sexuality on the whole, for the romance narrative between Hal and Sarah is quite classically defined by bodily desire, even if of the PG-rating kind. But their status as a (nearly) postreproductive couple disengages sexual from procreative activity. It is for this reason, I believe, that the film labors through a potential sex scene with Zora and Diego, a Latino who works at Hal's dealership. By raising the specter of *this* interracial activity, which because of their ages is also potentially procreative, *Made in America* confirms its narrative refusal to challenge U.S. ideologies about the naturalness of race at the level most intimate and threatening.

Zora's date with Diego also demonstrates that while the film's primary couple form, via Sarah and Hal, is black-white, its racial imaginary is not uniformly fixed on this binary configuration. Indeed, the secondary cast of characters affirms a representational multiracialism, with named Latino, Asian American, and African American bit players. But while Hal Jackson's world is peopled with racial "diversity," it is significant that the film offers no other named white male character, which means that the crisis of subjectivity being explored in *Made in America* is precisely that of a now singular white masculinity facing the possibility of its own erasure. Hal's sentimentality is ultimately the means by which the film manages this subjective crisis, and it is in the nature of his kinship feeling that he comes to be rescued from a vacuous, dead-white life. While such a narrative in which black people give soul to whiteness is nothing new, its reiteration here rewrites the threat of white subjective disintegration in the context of a liberal, multicultural public discourse that defines racial diversity and inclusion as coextensive with national democratic achievement. That the film offers as cultural difference only a commodified representation of Afrocentrism (via Sarah's ownership of "African Queen," a book and novelty store) is less a contradiction than a strategic redeployment of all signs of difference into the discourse of class and consumption. And it is this redeployment, in which the political economy of historical processes of racialization are rendered secondary to the property forms of contemporary identity discourse, that functions to make equality the founding sensibility of the language (and leger) of personhood characteristic of the multicultural national imaginary.[31]

In the narrative movement that I have now charted—where the initial specter of sexual coupling is denounced in favor of a discourse of cross-racial feeling—we witness the film's ambivalence about the genre conventions of romance that it seems to reiterate: the couple form here must struggle to define itself outside the very conventions of embodied intimacy that locate the romance genre in a narrative discourse about the origins of kinship. In *Made in America*, the ambivalence arises precisely from the potential violation of romance's unspoken affiliation with racial sameness—an affiliation that becomes apparent by noticing how narratives of interracial love are more often organized under the genre terms of tragedy or sentiment than of romance itself. Tragedy witnesses the inability of interraciality to sustain itself, often in narratives that feature passing characters whose "real" blood identity is ultimately discovered and the lovers must part. Sentimentalism, on the other hand, negotiates the consequences of interracial sexuality by emphasizing not sexual but familial love and founding that love in a broader discourse about moral and national responsibility. In popular texts of the nineteenth century, including some of the most canonical slave narratives, for instance, sentimental discourse defines family and equality as coextensive in order to link black humanity to blood ties and rewrite slavery as the horror of enslaving one's own kin. While sentimental rhetoric was less a challenge to the economic structure of slavery than to its affective economy, it worked by naturalizing, as a form of feeling, the familial discourse that underwrote the monogenetic Christian belief in the total unity of man. Its strategy was a powerful, if not unproblematical, counter to the slavocracy's legal armature that substituted property for personhood and repeatedly consigned the slave woman's reproduction to accumulation as a desexualizing and defamilializing economic end. And yet precisely because of its tie to the violence of slavery, sentimental discourse in the nineteenth century turned to cross-racial feeling not to inaugurate a national discourse about multiracialism as the essence, if you will, of national identity but, rather, to right the wrong of slavery, understood primarily through the specter of interraciality as the domain of violation and violence.[32]

Made in America both lives up to and departs significantly from this description of sentimental narrative. On one hand, its narrative trajectory is aimed toward establishing cross-racial feeling and a sense of the implicit kinship between racially differentiated groups. On the other hand, it works to obviate altogether the possibilities that interracial sexuality might serve as the foundation for inculcating the affective economy of kinship. In this contradictory dynamic between biogenetic and social relatedness, it works to extradite Hal, as the emblem of white masculinity, from the history of racialized property relations while simultaneously ensconcing him in the domain of sentimental feeling. These narrative moves are made possible by the presence of new reproductive technologies that enable a vision of social reproduction not dependent on the biogenetic encounter that has come to be written as the originating moment of both nation and culture in sex. We are left, then, with a discourse of cross-racial feeling that sanitizes affect and separates it from embodiment, thereby rewriting the nineteenth-century sentimental tradition from a recognition of inequality and violence into nonsexual romantic comedy, which is to say that *Made in America* achieves the multiracial feeling necessary to the liberal consciousness of multiculturalism itself. In doing so, the film repeats what the legal cases of artificial insemination and accidental in vitro fertilization seem to assume with all the confidence that DNA provides for anchoring the truth of blood and nature: that racial categories are distinct. As the newspaper reports of the Rogers-Fasano case attest, one baby was unquestionably white and the other black.

Critical Kinship

I have used the Rogers-Fasano story as the occasion for considering the messiness of affect, personhood, property, and kinship that disorganizes the racialization of reproduction in contemporary U.S. culture today. My archive is eclectic, even idiosyncratic; and my argument is less comprehensive than mosaic; it proceeds by exploring three points: 1) how the feminist archive has failed to render a nuanced reading of the racial politics of contemporary reproduction by insisting on an analogy between surrogacy and slavery as its chief analytic; 2) how this insistence ignores the contract that serves as the defining feature not only for new reproductive kinship relations but of liberal personhood as the dominant subject formation within which racialization now takes place; and 3) how in the popular imaginary, new reproductive technologies provide the technical assistance to imagine multiracial families without engaging the living horror of miscegenation as the fleshiness of interracial sex. In all of this, I have been concerned with the way new reproductive technologies question our critical understanding of American culture's most cherished kinship terms—family, mother, father, brother—in ways that force us to rethink their present and past naturalization.

At the same time, I have tried not to place the issue of reproductive technologies in the context of temporal historical progress, as if the discursive operations of culture enable the seemingly new ever to replace without a living trace the old. Instead, I have used the Rogers and Fasano case to read the realm of reproductive technologies as an incoherent primal scene where embodied relatedness mingles with the genetic scientific imaginary that has now set Nature in conflict with Life and remapped the body as an engine of replication (the gene) and not reproduction (gestation). In this primal scene, the scientific worldview struggles to establish its legal authority, already consecrated in academic knowledge regimes, over everyday life. Understood, then, as contestatory knowledge projects, new reproductive technologies function at the incoherent intersection of various cultural discourses and domains and make possible, in their articulation in and through cultural imaginaries, our consideration of how race is being reanimated as nature in thoroughly contradictory ways in the United States today.

In making this claim for reading reproductive technologies as implicated in contestatory knowledge projects about race and nature, I do not mean to suggest that such technologies are more troublesome objects of study than those we otherwise encounter in critical work. But I am interested in how their analysis across the disparate domains of law, popular culture, and academic feminist criticism fails to identify with precision a consistent or paradigmatic operation for understanding contemporary racialization in the context of assisted conception. This is the case, in part, because racialization, as I noted at the outset, is itself an incoherent process. And it is for this reason that I have made no critical claim to provide an analytically consistent or methodologically coherent linkage of the discursive sites that I have assembled. In this failure to commit to the epistemological optimism (otherwise known as closure) provided by method and secured through a disciplinary apparatus that can claim for itself critical comprehension, I have tried to inhabit what I think of as the antidisciplinary productivity of an interdisciplinary study of race, which is constituted not by making a claim for the radical particularity of my critical sites (and hence for a critical practice borne of the objects of study under consideration) but by trying to resist the normalizing effects of humanistic knowledge production that are secured by reproducing the individual as historical subject.

Such resistance is of course never complete, never more than a failed attempt, if for no other reason than that our critical act cannot *not* be invested in understanding *something* about the specificity of the human in the making and unmaking of culture. How, after all, can I not want to account for the affective complexity, not to mention historical and political strangeness, of the images of maternity that the Rogers-Fasano case offers us: the theft of the body that Deborah Perry-Rogers experiences in the presence of the white woman who nurtured and birthed her genetic son; the embodied maternity that Donna Fasano powerfully feels as she who quite literally nurtured the "mistake" of misbegotten property. But it is precisely because agency is so fully awry in this case and the legal apparatus of liberal personhood called on to correct it so completely unable to bring reproduction back into the authority of embodied heteronormativity that one cannot turn to humanistic inquiry's desire for the individual's self-reflective articulation to settle the cultural implications and historical determinations raised by the case. There can be no justice, to put it in the language of political obligation so familiar in feminist knowledge production, for either the Fasanos or Rogerses here, no account in this critical act that can render their implication in the contestations of race and nature individual in the sense that we might partake comprehensively in the knowledge of the experiential pain that the mistake inaugurated for them. What, after all, do we want *that* knowledge for? Critical kinship with the objects we study?

This is perhaps a long and rather complicated way to explain my own resistance to any critical project that seeks kinship with its objects of study through the promise of methodological knowledge production. Instead, I have tried to demonstrate how the recursivity and relationality among my disparate discursive sites performs the cultural work of "nature" in the absence of knowing human subjects who can constitute themselves as such, even—indeed especially— in the context of liberal personhood's ideological pretensions to the contrary. By reading the technological "nature" of reproduction as it seeks to anchor itself as the contemporary epistemological foundation of both culture and bodies, and by linking this to heteronormativity; liberal notions of law, personhood, and property; contractual entitlements; maternal affect; white masculine sentiment; and national belonging in a multiracial cultural imaginary, I have tried to say something about the powerful effects and contradictory knowledge projects that attend the unstable regimes of naturalized race and racialized nature as they are articulated in and through reproductive technologies in the United States today.

Duke University

Notes

My thanks to Bill Maurer and Donald Moore for their pedagogical engagements with the anthropologically untrained, and to audiences at the Dartmouth Institute on American Studies; the University of California, Riverside; the University of California, Berkeley; the University of West Virginia; the University of Illinois, Chicago; and the MLA for their productive engagements. My additional thanks to Elena Glasberg for her astute readings of earlier drafts and to Brian Carr for his intellectual engagement and research assistance.
1   I draw my information on this case from four newspaper sources: Jim Yardley, "Health Officials Investigating to Determine How Woman Got the Embryo of Another," *New York Times*, 31 March 1999, B3; Michael Grunwald, "In Vitro, in Error—and Now, in Court; White Mother Given Black Couple's Embryos Will Give One 'Twin' Back," *Washington Post*,

31 March 1999, A01; Jim Yardley, "Sharing Baby Proves Rough on 2 Mothers," *New York Times*, 30 June 1999, B1; and David Rohde, "Biological Parents Win in Implant Case," *New York Times*, 17 July 1999, late edition, B3.

2   In various newspaper accounts, reporters simultaneously use and euphemize the word *twin*, putting it in scare quotes and defining one boy as black and the other as white. While the dictionary understanding of the word *twin* indicates the emergence of two new persons in a single birth, it is important to chart how the new reproductive technologies are making legible the naturalized assumptions about kinship and social relation on which twinship (and other terms) has long depended.

3   Donna Fasano; quoted in Grunwald, "In Vitro."

4   Throughout this essay, I use both Akiel and Joseph to refer to the contested child, depending on the family scenario I am discussing at the time.

5   Yardley, "Sharing Baby."

6   David Cohen; quoted in Grunwald, "In Vitro."

7   Donna Fasano; quoted in Yardley, "Sharing Baby."

8   Rudolph Silas; quoted in Yardley, "Sharing Baby."

9   Fasano is not, however, the first white woman to give birth to two children genetically classified as racially different. In 1995 a Dutch fertility clinic mistakenly fertilized a woman's eggs with the sperm of both her husband and a black man. She gave birth to twin boys and the white couple is now raising both of them (see Dorinda Elliot and Friso Endt, "Twins—with Two Fathers; The Netherlands: A Fertility Clinic's Startling Error," *Newsweek*, 3 July 1995, 38). The case is also referenced by Yardley, "Health Officials," and discussed briefly by Dorothy Roberts, *Killing the Black Body: Race, Reproduction, and the Meaning of Liberty* (New York: Vintage, 1997), 252. Further references to *Killing the Black Body* will be cited parenthetically in the text as *KBB*.

10 On the figure of the vampire as it relates to race and reproduction, see Donna Haraway, "RACE: Universal Donors in a Vampire Culture," *Modest_Witness@Second_Millennium. FemaleMan©_Meets_OncoMouse: Feminism and Technoscience* (New York: Routledge, 1997), 213–65.

11 See my "Whiteness Studies and the Paradox of Particularity," *boundary 2* (fall 1999): 115–50.

12 Because my essay was written in the context of this larger project on liberal whiteness, my focus in its latter stages tends to emphasize the racial affect of the Fasanos and their symbolic occupation of what I want to define as white multiracial desire. Readers more interested in the complexity of the Rogerses' response will, I hope, understand the analytic purchase this paper seeks.

13 I have decided not to "scare quote" my usage of parent, mother, father, brother, even reproduction and the human in this essay, in part because such marks cannot unwrite the power of these terms to renaturalize

themselves even in the context of critical attempts at rendering their social construction.

14 Scholarship on new reproductive technologies is by now too lengthy to comprehensively list. Some of the most widely cited studies include Jeanette Edwards, Sarah Franklin, Eric Hirsch, Frances Price, and Marilyn Strathern, *Technologies of Procreation: Kinship in the Age of Assisted Conception*, 2d ed. (London: Routledge, 1999); Sarah Franklin, *Embodied Progress: A Cultural Account of Assisted Conception* (London: Routledge, 1997); Sarah Franklin and Helen Ragone, eds., *Reproducing Reproduction: Kinship, Power, and Technological Innovation* (Philadelphia: Univ. of Pennsylvania Press, 1998); Valerie Hartouni, *Cultural Conceptions: On Reproductive Technologies and the Remaking of Life* (Minneapolis: Univ. of Minnesota Press, 1997); Maureen McNeil, Ian Varcoc, and Steven Yearley, eds., *The New Reproductive Technologies* (London: Macmillan, 1990); Michelle Stansworth, ed., *Reproductive Technologies: Gender, Motherhood, and Medicine* (Cambridge, Eng.: Polity Press, 1987); and Marilyn Strathern, *Reproducing the Future: Anthropology, Kinship, and the New Reproductive Technologies* (London: Routledge, 1992).

15 Sarah Franklin, "Romancing the Helix: Nature and Scientific Discovery," in *Romance Revisited*, ed. Lynne Pearce and Jackie Stacy (London: Lawrence & Wishart, 1995), 64.

16 George Annas, Professor of Health Law at Boston University; cited in Grunwald, "In Vitro." This standard seems to have arisen in relation to surrogacy cases in which the gestational mother and the biogenetic mother are the same.

17 *Anna J. v. Mark C. et al.*, 286 Cal. Rptr., 372 (Cal.App.4 Dist. 1991) and *Johnson v. Calvert*, 19 Cal. Rptr.2d, 506–18 (Cal.1993); cert. Denied, 113 S.Ct 206 (1993). For critical conversation about this case, see Deborah Grayson, "Mediating Intimacy: Black Surrogate Mothers and the Law," *Critical Inquiry* 24 (winter 1998): 525–46; Valerie Hartouni, "Breached Birth: Reflections on Race, Gender, and Reproductive Discourse in the 1980s," *Configurations* 1 (winter 1994): 73–88; Randy Frances Kandel, "Which Came First: The Mother or the Egg? A Kinship Solution to Gestational Surrogacy," *Rutgers Law Review* 47 (fall 1994): 165–239; and Mark Rose, "Mothers and Authors: *Johnson v. Calvert* and the New Children of Our Imaginations," *Critical Inquiry* 22 (summer 1996): 613–33.

18 Grayson, "Mediating Intimacy," 538.

19 In arguing that natural motherhood resided with the woman whose intention to donate the ova and to raise the child had initiated the surrogacy contract in the first place, the court made a distinction between what Laura Doyle examines as a familiar racial trope, the "ruling 'head' and the laboring 'body'" (*Bordering on the Body: The Racial Matrix of Modern Fiction and Culture* [New York: Routledge, 1994], 21). The lone dissenting opinion by Justice Joyce Kennard argued that the use of "intention"

to ground the majority decision suffered from a problematical equation between children and intellectual property (*Johnson v. Calvert*, 514). See also Grayson, "Mediating Intimacy," 534–36.

20 Franklin, "Romancing the Helix," 70.

21 Grayson, "Mediating Intimacy," 529 n 10. Significantly, the "model minority" label is itself unevenly distributed within the many ethnicities that coalesce under the sign Asian American, with Japanese and Chinese taking cultural precedence over Southeast Asians and Pacific Islanders, including Filipino/as. In fact, in a recent assessment of education in the state of California, Filipino/as were found to be more on par (which is to say similarly economically and racially oppressed) with Latinos than with several of the ethnic groups within the category Asian American. At the University of California-Irvine, as elsewhere in the state, there has been some student interest in detaching Filipino/a from Asian American, which has politically controversial implications for Asian American studies as a program and field.

22 Grayson, "Mediating Intimacy," 545. This comment is preceded by Grayson's deliberation on Crispina Calvert's statement, quoted routinely in the press, that the baby "looks just like us." Grayson interprets this statement as indicating not only "rights to parentage" but also "as a sign for blood—for the closed, racialized membership of family and race" ("Mediating Intimacy," 545). Here, again, is the condensation of the interraciality of the Calverts into a discourse of white racial homogeneity, one that functions in Grayson's text as the vehicle for rendering temporal continuity between the practices of slave culture and those of reproductive technologies.

23 Saidiya Hartman, *Scenes of Subjection: Terror, Slavery, and Self-Making in Nineteenth-Century America* (New York: Oxford Univ. Press, 1997), 9. Focusing on the official transformation from slavery to freedom, Hartman argues that "the vision of equality forged in the law naturalized racial subordination while attempting to prevent discrimination based on race or former condition of servitude" (9). In doing so, she "illuminates the double bind of equality and exclusion that distinguishes modern state racism from its antebellum predecessor" (9).

24 In writing this teleology, I do not mean to suggest that in the antebellum period black hyperproductivity raised no fear for the white national imaginary. The point is rather that while slavery structured a racialized division between persons and things, legal enfranchisement marked a process of reordering that offered little conscious or material reward for whites to value the reproduction of black persons.

25 See David Schneider, *American Kinship: A Cultural Account* (Englewood Cliffs, New Jersey: Prentice-Hall, 1968); and Sylvia Yanagisako and Carol Delaney, eds., *Naturalizing Power: Essays in Feminist Cultural Analysis* (London: Routledge, 1995).

26 In the "Baby M" case, the court awarded legal custody to the contractual father-sperm provider, giving the birth mother, who was also the biogenetic mother, visitation rights; see Anita Allen, "Privacy, Surrogacy and the Baby M Case," *Georgetown Law Journal* 76 (June 1988): 1759–92.

27 See George Lipsitz, *The Possessive Investment in Whiteness: How White People Profit from Identity Politics* (Philadelphia: Temple Univ. Press, 1998).

28 It is perhaps not coincidental that the major cultural text I read in my "Whiteness Studies and the Paradox of Particularity" is the popular 1994 film *Forrest Gump*, which while set in the South and in some ways overdetermined by the historical racial discourse of slavery, nonetheless pairs a white male and an Asian American woman as the model for a nonviolent, multicultural future. This alignment has a great deal to do with the film's articulation of a compensatory narrative concerning U.S. involvement in Vietnam, but it is a significant aspect of contemporary racial discourse that the power of whiteness does not secure itself through a segregation discourse or representational imaginary, as was clearly the case in the slave South. Rather, the fantasy that white supremacy ended with the official disestablishment of segregation is anxiously and hence repeatedly reproduced in images of interracial solidarity and (increasingly) sexuality. That Asian American female subjectivity mediates the racial dynamic of black-white is an important critical component to rendering the intersecting dynamics of racialization.

29 I am not claiming that the sentimentalizing of white masculinity is the only way in which liberal whiteness currently operates as a representational project in the national imaginary. Indeed, the national imaginary is not itself unitary, as the contestation between the far right and the multicultural left, to use the inadequate language of the public sphere, might best indicate.

30 Significantly, Hal's reconstruction is accompanied by financial success (commercials that inadvertently feature Sarah generate boom times at his car dealership). The ultimate liberal fantasy, of course, is that personal transformation is materially advantageous as well.

31 To trace various assessments about the radical and recuperated aspects of multiculturalism's deployment in the public sphere, see David Theo Goldberg, ed., *Multiculturalism: A Critical Reader* (Oxford, Eng.: Blackwell, 1994); Avery Gordon and Christopher Newfield, eds., *Mapping Multiculturalism* (Minneapolis: Univ. of Minnesota Press, 1996); Amy Gutmann, ed., *Multiculturalism: Examining the Politics of Recognition* (Princeton, N.J.: Princeton Univ. Press, 1994); Jeff Escoffier, "The Limits of Multiculturalism," *Socialist Review* 21.3/4: 61–73; Gayatri Spivak and Sneja Gunew, "Questions of Multiculturalism," in *The Cultural Studies Reader*, ed. Simon During (London: Routledge, 1993), 193–202; and Henry A. Giroux and Peter McLaren, eds., *Between Borders: Pedagogy and the Politics of Cultural Studies* (New York: Routledge, 1994).

32   As a literary-cultural critic whose primary training focused on U.S. narrative traditions, I am well versed in the family romance plot and its reworking in sentimental discourse. But rarely in the literary archive is the social constructionist analytic sustained in rigorous enough terms to yield an interrogation of sexual reproduction as the founding act of humanity and culture. For this reason, Yanagisako and Delaney's collection, *Naturalizing Power*, provides an important set of critical models for historicizing the family plot's ideological origins at modernity's intersections of industrialization, secular humanism, scientific Nature, and liberal personhood.

Stephanie S.
Turner

Jurassic Park Technology in the Bioinformatics
Economy: How Cloning Narratives Negotiate the
Telos of DNA

> The problem was that all known dinosaurs were fossils, and
> the fossilization [had] destroyed most DNA. . . . So clon-
> ing was therefore impossible. There was nothing to clone
> from. All the modern genetic technology was useless. It
> was like having a Xerox copier but nothing to copy with
> it. —Michael Crichton, *Jurassic Park*

In her book *How We Became Posthuman*, N. Kather-
ine Hayles argues that "a defining characteristic of the present cultural moment is the belief that information can circulate unchanged
among different material substrates," which she alternately describes
as the "condition of virtuality" and the "computational universe."[1]
The material substrates Hayles considers range from research in artificial life to science fiction novels. Her examples have in common
the contemporary concern with bringing explanations of organic processes into alignment with theories about complex systems or, to be
more specific, with treating living things as information-processing
systems. The historical precedent for this view of living things can be
traced to twentieth-century physicists' perplexity over how to account
for self-organization in life given the second law of thermodynamics, entropy. Some historians of science have pinpointed the precise
arrival of this new issue in biology to Erwin Schrödinger's question,
which became the title of his 1943 lecture series, "What is Life?"[2] On
the one hand, Schrödinger was simply asking a physicist's question:
Why don't living systems succumb to dissipation, as do nonliving systems? On the other hand, Schrödinger's question cued scientists in

American Literature, Volume 74, Number 4, December 2002. Copyright © 2002 by Duke
University Press.

the emerging field of molecular biology to treat the concerns of biology more like those of physics. In doing so, they established a conceptualization of the DNA molecule as autotelic, that is, as an entity working toward its own self-contained end, through the use of such information metaphors as data, code, and program. More broadly, they laid the foundation for our present bioinformatics economy, in which the marriage of biology and information technology in postcapitalism has transformed the life sciences into a global network of commodity biological information.

The result of this metaphorization of DNA is a surplus of meaning associated with the "master molecule," well illustrated in proposals for bioprospecting projects that have cloning whole organisms as an ultimate goal, such as the mining of dinosaur blood from the bodies of ancient mosquitoes trapped in amber famously depicted in Michael Crichton's novel *Jurassic Park*. The Jurassic Park narrative is instructive in showing how the surplus of meaning surrounding DNA is contested and how cloning serves as a fulcrum in the negotiation process. The premise of the novel is that cloning the DNA of ancient Tyrannosaurus Rex "should" replicate the dinosaur, much as a photocopy machine reproduces an image. Yet at the same time, it is a foregone conclusion in the novel that this formula is inherently flawed; having something to clone from is not enough to resurrect dinosaurs. The Jurassic Park narrative raises two important questions about the information metaphor of DNA: what is the cultural significance of the conceptualization that DNA has agency, and what do cloning narratives reveal about DNA's presumed telos? Although much has been written about *Jurassic Park*'s failed capitalist critique of cloned, genetically modified dinosaurs running amok, rather than turning a profit for their creators, the central role that cloning itself plays in this turn of events has been largely overlooked.[3] A closer look at how information metaphors of DNA operate in the Jurassic Park narrative will show how genetic engineering works both with and against the telos of DNA and, more crucially, how cloning scenarios negotiate this ideological traffic.

To return to the historical context of the metaphoricity of DNA for a moment, Shrödinger's speculation that chromosomes must contain "some kind of code-script"[4] is a fusion of terms that has the effect of casting the DNA molecule as somehow the product of its own making. Again, Schrödinger's confrontation with the inexplicable resistance of life to the second law suggests how this idea of DNA as autotelic came to pass. Concluding, paradoxically, that "the term code-script is ... too narrow," he enlarges upon his sense of how organisms manage to side-step entropy: "[C]hromosome structures are at the same time instrumental in bringing about the development they foreshadow. They are law-code and executive power—or, to use another simile, they are architect's plan and builder's craft—in one."[5] Although Shrödinger acknowledges the figurative language in his representation of the DNA code-script, he seems to have no recourse in his effort to explain life itself but to engage nonliteral language, which achieves, in fact, more than a merely figurative comparison. In terms of *Jurassic Park*'s cloned dinosaurs, as I will show, this amounts to a "condition of virtuality" more real than their developers anticipated.

Considering the political climate surrounding science and technology in the United States during and immediately following World War II, the representational problems presented by Shrödinger's code-script metaphor were not likely to be resolved. With a practical need to develop information technologies and to establish their associated research as full-fledged disciplines, the code-script metaphor—which was, after all, useful—gained acceptance. James Watson and Francis Crick's 1953 description of the DNA molecule's double helical structure as a kind of linear code carried out the strange logic that Schrödinger first articulated ten years prior. Among other benefits, the rhetorical momentum established by the code-script soon established a ruling paradigm in molecular biology: the so-called Central Dogma of DNA first set forth by Crick in 1958, which stipulates the unidirectional flow of "information" in a cell from DNA to RNA to protein, never the reverse. Although the Central Dogma is not unqualifiedly true, as Evelyn Fox Keller demonstrates, it was historically important in the development of the discipline.[6] Keller has assessed the conceptual impact of Watson and Crick's famously understated description of the double helical structure of DNA as a "critical shift" in the history of biology from observation to experimentation, that is, from representation to intervention to, most significantly, control.[7]

Any assessment of this notion of control in the bioinformatics economy, however, must be qualified, because sometimes information seems to flow back into DNA. The cloning projects in Crichton's novels *Jurassic Park* and *The Lost World* illustrate this permeability. For the computer-mediated quality control of the genetically altered clones and the safety of their sanitized park in the first novel disintegrate, and the replicated dinosaurs seem to regress en masse in what a computer software writer might describe as an "unrecoverable program error" to a breed status that a field biologist might describe as a "wild type." In the involutionary, and thus cautionary, tale of irretrievable origins portrayed in the first novel, the creation becomes "lost" in the second novel not by returning to what it was "in the beginning"—as *The Lost World* title implies but which, as a simulacrum, it cannot do—but by evading the human controls so carefully engineered to contain it. As the *Jurassic Park* reader discovers in *The Lost World*, although the theme park and its inhabitants have been destroyed, a second island and its cloned inhabitants, "Hammond's dirty little secret," the "dark side of his park," remain intact.[8] Unlike the tidy research facility designed for Jurassic Park visitors, the offsite facility is a "giant industrial operation" with a production capacity far exceeding the needs of the theme park (*LW*, 142). The control problem in reprogenetics narratives such as *Jurassic Park* and *The Lost World* is the same one that Hayles sees in the history of cybernetics—the persistence of embodiment—yet with one important difference: a "mania for origins" and a countervailing fear of "involution" derived from a view of history as a totalizing account. According to Jean Baudrillard, the "mania for origins" so characteristic of mass culture at the turn of the millennium, with its repeated attempts to "restore everything," is symptomatic of an obsession with the "end of history," which, of course, never comes.[9] Similarly, in "reviewing," "rewriting," and "face-lifting everything" to produce a "perfect set of accounts," we are, in effect, "putting an end to natural selection" and thus "ushering in involution," he claims.[10] Bioprospecting with intent to clone and genetic engineering with intent to upgrade, as illustrated in the Jurassic Park narrative, are two manifestations of these countervailing forces that Baudrillard emphasizes.

Here is what Lily Kay calls the "key conundrum" of the code-script metaphor.[11] On the one hand, the information and linguistic metaphors that have sprung up around the description of DNA as a code-script have created the perception that the DNA molecule, though immutable, is infinitely adaptable in various contexts. This perception of DNA's adaptability is, in fact, the basis of the bioinformatics economy, with its capitalist imperative to innovate. Yet by leading to the metaphorization of a metaphor (*OBL*, 4), the code-script idea renders the "genetic text" a "signification without a referent" with "profound social consequences for the knowledge-claims" that result, according to Kay.[12] Among these consequences are the questions of authenticity that cloned organisms embody, and whose version of authenticity predominates. Thus we see that the problem of cloning extinct animals perceived by *Jurassic Park* paleontologist Alan Grant—that "all known dinosaurs were fossils, and the fossilization [had] destroyed most DNA. . . . So cloning was therefore impossible"—is never for a moment viewed as a problem by InGen CEO and Jurassic Park mastermind John Hammond.[13] Rather, for him, resurrecting extinct species and restoring paleohabitat is purely a matter of stockpiling the right resources and buying enough time from the project's investors to modify those resources to fit his purposes. Long before starting the actual work required to test his far-fetched hypothesis that dinosaur blood could yield viable nucleic acid, Hammond has set his plan in motion. For several years, the Hammond Foundation has been funding a number of dinosaur digs by well-known academic paleontologists, amassing "the largest privately held stock" of amber anywhere (in hopes of mining it for fossilized, dinosaur-biting insects, which might contain enough saurian blood to clone) and setting up "one of the most powerful genetic engineering facilities in the world in an obscure Central American country" (*JP*, 35–39). Of course dinosaurs can be cloned; Hammond is certain of it, even if it means augmenting the fragmented saurian DNA sequences extracted from dinosaur blood found in prehistoric mosquitoes with contemporary avian, reptilian, and amphibian DNA (*JP*, 168, 210). So although they are created by a cloning technique, the *Jurassic Park* dinosaurs cannot, strictly speaking, be described as genetic copies. They are only dinosaurs in a metaphorical sense, just as the code-script paradigm that makes possible the hypothesis of their resurrection is metaphorical.

The creation of the life forms in *Jurassic Park* supports the tenet of evolutionary theory that the adaptability of DNA does not reside within the molecule itself or even within genes but rather relies on material forces, which are always already ideological. In addition to the need for supplemental DNA sequences of anachronistic species, the *Jurassic Park* dinosaurs could never have been created without a number of high-powered computers capable of processing an enormous amount of biological data—"an incredibly powerful genetics factory," in the words of Jurassic Park's geneticist Dr. Wu (*JP*, 100).

Yet rather than manufacturing from scratch these "consumer biologicals"—Hammond's term—this factory is more precisely in the repair and refurbishing business.[14] Wu explains the role of the computers in the manufacturing process during a tour of Jurassic Park's research facility: "Much of the DNA we extract is fragmented or incomplete. So the first thing we have to do is repair it—or rather, the computer has to. It'll cut the DNA, using what are called restriction enzymes. The computer will select a variety of enzymes that might do the job" (*JP*, 101). Considering that the DNA molecule consists of more than three billion base pairs, it would take too long even for Hammond's considerable collection of supercomputers to analyze an entire strand. As it is, the research and development phase of the park is now in its fifth year (*JP*, 123). So, Wu continues, "We look only at the sections of the strand that differ from animal to animal, or from contemporary DNA" (*JP*, 103). The Jurassic Park "genetics factory" exemplifies W. J. T. Mitchell's description of "the age of biocybernetic reproduction," an era that is "beyond the machine and the assembly line," its factories places "where machines do the thinking, and the commodities coming down the assembly line are living creatures or organisms" (*LDB*, 216). In this version of the posthuman, information about dinosaur bodies precedes and influences their eventual embodiment, though the human motives of greed and scientific hubris persist in the island's dinosaur manufacturing economy.[15]

In itemizing the types of "repairs" being made to dinosaur DNA during the tour of the facility, however, Wu glosses an important detail about the manufacturing history of the dinosaurs that not only further compromises their credibility as copies but also complicates the notion of the original. "[S]ometimes," Wu allows, "we think we have an animal correctly made—from the standpoint of the DNA, which is our basic work—and the animal grows for six months and then something untoward happens. And we realize there is some error. A releaser gene isn't operating. A hormone not being released. Or some other problem in the developmental sequence. So we have to go back to the drawing board with that animal, so to speak" (*JP*, 111). As a matter of fact, Wu has spent a lot of time back at that drawing board. By the time the island theme park is ready for the "sneak preview" he gives Hammond's hand-picked visitors touring the facility, the virtual dinosaurs, like so much computer software, are already in their fourth "release version" (*JP*, 120).[16] Nevertheless, Wu, who sets a high standard for his work, finds that he needs to surpass even that. Wu knows that Hammond wants Jurassic Park "to be as real an environment as possible—as authentic as possible" (*JP*, 111), but in Wu's estimation, the achieved authenticity has backfired; the dinosaurs must be upgraded yet again. Seeing his creations through the eyes of the astonished and frightened visitors has convinced him of this; they move too fast for animals so large. After the tour, he explains the situation to Hammond as diplomatically as he can: "The dinosaurs we have now are real . . . but in certain ways they are unsatisfactory. Unconvincing. I could make them better" (*JP*, 121). Wu's evaluation of the dinosaurs as "unconvincing" presupposes a template, a universally accessible model after which true types can be molded. In fact, many such models of dinosaurs exist, as Mitchell points out in his ironically titled *The Last Dinosaur Book*.[17] There's the "terrible lizard" model attributable to nineteenth-century paleontologist Richard Owen; there's the dim-witted, slow-moving monster-doomed-to-extinction model of the early twentieth century; and there's the bird-like model of Victorian T. H. Huxley that Gregory Paul revived a hundred years later depicting, among other dinosaurs, Tyrannosaurus Rex looking, according to Mitchell, "very much like a large and rather dangerous plucked chicken" (*LDB*, 103–4, 54). In short, representations "evolve," Mitchell claims, and they sometimes do so dialectically, "taking a very long step back to move forward" (*LDB*, 104). In his painstaking, hit-or-miss process of cloning dinosaur DNA, Wu is discovering this the hard way; he will have to "retool" the biocybernetic reproduction "machinery" to create a more aesthetically pleasing representation of the dinosaur. Mitchell's analysis of the dinosaur as a national icon whose various representational phases reflect American modes of production emphasizes the hyperreality of representing prehistoric things.[18] As "a mere copy of a fragment of a corpse or [a] skeleton [or] a fossil imprint" (*LDB*, 266)—or, for that matter, of a DNA sequence—the fully assembled, museum- or amusement-park-ready dinosaur, with its equally conjectural habitat, displaces the idea of "the original" as the first thing from which everything else proceeds.[19] *The Lost World*'s open-ended narrative of "what happens next" to the abandoned dinosaur colony on the second island, an involutionary tale of an unharnessable mania for molecular origins, is sure to follow the saurian simulacrum of *Jurassic Park*.

Together, then, *Jurassic Park* and *The Lost World* show how the bioprospecting narrative functions as just another humanist tale of the tendency of capitalist commodity production to exploit resources and labor, engage in short-range planning, and emphasize conspicuous consumption. Hammond's scheme to mine, engineer, and clone from the "raw material" of saurian DNA sequences is too successful; the engineered life forms take on an unpredictable life of their own, becoming a danger to themselves and others. Mitchell, in fact, views *Jurassic Park* as an "extinction scenario" about the ultimate threat to homo sapiens. No longer, he claims, is the "threat to human life" "mass destruction"; it is the "overproduction of life itself, life out of control" (*LBD*, 226). But the cloning component in the novels shows how the bioprospecting narrative also functions as a posthumanist tale of the commodity value of disembodied genetic information, which lives on long after the "original" body itself, along with all of its descendants, has disintegrated. Hayles's emphasis on the reification of information after it has been decontextualized is just as relevant in the bioinformatics economy as it is in the history of cybernetics: even though it is embodiment that makes information possible and meaningful,[20] information is privileged over the material in narratives of bioprospecting with intent to clone.

The two novels also illustrate how the binary of perfection-degeneration that underpins cloning projects is analogous to the "perfection of 'planned obsolescence'" in the post-Fordist economy. The state-of-the-art automobile that begins to fall apart as soon as it's paid for, the exquisitely biocrafted dinosaurs that nevertheless require serial upgrading—such "'problems' or 'defects' in contemporary economic systems" are really, Mitchell contends, "the very basis for the proper functioning of those systems. Things have to break down and turn into junk, or else 'our [American] way of life' will [do so]" (*LDB*, 219). Part of the appeal of *Jurassic Park* is, after all, the domestication via bioengineering of the cloned dinosaurs; what new things can they be genetically made to do, or kept from doing, to keep park visitors entertained? Yet despite even periodic upgrades to the virtual flora and fauna, Hammond's Jurassic Park is likely to lose its novelty for the narrow target market that can afford to consume it, or be beaten out by a competitor who has an idea that is, for the moment, better. And besides, since the theme park is but a façade for Hammond's unspecified "dark side," it is expendable. Thus the cycle of planned obsolescence in capitalist production begins anew in *The Lost World* with "results-oriented" bioprofiteer Lewis Dodgson's plans for a hostile takeover of the abandoned industrial operation that the Japanese investors refuse to relinquish. Dodgson's plans for the dinosaur clones gone wild include a different sort of domestication—marketing them as research subjects. His reasoning for the preferability of dinosaurs over the usual lab mice, dogs, and monkeys is based on Baudrillard's logic of the third-order simulacrum, the copy for which no original exists.[21] "[A]n animal that is extinct, and is brought back to life, is for all practical purposes not an animal at all. It can't have any rights. It's already extinct. So if it exists, it can only be something we have made. We made it, we patent it, we own it," according to Dodgson (*LW*, 107). Outside of the law, "these animals are totally exploitable" as biological research commodities. To Dodgson's way of thinking, the virtual saurian bodies can serve as models for humans just as easily as their more cuddly counterparts, and with a lot less protest from those pesky animal rights activists, because, as he puts it, "nobody loves a lizard" (*LW*, 108, 107). Here, Dodgson is making the mistake of not paying attention to the real impact of countercultural forces on the market, for as some animal rights activists are fond of pointing out, a rat is a pig is a dog is a boy. Given DNA's function as the great equalizer, the code-script common to all life, so too is a dinosaur.

Bioengineered life forms in "real life" tend to become objects for spectacular consumption as well in the bioinformatics economy. Dolly, the cloned sheep, is a prime example. According to her caretakers at Roslin Institute in Edinburgh, Dolly has become so accustomed to being photographed by her visitors that she actually poses for the camera.[22] Bioethicist Glenn McGee, in an interesting (though not totally unrelated) departure from the usual invocation of the code-script metaphor, describes Dolly as a "snapshot—not a snapshot of an adult sheep but one of that sheep's cells."[23] And plans have already been made to stuff, mount, and display Dolly in the Royal Museum in Edinburgh,[24] even though she may continue to live for a decade or longer and even though, by the time the taxidermist prepares her body, a variety of techniques for industrialized mammalian cloning will have become commonplace, making Dolly old news.[25] Wu's claim that he can make an already good product better, the clichéd banner of commercial competition, arises from his keen sense of the dinosaurs' mass appeal, which is less associated with how historic dinosaurs really looked and acted than it is with what contemporary dinosaurs look and act like in the popular imagination: how dinosaur consumers conceptualize them. Observing the visitors' discomfort on the tour, Wu is persuaded by their assessment that the dinosaurs "move too fast." "People aren't accustomed to seeing large animals that are so quick," he explains to Hammond. "I'm afraid visitors will think the dinosaurs look speeded up, like film running too fast" (*JP*, 121). Wu's comparison to visual media is apt. Not only does Wu make good dinosaurs, he also has a good grasp of what makes a good dinosaur theme park: what people experience there should correspond with what they have already experienced while viewing the parade of dinosaur images on television and at the movies. Indeed, the people-moving plan for the Jurassic Park experience is essentially a theater on wheels, a mega-mediated, safari-like "expedition" in which visitors view the creatures in their "natural habitat" from the air-conditioned safety of fully automated Toyota Land Cruisers that inch along the park's paved roads. If, as so often disappointingly happens at a zoo, the animals on exhibit are nowhere to be seen, Jurassic Park visitors need not peer fruitlessly into the "greenery [intended] to heighten the illusion of moving through real jungle" (*JP*, 136), because on-board video screens run a constant stream of live images of the animals while a voice-over provides additional information about them. Reminding Hammond that "entertainment has nothing to do with reality," that it is, in fact, "antithetical to reality," Wu argues for the development of more "domesticated" dinosaurs (*JP*, 121). Although Hammond unwisely, from a business point of view, resists Wu's argument, it hardly matters, as this first batch of visitors to the park functions as the last straw in a series of unforeseen and uncontrollable variables in the park's development that tips the whole island over into chaos. Despite Wu's considerable scientific skills, the "too real" dinosaurs suffer from "skin problems," "blisters on their tongues," and diarrhea (*JP*, 137, 139). Not only that, they are out of synch with their restored habitat, lacking the bacteria needed to break down their feces, appearing, in the case of the stegosaurs, to be poisoned, coexisting with certain other species uneasily, at best (*JP*, 112, 154–57, 146–47, 278), and thus—not surprisingly—attempting to migrate off the island by the end of the novel. Worst of all, though, the dinosaurs have been resisting their own bioengineering, managing to breed even though they are created to be sterile and to find food when they are designed to be dependent on their human caretakers for it. The Jurassic Park dinosaur clones demonstrate that although genetic information and its high-tech mediation may be privileged over the material, the material nevertheless insinuates itself into the bioinformatics narrative.

Wu is ambivalent about this adaptation. Although he "would never admit it, the discovery that the dinosaurs are breeding represents a tremendous validation of his work. A breeding animal is demonstrably effective in a fundamental way; it implies that Wu has put all the pieces together correctly," that is, they exhibit the kind of authenticity associated with autonomy (*JP*, 334). Yet at the same time, their behavior makes him uncomfortable. Significantly, it is Wu, the scientist, not Hammond, the entrepreneur, who wants to modify the dinosaurs so that they will seem less real. In this regard, Wu typifies the new, entrepreneurial style of scientists like human genome sequencer Craig Venter, who conduct their work with an eye on the profit margin. Indeed, it could be argued, Wu's employment by Hammond requires that he adapt an entrepreneurial outlook. As the two novels together make clear, however, for-profit science is not so much a matter of "selling out" as it is the "only alternative" for many scientists and engineers. "Universities simply aren't where it's happening anymore," Hammond tells Wu. "And they haven't been for forty years. If you want to do something important in computers or genetics, you don't go to a university. Dear me, no" (*JP*, 123–124). If a scientist who elects to stay in academia has any hopes of distinguishing herself, she must become a consultant to industry: "It's part of the deal" (*LW*, 31).[26] Wu's revisionary impulse is thus a product of both his scientific training, which mandates replicating an experiment to prove its reliability, as well as his indebtedness to the profit margin, which mandates going beyond mere replication and subsequent innovation. The capitalist economy's "science as usual" approach is what drives reprogenetics, which, because it emphasizes reproduction in the first place, contributes to the naturalization of the commodity production and consumption of bioengineered life forms, regardless of any discomfort that people might feel about them.[27] This is the same ambivalence that undercuts the capitalist critique Crichton attempts in *Jurassic Park* and *The Lost World*. As Baudrillard has said, "production is dead, long live reproduction (*S*, 126), which the always already reproducibility of the clone perfectly carries out.

The abject resistance of Jurassic Park's dinosaurs to their biomanipulation, the forcible adaptation of reprogenetics' extreme breeding programs, leads to the "on the other hand" regarding Kay's observation of the "key conundrum" of the code-script metaphor. Notwithstanding the metaphor's invitation to "crack the code" and "revise the script," it has simultaneously created the perception that the DNA molecule is self-authoring and therefore not completely accessible to the scientific gaze, even as the resolution becomes finer and finer, that is, as scientists learn more and more about how the molecule works. This paradoxical inscrutability, Richard Doyle claims, makes DNA "the sublime object of biology" (*OBL*, 20). As Doyle explains it, Shrödinger's interpolation of "code" and "script" opened up the space of the postvital, "a dynamic space where the implosion between the animate and the inanimate" negates the need for translation between the organic and the molecular. This space "is a space of no difference: . . . [B]odies, codes, and molecules all glide together in a universal language" (*OBL*, 42). Baudrillard uses similar terms in describing the "DNA model" with which to "imagine TV" and other third-order simulacra: "[O]pposing poles of determination vanish" in this model; "there is just a sort of contraction into each other, a fantastic telescoping, a collapsing of the two traditional poles into one another: an IMPLOSION" (*S*, 56–57). Both Doyle and Baudrillard, in ascribing the concept of implosion to the "DNA model," are describing a transparency of mediation central to the implicit agency of the gene. Just as the adaptability of DNA across various material substrates positions it within Hayles's analysis of the posthuman condition of virtuality, so does its implicit agency, or telos. What makes this possible can be seen in Doyle's reference to "a universal language," which idealizes translation as a "true copy."

The idea that genome mapping amounts to using the same language that God used to create life will help to illustrate the problematic allure of the metaphor of the DNA code-script as self-authoring. Implicit in sacral metaphors in genetics is that DNA is somehow original to life itself. The story goes something like this: before creation, there was this god, God, and this language, DNA. In the logocentrism of Western metaphysics, from there it is but a short step to the idea that the language of DNA might even precede a creator, for one might wonder whether the two had always coexisted, or whether in fact DNA, which is itself construed as a creative force, was what created God. This is the conundrum expressed in the opening observation of the gospel of St. John: "In the beginning was the Word." Kay notes the bewildering

implication of John's observation, asking, "How can a word, a signifier, precede what is signified?" (*WW*, 31). Not even God knows what
DNA is really up to, it seems—not, that is, unless DNA *is* God, as could
be inferred from John's equation "the Word was God." The assumption that DNA is a prime mover, with its "theistic implications" (*WW*,
295), permeates the rhetoric surrounding the two key achievements
in the bioinformatics economy, the mapping of the human genome and
the cloning of Dolly, and for similar reasons: both technological feats
reconfigure human ideas about the origin and evolution of life by signifying human fluency in the "language of life." Simply stated, mastery over the DNA code-script enables a new kind of narrative of life
in which neither beginnings nor endings are fixed and humans "play
God" with their computers. Watson's rhetorical question mandating
the Human Genome Project—"'If we don't play God, who will?'"[28]—
and the panicky uproar over nuclear transfer cloning as "playing God"
following the announcement of the creation of Dolly dramatize the
mania for origins and fear of involution that arise simultaneously in
the metaphysics of DNA, when God is found to be nothing more, or
less, than code.

In Doyle's analysis of the paradigm shift constituted by molecular biology, summed up in biologist Walter Gilbert's declaration that
"'Molecular biology is dead—Long live molecular biology,'"[29] Doyle
affirms the connection between this new narrative and its computerized mediation:

> No longer about "life," life science is now about the fact that there
> is nothing but story, nothing but information. . . . A researcher will
> begin with the end of narrativity, with the idea that "all there is"
> to know about an organism can be found in its electronic database
> sequence, the notion that such information is the timeless and per-
> haps indestructible essence of the organism. But she will not stop
> there; the narrative of life will now be an exegetical one, where
> theorists scan databases and through "individual insight and inspi-
> ration," produce new knowledge, new stories of organisms that will
> themselves become a part of the worldwide [network of] databases.
> (*OBL*, 22–23)

In the digital logic of the computer database, the universal language
of life-as-molecular carries on in a postvital mode, self-possessed and
self-perpetuating, conducting some business of its own with no appar-

ent mediation. Jurassic Park embodies this digital-molecular vision of life. The island's elaborate, intricately networked automation and surveillance systems all but render human involvement unnecessary; it is not too difficult to imagine an all-saurian labor force, a handful of specialized platform and peripheral dinosaurs—cloned transgenic wetware—to run the island's computerized operations, maintaining the tourist attraction on their own. Whether this high-tech work force would refer to the "truth" of cloned dinosaurs, or whether it would refer to the "truth" of the technology that creates them, as Baudrillard asks about the subjects of TV-vérité (S, 51), is the question. (And whether these saurian workers would be able to organize to resist the inevitable downsizing that would occur when Hammond gets his industrial cloning operation on the other island up and running is the next question.) In his discussion of the film version of Crichton's novel, Mitchell praises *Jurassic Park* movie producer Stephen Spielberg for providing the "most up-to-date contemporary representation" of dinosaurs—as "pure creations of information science." In the informational model, the "species becomes a message, an algorithm; the boundary between organism and machine, natural and artificial intelligence, begins to waver" (*LDB*, 213).[30] But even in the informational model, embodiment remains crucial, as Hayles insists. More than just a cover-up for Hammond's industrial cloning operation, the park also functions as a prototype, an experiment that is bound to contain some instructive bugs, the dinosaurs functioning as the necessarily expendable research subjects. The genetic code-script does not "circulate unchanged among different material substrates," as Hayles says of information narratives generally, nor is it scientifically efficacious to expect otherwise.

Enterprising scientists like Celera Genomics's Craig Venter and the fictional Henry Wu seem god-like in their fluency in the code-script of DNA, knowing how to translate its seemingly self-authored messages. What is more, they know that they know, which can be a source of hubris. Chicago physicist Richard Seed, for example, fully intended to provoke the ire of morally upright, law-respecting citizens everywhere in his statement that "[c]loning and the reprogramming of DNA is the first serious step in coming to one with God,"[31] and in his on-the-air threat to clone television's *Nightline* host Ted Koppel without his permission (to which Koppel replied that it would make "an interesting lawsuit"[32]). That such scientists occupy strategic posi-

tions in what Doyle views as the bioinformatics economy helps to clar-
ify Hayles's apprehension over the liberal humanist subject persist-
ing in the "new knowledge" and "new stories" that come about from
their exegetical accounts of life. Both the Human Genome Project and
the development of nuclear transfer somatic cell cloning technology,
for example, perpetuate the Western binary privileging complete over
partial knowledge of living things, even though a supposedly complete knowledge is just as subject to the challenge of some other "complete" knowledge as are partial knowledges. Venter's disputed shotgun approach to genome mapping and the controversy in cloning over
the molecular fidelity of the clone to its progenitor illustrate the technological basis of this binary.[33] Which version of the total knowledge
is determined to be more true often hinges on the material contin-
gencies of the technique that is used to attain it. Despite, or perhaps
because of, the corporatization of knowledge production, scientists
today occupy a more privileged and powerful place in society than
ever. Hayles's apprehension over the persistence of the liberal humanist subject in the development of the posthuman subject is under-
standable considering how quickly these new stories are reabsorbed
into the ideological manifestations of DNA as code-script. The potential intelligibility of DNA is not compromised by Venter's shotgun
sequencing approach because faster equals better in free enterprise;
likewise, the genetic redundancy of industrial cloning poses no threat
to "meaningful" DNA code-scripts in commodity production's pre-
mium on quality control. Yet scientists can also use their influential
positions to leverage ethical decision making in technoscience policy.
Dolly's creator, Ian Wilmut, assuming nearly the same celebrity status
as the world's first cloned mammal herself, has risen to the occasion
by routinely weighing in on the ethical aspects of developments in
cloning.[34] Similarly, the fictional character Ian Malcolm in the Jurassic
Park novels provides the novels' moral ballast as the mathematician-
turned-philosopher.

Doyle's discussion of the idealization of a universal language underlying the concept of translation in reprogenetics further elucidates
the problems and possibilities surrounding who gets to translate and
what gets to be translated. How molecular biologists understand the
concept of translation obviously differs from how linguists understand it, but these discursive fields are interpenetrating. Like Baudrillard, Doyle turns to Walter Benjamin to examine reproduction under

the molecular regime. Allowing that Benjamin's essay "The Task of the Translator" has nothing to do with the "frenzied [contemporary] attempts to describe the mechanisms by which DNA is 'translated,'" Doyle argues convincingly for an analogy between the translator and the genetic engineer on the basis of Benjamin's essay. The crux is Benjamin's assumption of an a priori and ahistorical kinship among all languages; thus, the task of the translator is to "release in his own language that pure language which is under the spell of another."[35] In the metaphor of the code-script, the genetic engineer performs just such an operation when he "release[s]" the "pure language" of DNA from the "spell" of an organism's particular, embodied genotype. Translation occurs in *Jurassic Park* when Wu clones various "release versions" of prehistoric species—a series of failed attempts to make perfect representatives of their type—from the DNA of particular organisms that has been suspended in fossilized insect blood. As Benjamin stresses, and as cloning scenarios typically demonstrate, not all texts translate equally well; that is, not all texts have a vital connection to the universal, univocal language, even though they may all derive from it. On the face of it, cloned organisms would seem to have this vital connection; indeed, cloning technology seems to bypass translation altogether in the code-script metaphor, since DNA, in the case of the clone, seems to function not only as its own author but as its own translator as well, in the indefinite replication of the cloned organism. Nevertheless, the materiality, or text, of the clone, which can only be a technocultural product of the lab, as opposed to an instance of life itself doing "what comes naturally," renders it a poor translation, containing either too much or too little of the organism that preexisted it, as Wu's "release versions" throw into stark relief. In this view, the clone is destined to be a bad copy. More important in terms of the ideology of DNA and the role of the scientist in maintaining it, the code-script metaphor's assumption of DNA as the prototypical language of life contributes to the naturalization of reprogenetics technologies in the bioinformatics economy. This naturalization of the "master molecule" concept helps to explain why metaphor (which one might argue is a particular instance of translation) is so often "'take[n] . . . for the concept,'" as Jacques Derrida famously puts it, in the life sciences.[36]

The cloning narratives of *Jurassic Park* and *The Lost World*, then, when examined from the viewpoint of DNA as the "sublime object of biology," illustrate the humanistic idealism of a molecular protolanguage, with its illusions of a master engineer, true copies, and universal kinship. By seeming to critique profit-driven science, bad copies, and unlikely alliances, the novels serve as a reminder of the illusory aspect of this idealism. At the same time, however, the novels cannot avoid capitalizing on the speculative mode of "information thinking" (*WW*, xv) that the DNA code-script metaphor invites. An obvious source of the failure of the novels to carry out an unimplicated critique of the bioinformatics economy, for example, is their circulation as commodities within the same mass culture that maintains the ideology of DNA as a consumable object. *Jurassic Park* the novel is made into *Jurassic Park* the movie, with the inevitable book and movie sequels duly following.[37] It is as if the Jurassic Park narrative were being cloned repeatedly.

In the Jurassic Park narrative itself, this critical failure is located in the tension between the dinosaurs' self-selected breeding and their likely exploitation, somewhere down the line, as some sort of consumer biological. Beginning in *Jurassic Park* and continuing in *The Lost World*, the dinosaurs demonstrate an impressive capacity to reproduce outside of the "law" governing their creation and behavior—the combined vision of Hammond and Wu and the generous backing of their Japanese investors. By the time the electronic gears disconcertingly grind on the customized Land Cruisers' first trek around the island, the more pressing engineering problem of unauthorized saurian reproduction is already well underway, the population having increased, on its own somehow, by 23 percent (*JP*, 164). Five years later, by the time humans revisit Hammond's abandoned manufacturing facility, the situation has worsened: there is a disproportionate ratio of adults to infants and of predators to prey (*JP*, 237, 299); and disorderly nest building, cannibalism, and violent behavior are now rampant among the velociraptors (*JP*, 355, 238). Demonstrating what Judith Roof calls the "lawless immorality . . . of the genetically engineered,"[38] the dinosaurs have become bad citizens by being bad copies.

But what exactly constitutes a bad copy? By failing to acknowledge DNA as the sublime object of biology and, more important, by ignoring biology as a naturalizing force in the bioinformatics economy, the novels resort to a "copy problem" representation of cloning that reproduces cultural norms and prejudices. Malcolm's rumination upon adaptive behavior constituting "a kind of morality" (*LW*, 361–62)—because it fosters cooperation in the social order, in hunt-

904 American Literature

ing, and in raising young—points to the anthropomorphizing strain in reprogenetics narratives. In this view, the maladapted velociraptors function as the requisite criminal class that has degenerated perhaps even beyond the reach of eugenic adjustment, justifying Dodgson's plan to sell the cloned dinosaurs as research animals and market the Lost World island as a game preserve. The Japanese investors funding this mess, whom the reader never sees, serve as the novels' behind-the-scenes scapegoat, Crichton's reference to Reagan-era hostility toward Japan's considerable share of the American automobile and electronics markets. Indeed, the reengineered Toyota Land Cruisers, their faulty transmission apparent from the start, are the bad copies signifying this social disorder.

Yet as I have shown, cloning scenarios such as the Jurassic Park narrative negotiate the telos of DNA in a number of ways that suggest the possibility for all kinds of copies, not just bad consumer biologicals. The kind of authenticity associated with autonomy that the cloned transgenic dinosaurs exhibit in self-selective breeding, for example, need not be limited to that function; indeed, my hypothetical "all-saurian labor force" organized to resist downsizing indicates that a self-correcting, creative force is also associated with the code-script metaphor for DNA. In real life, Jurassic Park technology, though still largely hypothetical, is already being seriously considered as a means of "bringing back" recently extinct species, like the thylacine, an Australian wolf, and not-so-recently extinct species, like the Siberian woolly mammoth.[39] The controversy over the meaning of DNA among conservationists, adventurers, and entrepreneurs surrounding these speculative cloning scenarios justifies Hayles's misgivings about the "belief that information can circulate unchanged among different material substrates." As it turns out, there is plenty to "clone from," and that is strong support for representations of reprogenetics technologies that also function as productive interventions in the surplus of meaning surrounding DNA.

Cornell University

Notes

N. Katherine Hayles, *How We Became Posthuman: Virtual Bodies in Cybernetics, Literature, and Informatics* (Chicago: Univ. of Chicago Press, 1999), 1, 14, 239.

2   See, for example, Richard Doyle, *On Beyond Living: Rhetorical Transfor-mations of the Life Sciences* (Stanford, Calif.: Stanford Univ. Press, 1997), 27–35; and Evelyn Fox Keller, *Refiguring Life: Metaphors of Twentieth-Century Biology* (New York: Columbia Univ. Press, 1995), 45–47. Fur-ther references to Doyle's *On Beyond Living* will be cited parenthetically as *OBL*.

3   Typical examples include Paul Lauter's analysis in *From Walden Pond to Jurassic Park: Activism, Culture, and American Studies* (Durham, N.C.: Duke Univ. Press, 2001), 109–10; W. J. T. Mitchell's examination in *The Last Dinosaur Book: The Life and Times of a Cultural Icon* (Chicago: Univ. of Chicago Press, 1998), 221–27; and Joe Sartelle's critique in *"Jurassic Park,* or, Sympathy for the Dinosaur," *Bad Subjects* (May 1993), <*http:// eserver.org/bs/06/Sartell.html*>. Further references to Mitchell's *The Last Dinosaur Book* will be cited parenthetically as *LDB*.

4   Erwin Shrödinger, "What Is Life?" in *What Is Life? The Physical Aspect of the Living Cell* (Cambridge, Eng: Cambridge Univ. Press, 1945); quoted in Keller, *Refiguring Life*, 47.

5   Ibid.

6   See Evelyn Fox Keller, "Between Language and Science: The Question of Directed Mutation in Molecular Genetics," in *Secrets of Life, Secrets of Death: Essays on Language, Gender, and Science* (New York: Routledge, 1992), 161–65.

7   In concluding their 1953 *Nature* article "Genetical Implications of the Structure of Deoxyribonucleic Acid" describing the double helical struc-ture of DNA, Watson and Crick state: "It has not escaped our notice that the specific pairing we have postulated immediately suggests a possible copying mechanism for the genetic material"; quoted in Alan G. Gross, *The Rhetoric of Science* (Cambridge: Harvard Univ. Press, 1996), 64. See Keller, "Fractured Images of Science, Language, and Power: A Postmod-ern Optic, or Just Bad Eyesight?" in *Secrets*, 96–97.

8   Michael Crichton, *The Lost World* (New York: Ballatine, 1995), 143; fur-ther references to this source are to this edition and will be cited paren-thetically as *LW*.

9   Jean Baudrillard, *The Illusion of the End*, trans. Chris Turner (Stanford, Calif.: Stanford Univ. Press, 1994), 12.

10   Ibid., 84.

11   Lily E. Kay, *Who Wrote the Book of Life? A History of the Genetic Code* (Stan-ford, Calif.: Stanford Univ. Press, 2000), xvi–xvii; further references to this source will be cited parenthetically as *WW*.

12   Lily E. Kay, "Cybernetics, Information, Life: The Emergence of Scrip-tural Representations of Heredity," *Configurations* 5 (winter 1997): 23–91.

13   Michael Crichton, *Jurassic Park* (New York: Ballantine, 1990), 85; further references to this source are to this edition and will be cited parentheti-cally as *JP*.

14 The reader is introduced to Hammond as an entrepreneur in "consumer biologicals" when he presents, as his calling card to interest potential investors, a tiny dwarf elephant as an example of his proposed stock of genetically engineered life forms. But the miniature elephant is not genetically engineered (it is merely bioengineered via hormonal manipulation, never to grow to full size), nor is it cloned. It is not even, in fact, a "perfected" version of an endangered wild animal via domestication. It is "prone to colds" and "infections around the tusk line" and "act[s] like a vicious rodent," nipping the fingers of anyone who attempts to pet it (*JP*, 59–60). In this way, *Jurassic Park* presents Hammond as a sort of reprogenetics huckster.

15 In Sartelle's Marxist analysis of the Jurassic Park dinosaur manufacturing economy, the cloned dinosaurs constitute "a class of beings created by capital in order to serve capital" ("Sympathy for the Dinosaur," paragraph 6). Thus InGen's abandonment of the saurian labor force to an unclear evolutionary fate on an obscure Costa Rican Island unaffected by U.S. law is analogous to the corporate liquidation of an unsuccessful manufacturing outpost in a developing region leaving minimally trained workers to fend for themselves in a destabilized economy.

16 In the "release version" logic of the Jurassic Park experiment, Fibro, the first male mammal to be cloned, is an upgrade of the cloned mouse Cumulina's clones, who together constitute an upgrade of Dolly, the prototypical cloned sheep. Also similar to the loss of life in "real-life" cloning experiments, "the survival rate [of cloned dinosaurs] is somewhere around point four percent" (*JP*, 106).

17 What makes Mitchell's title suspect is summed up by one of the book's image captions: "The time when dinosaurs ruled the earth is now, and their rule is synonymous with the global dominance of American culture" (*LDB*, 265). Despite what he claims about the movie version of *Jurassic Park*—that in thoroughly exploiting the cultural image of the dinosaur on multiple levels of signification it "is smarter than any 'critique' that might be brought to bear on it" (226)—given the global dominance of American mass culture, a preponderance of dinosaur books of all kinds is sure to follow Mitchell's. Perhaps his is merely the last dinosaur book anyone will ever *need*.

18 Mitchell's take on the Sinclair dinosaur is an apt example, describing Sinclair Oil Company's successful advertising campaign based on the unsupportable claim that Sinclair's fossil fuels were superior to its competitors' by virtue of some sort of paleontological aging process—rhetorically speaking, an appeal to tradition. The company's now obsolete business practice of controlling all phases of production "from the wellhead to the pump" probably contributed to the perception that it was privy to all the details of this process (*LDB*, 167–68).

19 Jennifer Andes, "Plastic Dinosaur Better Than Real," *Journal and Courier*

[Lafayette, Ind.], 23 August 2000, A3. The Smithsonian Natural History Museum's recent Triceratops "upgrade" provides an interesting example of the digitized-replica-as-simulacrum: how is it that a laser scan of the museum's model can produce a replica "better than real"? The question of what is being scanned remains ambiguous.

20   See Hayles, *How We Became Posthuman*, 54.

21   Baudrillard, *Simulations*, trans. Paul Foss, Paul Patton, and Philip Beitchman (New York: Semiotext[e], 1983), 100–101; further references to this source are to this edition and will be cited parenthetically as *S*.

22   See Gina Kolata, *Clone: The Road to Dolly, and the Path Ahead* (New York: Morrow, 1998), 223–24.

23   Glenn McGee, quoted in "Experts: Cloning Could Not Duplicate Humans," Associated Press, 16 March 1997.

24   See "Media and Public Interest" on the Roslin Institute's Web site: <*http://www.roslin.ac.uk/publications/9798annrep/review.html#media*>.

25   The body of Morag, a sheep cloned from differentiated embryo cells prior to the somatic cell cloning of Dolly, is already on display at the Royal Museum in Edinburgh, and the remains of Cumulina, the world's first cloned mouse, are destined for the same treatment at the new Institute for Biogenesis Research in the United States. The museumization of Dolly and other prototype clones dramatizes the unique amnesia that cloning begets. While her own biological mother, a six-year-old ewe living on a farm some distance from Roslin Institute, was butchered and eaten by persons unaware of the sheep's role in reprogenetics history (see Kolata, *Clone*, 27), Dolly too will become lost to history despite her museumization. Her metaphoric progeny—the genetically modified clones of which she is the prototype—will revise the very notions of the spatiotemporally defined body that figure into her museumization in the first place. Dolly's museumized body thus exemplifies the "fear of some imminent traumatic loss," a surplus of meaning that Andreas Huyssen argues fueled the building of museums and memorials in the late twentieth century (*Twilight Memories: Marking Time in a Culture of Amnesia* [New York: Routledge, 1995], 5, 15).

26   Unfortunately, Crichton's mostly matter-of-fact commentary on the corporate imposition on "disinterested" knowledge production occasionally stoops to academy bashing and just plain anti-intellectualism. This is especially obvious in his characterization of the former professor of applied engineering, Jack Thorne, who is "popular with his students" and "advocate[s] general education" but who finds that his "interest in real-world problems [is] proof of [his] intellectual poverty" (*LW*, 66).

27   I revise Thomas Kuhn's idea of "normal science" in this allusion to "business as usual" reprogenetics research, for as Kuhn himself says, although "[n]ormal science . . . often suppresses fundamental novelties because they are necessarily subversive of its basic commitments, . . . so long as

those commitments retain an element of the arbitrary, the very nature of normal research ensures that novelty shall not be suppressed for very long" (*The Structure of Scientific Revolutions* [Chicago: Univ. of Chicago Press, 1970], 5).

28 James Watson, "Values of a Chicago Upbringing," in *DNA: The Double Helix: Perspective and Prospective at Forty Years*, ed. Donald A. Chambers (New York: New York Academy of Science, 1995), 197; quoted in *WW*, 37.

29 Walter Gilbert, "Towards a Paradigm Shift in Biology," *Nature* 349 (10 January 1991): 99; quoted in *OBL*, 22.

30 See Stephen Spielberg, *Jurassic Park* (Universal, 1993).

31 Richard Seed, National Public Radio, 6 January 1998; quoted in Joanne Silberner, "Seeding the Cloning Debate," *Hastings Center Report* (March–April 1998): 5.

32 Ted Koppel, quoted in Lori B. Andrews, *The Clone Age: Adventures in the New World of Reproductive Technology* (New York: Holt, 1999), 134.

33 On Venter's approach, see Tim Beardsley, "An Express Route to the Genome?" *Scientific American*, August 1998, 30–32; on the cloning controversy, see M. J. Evans et al., "Mitochondrial DNA Genotypes in Nuclear Transfer-Derived Cloned Sheep," *Nature Genetics* 23 (September 1999): 90–93; and Paul G. Shiels et al., "Analysis of Telomere Lengths in Cloned Sheep," *Nature* 399 (27 May 1999): 316–17.

34 See, for example, Andrews, *The Clone Age*, 251; Ian Wilmut, Keith Campbell, and Colin Tudge, *The Second Creation: Dolly and the Age of Biological Control* (New York: Farrar, 2000), 267–74; and Ian Wilmut, "Cloning for Medicine," *Scientific American*, December 1998, 58–63.

35 Walter Benjamin, *Illuminations*, trans. Harry Zohn, ed. Hannah Arendt (New York: Schocken, 1986), 80; quoted in *OBL*, 46.

36 Jacques Derrida, *Margins of Philosophy*, trans. Alan Bass (Chicago: Univ. of Chicago Press, 1982); quoted in *OBL*, 86.

37 Crichton's *The Lost World* was followed by Spielberg's film version in 1997. *Jurassic Park III*, a film sequel to *Jurassic Park* and *The Lost World* directed by Joe Johnston, was released in 2001 by Universal Pictures.

38 Judith Roof, *Reproductions of Reproduction: Imaging Symbolic Change* (New York: Routledge, 1996), 177.

39 California Polytechnic State University microbiology professor Raul Cano's successful extraction of DNA from fossilized insects trapped in amber coincided with the premier of the film *Jurassic Park*, and Cano since then has obtained a patent for the technique. Following the death of the last known thylacine, "Benjamin," in Australia's Hobart Zoo in 1936, the bodies of seven thylacines preserved in alcohol have been located in museums around the world. According to the Australian Museum director Mike Archer, this meager assortment of tiny pickled wolf bodies presents an opportunity to reverse extinction and redress the immorality of the human extermination of the Tasmanian tiger through clon-

ing; quoted in "A Conversation with Professor Mike Archer, Director of the Australian Museum," <*http://www.Amonline.net.au/thylacine/archer. htm*>. The thylacine cloning project does not look promising, however, due to poorly preserved DNA, according to Robert P. Lanza, Betsy L. Dresser, and Philip Damiani, in "Cloning Noah's Ark," *Scientific American*, November 2000, 84–89. Through DNA retrieval from frozen tissue and interspecies embryo transfer, some scientists think that they might be able to "resurrect" a woolly mammoth in the womb of a modern elephant; see Richard Stone, "Cloning the Woolly Mammoth," *Discover*, April 1999, 56+.

Wai Chee Dimock   Non-Newtonian Time: Robert Lowell, Roman History, Vietnam War

What is non-Newtonian time? No ready answer comes to mind. Its opposite—Newtonian time—hardly fares better. Neither term is idiomatic or even vaguely recognizable because *time* is rarely qualified by these adjectives, or qualified at all. In more than just a grammatical sense, time seems to come all in one piece, in one flavor. It is an ontological given, a cosmic metric that dictates a fixed sequence of events against a fixed sequence of intervals. It is present everywhere, the same everywhere, independent of anything we do. It carries no descriptive label and has no need to advertise or to repudiate that label.

When seen as this uniform background, time is quantifiable. Its measurable segments are exactly the same length, one segment coming after another in a single direction. This unidirectionality means that there is only one way to line up two events, one way to measure the distance between them. Apparently, we need to imagine time in this concrete form—as a sort of measuring rod—to convince ourselves of its absolute existence. One year, one month, one minute—these unit lengths have to be "real" unit lengths, objectively measurable. And as proof of that objective measurement, they have to come already stamped with a serial number. And so we speak of one particular minute as, say, 10:10, followed by the next minute, 10:11, just as we speak of one year as, say, 1965, followed by the next year, 1966. This serial designation puts time completely under the jurisdiction of number.

Most of us take this step quite innocently. Without much thought, we refer to a particular year as 1965, because a numerical bias is so

American Literature, Volume 74, Number 4, December 2002. Copyright © 2002 by Duke University Press.

deeply entrenched in our thinking that it works as a kind of mental reflex. Dates thus acquire a summary authority, with great descriptive and explanatory power. We don't doubt that a number, 1965, can be assigned to one particular slice of time and that this meaningful numerical designation exercises a binding power over all the events that happen within its duration. Number, in this way, works as a kind of automatic unifier: it imposes an identity across-the-board. Because this numerical chronology standardizes time into a sequence of equal units, the location of any event and its proximity to any other is fixed by this sequence. 1965 is separated by only 20 years from 1945, and so it has got to be closer to this year than to the year 65, from which it is separated by 1900 years.

This numerical bias is the unspoken norm for humanists no less than for scientists. Under new historicism, this norm has sometimes turned into a methodological claim, producing a spate of scholarship whose very ground of analysis is numerical time. It is routine for us to seize upon one particular number—the date of a text's composition—and use it to set the limits of an analytic domain, mapping the scrutinized object onto a time frame more or less standardized. One year, five years, ten years: these are the numerical units we use, as a matter of course, when we try to contextualize. Defined in this way, contextualization is based almost exclusively on synchrony. Events are deemed pertinent to one another only if they fall within the same slice of time, which is to say, if they are bound by two serial numbers so close to being consecutive that the distance between them is measurable by single digits. This short duration is supposed to be adequate, to capture both cause and consequence: the web of relations leading to the making of the text and the web of relations flowing from its presence in the world.

Elsewhere I have argued against this synchronic model, offering instead a conception of literary history based on extended duration, what I call "deep time."[1] Here I want to take issue, more specifically, with the numerical bias at work in a synchronic model. What does it mean to construct an analytic domain bound by two serial numbers with a minimum degree of separation? As a time frame, how adequate is this brief duration and serial alignment? What sort of phenomena falls within its purview, and what falls outside? What effect does this conception of time have on the institutional shape of literary studies? And what effect does it have elsewhere, in other disciplines? How far

should we go, how interdisciplinary should we get, to put our synchronic model into perspective?

It is worth taking a risk here, looking beyond our usual intellectual allies, because the question of time—its ontology and numerical
measurement—turns out to be a central issue in one field ordinarily
seen as quite remote from the study of literature: physics. Exchanges
between these two fields stretch the limits of both. Currently located
on two ends of our intellectual spectrum, literary studies and physics
can come into contact only through a long backward extension, a
reengagement with some longstanding and as yet unsettled disputes.
Plato, Aristotle, Newton, Einstein: these are not names one routinely
sees in the pages of *American Literature*. In this essay, I invoke them,
not only to frame a specific argument about time but also to propose
an analytic horizon broadly conceived: not coinciding with our usual
disciplinary boundaries, and not coinciding with the chronological and
territorial borders of the adjective *American*.

I begin with a debate between Plato and Aristotle. This is a debate
over two different conceptions of time, two ways of mapping time
against number. Plato, with his belief in the transcendent reality
of mathematics, argues, not surprisingly, for the priority of number
over time. Time, for him, is an effect, an epiphenomenon deduced or
derived from number. Past and present, Plato says in the *Timaeus*,
are no more than shadows cast by an everlasting and ever unchang-
ing mathematical structure. They are a "moving image of eternity,"
"moving according to number."[2] For Plato, number is a preexisting
order of reality; it is a structural antecedent that grounds all events,
giving the world an eternal sequence. Aristotle is not so sure. Book 4
of his *Physics* is devoted to complicating and qualifying Plato's formulation. "Time is a number," Aristotle concedes, but he quickly adds a
caveat that sharply limits the operative parallel between the two: "But
'number' may mean either that which is numbered, or that by which
we number it; time is number in the former sense."[3] This point might
seem like hairsplitting, but Aristotle does not think so. The distinction
between what does the numbering and what is being numbered is crucial. For him, "Time is not the number we count with but the number
counted" (*P*, 388). In other words, time can perhaps be enumerated,
but it is not the vehicle with which we do the enumerating. A measuring rod can perhaps be put to it, but time itself does not generate that
measuring rod.

Having made this operative distinction, Aristotle then goes one step farther to insist on an ontological difference between time and number. Number is sharp-edged and clear-cut; time is not: "Time is a number not as a self-identical point has a number in respect of its being both beginning and end" (*P*, 387). Every number is a discrete entity: it is self-contained, self-identical, ending exactly where it begins. It is a modular unit, point-like in its ontology. Time is anything but that. The relation between any individual instant and time in its totality is not a discrete relation at all. Instead, it is an overlap, a fold within a voluminous fabric, an interplay that goes backwards as well as forwards, producing adjacencies between what was and what will be: "Being the number of what is continuous, it is itself continuous" (*P*, 387). Clean resolution, in other words, is not at all possible given the ontology of time. Years, decades, and centuries are endlessly connected even when they are discretely numbered. There can be no secure partitions here, and no clean breaks.

Rather than segmenting evenly along lines fixed by serial numbers, time, for Aristotle, is a continuum that can be cut in any way at any given moment. These "cuts"—their lengths, their angles of incision, the folds being gathered together as a result—are generated strictly under the shaping hand of particular events. As these resonate with the past, drawing it into the orbit of the present, distance can become radically foreshortened. Events otherwise far apart can find themselves suddenly side by side, rendered simultaneous for the moment. This "simultaneity" is not the effect of a fixed coordinate. It does not come stamped with a serial number. As a conjunctive relation created when the distance between two events collapses, it owes its existence to something like a gravitational pull, drastically altering the numerical length of temporal separations. Aristotle does not mince words on this point: "[I]f to be simultaneous in time is to be in the same now, then if both what is earlier and what is later are in one particular now, the events of 10,000 years ago will be simultaneous with those of today, and no event will be earlier than any other" (*P*, 385).

This is, of course, a scandalous thing to say. In espousing it, in the teeth of Plato's numerical determinism, book 4 of *Physics* challenges anyone who wants to think seriously about time. Unfortunately, that challenge has gone largely unheeded. In the centuries that followed, it was not Aristotle's conception of time but a new version of Plato's— Newton's version—that would dominate the field of physics as well as a broad swath of Western culture outside physics, as Peter Gay, Mar-

garet Jacob, Garry Wills, and I. Bernard Cohen have shown.[4] Newton's
descent from Plato (and our descent from both) can be gleaned from
the opening pages of the *Principia*:

> Absolute, true, and mathematical time, of itself, and from its own
> nature, flows equably without relation to anything external, and by
> another name is called duration. . . . Absolute space, in its own
> nature, without relation to anything external, remains always simi-
> lar and immovable. . . . As the order of the parts of time is immutable,
> so also is the order of the parts of space. . . . All things are placed in
> time as to order of succession; and in space as to order of situation.
> It is from their essence or nature that they are places, and that the
> primary places of things should be movable, is absurd. These are
> therefore the absolute places.[5]

Time is "mathematical" for Newton: expressible as a numerical constant. It flows everywhere at the same pace, in the same direction,
and everywhere yields the same number. It is an immutable sequence
grounded in an immutable metric. But to say this is to realize, with
a shock, that Newtonian time is simply time for most of us, general-
ized and naturalized, not called "Newtonian" at all, because no attribu-
tion is made to the individual who invented it. Instead, its numerical
nature is taken for granted as a fact, the stuff of common sense. We
are Newtonians precisely because we never carry that label.

Given this silent hegemony, this dominance of one conception of
time and the erasure of all competing versions, it is especially important to take a new look at Newton, bringing into the open his unstated
premises, the freighted corollaries locked into place by his numerical
model.[6] It turns out that, for Newton, "absolute, true, and mathematical time" does not come alone. It is part of a larger conceptual edi-
fice, inseparable from and, it would seem, all but interchangeable with
"absolute space." Time and space are mentioned in the same breath;
one dovetails the other. For Newton, space is not only parallel to time
but also the antecedent, the originating idea from which time derives
its shape, as a longitudinal "order of succession," just like a latitudi-
nal "order of situation." It is space that provides the mental image for
time, space that dictates the ontology of both.[7] Conceived in this light,
time functions in exactly the same way as a spatial coordinate. It is a
place, a location, a fixed term on a numerical sequence—and, for all
those reasons, a container to which any event can be assigned.

This image of time as a container is at the center of Newtonian physics. And so time is perhaps less a measuring rod than a filing cabinet. Any event can be automatically filed into one of an infinite number of slots—into a century, a year, a month. Placement is crucial: everything must be given a temporal address and locked into a uniformly numbered linear series. In one and the same gesture, then, Newton spatializes and standardizes time. Because time's vertical axis is represented as a series of synchronic planes, of numerical cross sections, events are assumed to be unified because they happen to fall on the same plane; they have a common identity because they have a common serial address. Newtonian physics thus assigns a tremendous regulative power to simultaneity, the condition of being at an identically numbered cross section.[8] And for Newton, this simultaneity is not a contingent fact, true within one particular frame of reference, but an absolute mathematical truth, eternally binding. What this means is that every event is permanently tied to two sets of synchronic neighbors: to one set of events that comes before it and to one set that comes after it, a sequence as immutable as a sequence of numbers.

This numerical chronology—probably the least examined dogma of modern thought—governs our sense of duration and the historical relations it permits. Because numbers are discrete and morphologically ironclad, there is always a dividing line—a clean break—between them, even when consecutive. One number comes after another, with no blending and no spilling over. This ontology is indeed the ground on which most of us envision history as well as our own life spans, as we assign historical events to absolutely numbered slots and ourselves to a duration the numerical length of our lives. This is what it means to be Newtonians. Most historians—Newtonians in this sense—thus divide history into numbered periods and speak of them as if they were objective units. And literary critics, Newtonians as well, lock a text into a brief duration, a numbered slice of time, as if that slice were an air-tight container.

What if we were to modify or reject this conception of time? The consequences for the humanities are far-reaching, especially for literary studies. In his well-known essay "DissemiNation: Time, Narrative, and the Margins of the Modern Nation," Homi Bhabha suggests that time has no phenomenal unity; it is a crucial analytic axis precisely because it is contested.[9] Lived memories and lived subjectivities do not line up as units of the same length, sequenced by the same unidirectional metric. Time, experienced through these individual filters, can take on any shape, beginning and ending in odd places, with strange extensions and juxtapositions. No numerical chronology can unify the subjective experience of time. And in escaping unification, experiential time works against the putative unity of any construct, including the one called the nation.

For Bhabha, then, the breakdown of a single, enforceable chronology stands as one of the most powerful challenges to the unity of the nation-state, directly contradicting the regime of "simultaneity," which Benedict Anderson posits as the hallmark of the nation. Against that regime—against Anderson's account of national time as "homogeneous empty time . . . measured by clock and calendar"[10]—Bhabha calls attention to many alternate temporalities: "disjunctive" narratives, written at the margins of the nation and challenging its ability to standardize, to impose an official ordering of events.[11] "Postcolonial time," Bhabha says, "questions the teleological traditions of past and present, and the polarized historicist sensibility of the archaic and the modern."[12]

Bhabha does not mention Newton in his essay. And yet the postcolonial time he describes marks a break not only from the synchronic plane of the nation-state but also from the numerical jurisdiction of Newtonian physics. It is helpful to bring the latter squarely into the foreground as we try to explore an alternate conception of time as something other than a serial line, something working, more immediately, against the chronology of the nation and, more deeply, against the chronology of number.

In "Newton and the Ideal of a Transparent Scientific Language" (1982), J. M. Coetzee probes Newton's quest for a purely mathematical language, untouched by the embedding, localizing, and contaminating effects of metaphor.[13] The *Principia*, its author a user of language like the rest of us, becomes, for Coetzee, a language experiment that tries to do away with the messiness of ordinary speech and replace it with the precision of number—unambiguous, universally true. It is a noble experiment but doomed to fail, Coetzee says. Because every time Newton tries to take a mathematical truth into an experiential realm—to translate numerical notation into verbal expression—an extra layer of meaning sets in: unintended, unwelcome, unstoppable. Ordinary language, it seems, is metaphoric by nature, always muddled by a semantic surcharge. The way human beings talk is different from the way mathematics talks. There can be no one-to-one mapping between the freighted particularity of words and the burdenless universality of numbers.

For Coetzee, then, Newton dramatizes the problem of translation: the impossible task of trying to unify two languages with different referential claims on the world. Taking Coetzee's point but putting a slightly different spin on it, we can think of Newton's problem not only as one of translation but also, in more pragmatic terms, of jurisdiction. How much of the world is under the rule of number? Not all, it would seem, if Coetzee is right. A mathematical description has its limits: it does not cover everything, and its sequential logic is not everywhere honored. What, then, is this other realm not fully collapsible into number? Can we give it a name? Can we define its habitat? What are the circumstances for its emergence? And what is the shape of time that unfolds in it? If numerical jurisdiction relies on the chronology of clock and calendar, how is time kept in this other, non–Newtonian, realm?

Here the history of physics can come to our aid. For in a remarkable turn, twentieth-century theorists—Einstein, in particular—have actually dismantled the Newtonian conception of time. In a dramatic moment in his "Autobiographical Notes," Einstein writes:

> Enough of this. Newton, forgive me; you found the only way which, in your age, was just about possible for a man of highest thought and creative power. The concepts, which you created, are even today still guiding our thinking in physics, although we now know that they will have to be replaced. . . .
>
> "Is this supposed to be an obituary?" the astonished reader will likely ask. I would like to reply: essentially yes.[14]

Newton's "obituary" has to be written, because all his assumptions about time—as uniform and numerical, as predicated on fixed simultaneity—have now been challenged. Indeed, the turning point in modern physics, for Einstein, comes from his "difficulty with all physical statements in which the concept 'simultaneous' plays a part."[15]

Rather than accepting simultaneity as a quantified given, Einstein asks if it is generalizable at all. Is there such a thing as a synchronized now, identical across the board, expressible as a numerical constant? Is synchrony itself an absolute fact that stands as an eternal relation between two temporal neighbors? Does the motion of an object make any difference to its space and time coordinates? And if so, what difference does *that* difference make to the concept of simultaneity? To answer these questions, Einstein considers the phenomenal world from two frames of reference in two different states of motion. Using a moving train as one frame of reference, and the railroad embankment as the other, he asks whether the timing for two flashes of lightning can be assigned to a unified synchronic plane. Can they be seen as simultaneous in both places?

With palpable satisfaction, Einstein writes that "the answer must be in the negative" (*R*, 30). The two flashes of lightning, A and B, might be simultaneous for the observer standing still on the embankment, but they will not be simultaneous for an observer on the train moving away from A towards B. Since this observer is shortening his distance to B and lengthening his distance to A, he "will see the beam of light emitted from B earlier than he will see the one emitted from A" (*R*, 30). And so:

> Events which are simultaneous with reference to the embankment are not simultaneous with respect to the train, and vice versa (relativity of simultaneity). Every reference-body (coordinate system) has its own particular time; unless we are told the reference-body to which the statement of time refers, there is no meaning in a statement of the time of an event. (*R*, 31)

Simultaneity turns out to be a nongeneralizable proposition. Two events might be simultaneous in one frame of reference but not in another. The now experienced in one location, then, cannot be the same as the now experienced in a location moving differently. These two nows cannot be unified; the relation between them is not an eternal relation and cannot be expressed as a numerical constant. Einstein thus turns Newton's absolute truth into a contingent truth, specific to one set of coordinates and not generalizable beyond them. This is what he calls relativity. Of course, for Einstein, relativity is itself a mathematical concept, derived from non-Euclidean geometry, the peculiar geometry exhibited by space-time when faced with the requirement that the speed of light be invariant.[16] And in making the invariance of light the foundation of physics, Einstein is as committed as Newton to a formalizable numerical language.[17] We are seriously mistaken if we imagine that there can be an easy translation from that language to ordinary speech.

Still, it is not impossible, even for the layperson, to have some experience of Einstein's basic idea, namely, that time is frame-dependent, that there can be no numerically unified now. At least one occurrence from everyday life allows that idea to make nonmathematical sense. I have in mind the occurrence of literature, routine enough, whose temporal ontology nonetheless upsets the coordinates of the routine, delivering not only a blow to Newton but also a tribute to Aristotle, giving his *Physics* an unimagined extension. Drawing on both Aristotle and Einstein, then, and translating their arguments into an argument about the temporal ontology of words, I propose an intersection between literature and science, based on what I call non–Newtonian time: a domain in which the reign of number is not absolute, in which experience is not bound by seriality. To the extent that it inhabits this domain, literature offers a temporal axis startling to contemplate: longer than we think, messier, not strictly chronological, and not chronological in a single direction. The most important claim to be made for literature, I argue, is the evidence it provides of a temporal order outside the jurisdiction of number.

I am thinking, in particular, of the experience of reading. What reading activates is what I call a "relativity effect": a telescoping of two time frames, each putting pressure on the other but remaining stubbornly apart, not unified by a number. This relativity effect comes about when we are drawn to words that came into being long before we did, not occasioned by us and not referring to us. In that sense, these words are entirely outside our life spans. But in another sense, they are not outside, because as a result of the temporal foreshortening created by reading, they are actually, literally, in our hands. They have been pulled into our gravitational field and grafted upon our immediate environments. Perhaps this is a case of temporal colonization, the domestication of an alien segment of time. But—and this is important to recognize—any domestication we undertake is bound to be limited by the paradox that these texts are ours and not ours, both in and not in our hands.[18]

In this paradox, two things happen. First, because domestication works only to a certain point, these strange words retain a good part of their strangeness. They are here, but they are not completely of the moment. Second, this unyielding, unstoppable strangeness says something about the imperfect naturalization of the nation-state, the insecurity of its territorial borders, occasioned, I argue, by an even more fundamental insecurity—that of chronology. A year, a decade, a century: these time slots are not ironclad. They are not made like file cabinets. They cannot lock events into a sealed box; they cannot make the world walk in a single file.

Reading, I want to suggest, is a common activity that can have an uncommon effect on the mapping of past and present, and on any kind of territorial sovereignty predicated on that mapping. Reading can generate bonds that deviate both from the national timetable and from the quantified metric of Newtonian time, because what brings a reader into the orbit of a text is certainly not numerical chronology—the clock and the calendar—but something much more chancy and much less regulated. Literary relations are idiosyncratic; they make time idiosyncratic. They bring distant words close to home, give them a meaningfulness that seems local and immediate even though they could not have been so initially, objectively. The distance between readers and the words they read is anything but a number. In this experiential domain, at least, time is composed not of quantified unit lengths but of distances variably and circumstantially generated by each reader in the intensity of the readerly attachment, or, as Roger Chartier says, in "the dialectic between imposition and appropriation, between constraints transgressed and freedoms bridled."[19] There can be no such thing as a numerical now, a synchronic plane enforceable across the entire nation.

Literary studies is currently dominated by a nation-based paradigm, defined, in the influential view of Anderson, as a domain of "simultaneity." I want to take issue once again with this paradigm, specifically as a Newtonian artifact based on uncritical premises about temporal homogeneity and standardization.[20] Against Anderson's Newtonian model, it is helpful to make a counterclaim on behalf of a mode of time that is the opposite of the standardized. Deviation from a national timetable surely matters as much as synchronization under the sign of the nation. Such deviation challenges any fixed sequence of events, whether dictated by a territorial entity or by a literary canon. These official narratives cannot serialize everything, for the effect of offbeat reading is to suggest a temporal axis at odds with the chronological progression of the nation, and at odds with the chronological succession of sanctified texts. What results is a kind of serial unpredictability—the unexpected contact between events numerically far apart. Nowhere is this more salient than in the reading and translating of ancient texts, written in "dead" languages centuries ago.

In the rest of this essay, I will explore one such instance of offbeat reading: Robert Lowell's twentieth-century translations from Latin. Time is out of joint for Lowell, stretching across the borders of many centuries and jurisdictions. It is not one with the nation because it is not one with the synchronic plane dictated by the territorial map. Perhaps it is not even one with itself. Rather than being unified by a chronological date, these translations are structured instead by the tension between two time frames uneasily juxtaposed, at home neither in the numerical now of the twentieth century nor in that of, say, the first century.

Lowell's interest in translation was longstanding, and he had many theories for its practice.[21] In his introduction to *Imitations*—his translation of Homer and Sappho, as well as Villon, Baudelaire, Rilke, and others—Lowell begins with a critique of those translators who aim only for fidelity to the original, who want only to head back to the century in which the text was written. Such people, he says, "seem to live in a pure world untouched by contemporary poetry. Their difficulties are bold and honest, but they are taxidermists, not poets, and their poems are likely to be stuffed birds."[22] Lowell, of course, had no desire to be a taxidermist. His principle of translation was different: "I have been reckless with literal meaning, and labored hard to get the tone. . . . I have tried to write alive English and to do what my authors might have done if they were writing their poems now and in America."[23]

For Lowell, translation means not a rendition of the past in its pastness but the recasting of past words into "alive English," words that are kicking and screaming right at this moment. Bringing the original texts "up to date" and shooting for a contemporary sound, translation is above all a temporal exercise that plays fast and loose with duration, compressing the numerical chronology into a newly scripted shape. Two steps, at least, are involved, something like a double alienation. First, there is a deliberate yoking of a moment from the present and a moment from the past, followed by a deliberate wrenching apart, a mutual tearing and dislodging effected by the very act of conjunction. This double alienation produces the relativity effect. It brings together two segments of time, each plied from its synchronic neighbors, within hailing distance of each other but not allowed to coalesce into a unified now. The temporal structure that results is clearly not expressible as a numerical constant, because not only are there two dates, two chronological numbers made adjacent, but they are made adjacent in such a way as to yield the maximum friction, a repulsive force equal to the conjunctive one.

This breakdown of the numerical constant is at work not only in Lowell's translation of the Latin authors but also in his many poems invoking Roman history, including "Caligula."[24] Caligula is, of course, Lowell's namesake. Since his schooldays at St. Mark's, he had called himself "Cal" after the notorious Roman tyrant, translating that name into his own person, so to speak.[25] The poem "Caligula" was probably written in or around 1962 or 1963, its first version published in the fall of 1964 in *For the Union Dead*:

> My namesake, Little Boots, Caligula,
> you disappoint me. Tell me what I saw
> to make me like you when we met at school?
> I took your name—poor odd-ball, poor spoiled fool.
>
> .   .   .   .
>
> Your true face sneers at me, mean, thin, agonized.
>
> .   .   .   .
>
> I live your last night. Sleepless fugitive,
> your purple bedclothes and imperial eagle
> grow so familiar they are home. Your regal
> hand accepts my hand. You bend my wrist,
> and tear the tendons with your strangler's twist.[26]

For Lowell, the Roman Empire is a contemporary phenomenon: Caligula is his classmate (they "met at school"); the Roman Emperor's palace is "home" to the American poet. The two are wedded to each other at this moment. But Lowell is careful to remind us who Caligula is. The Roman face is sneering; the Roman hand extended to meet his is one that mangles and lacerates: "You bend my wrist, / and tear the tendons with your strangler's twist." Caligula is here, he is on the run, a "fugitive" in the twentieth century, but this hardly tames his malice, his fury, his unexplained but unrelenting desire to harm his American offspring.

The possibility of being harmed—of having one's tendons torn and twisted—suggests that something odd has happened to the temporal distance of 1900 years supposedly separating the first-century emperor and the twentieth-century poet. That number has been shortened beyond recognition. Helen Vendler, struck by Lowell's habit of "keep[ing] ancient and contemporary history before him in one stereoptical view," argues that it stems from a "contemptuous indifference," a "mortmain equalizing of any event to any other event."[27] This may be. I want to call attention, however, to the tremendous repulsive force generated by this contact, which both couples and decouples the emperor and the poet. The hands of these two are not exactly fused. Far from being domesticated, Caligula remains a Roman tyrant, not assimilable, angry, ungrateful, evil-minded, mutilating the very hand that has brought him back to life. The fit between Roman history and Lowell's personal history is less than perfect. And that is precisely the point. Caligula might be in the United States, but he remains a nonresident alien, resisting any attempt to translate him. This does not, of course, stop Lowell from trying. For it is only through this attempted translation that the poet can give himself a name, even though, as he himself knows too well, it is a name that keeps lashing out at him, trying to cut him up.

The two published versions of "Caligula" are instructive. In the first version of the poem, published in 1964, Lowell ends with the line: "my namesake, and the last Caligula."[28] Five years later, in the much abbreviated version in *Notebook*, this last line has been changed to its exact opposite: "my namesake, *not* the last Caligula" (my emphasis).[29] The name, then, has no terminal point. It is the name of a Roman emperor; it is the name of an American poet; and no doubt it is the name of someone else just around the corner. It is these endlessly attempted and endlessly incomplete translations that make Rome both far and near, both ancient history and current drama.

And indeed, Rome is both ancient and current for others besides Lowell the poet. In the 1960s, the United States, flaunting its might as champion of the free world, seemed to turn itself into a ventriloquized version of Rome, repeating the excesses as well as the horrors of that ancient empire. No one was more aware of this ventriloquy than Lowell, deeply opposed to the war in Vietnam, and deeply convinced as well that this destructive course of action was not national but planetary in scope:

> Pity the planet, all joy gone
> from this sweet volcanic cone;
> peace to our children when they fall
> in small war on the heels of small
> war—until the end of time

to police the earth, a ghost
orbiting forever lost
in our monotonous sublime.[30]

This is Lowell's "Waking Early Sunday Morning," one of the best-
known antiwar poems of the 1960s, written during the summer of
1965, though hardly Lowell's only preoccupation that season.[31] Indeed,
those were feverish months for him, a political maelstrom clearly
gathering on the horizon. Earlier that year, in February, American
planes had started bombing Vietnam. In March, Johnson stepped
up the deployment of combat troops. By April, antiwar demonstra-
tions had spread across the nation, from Washington to many college
campuses. It was in this explosive climate that Johnson announced
a White House Festival of the Arts, to be held on 14 June, to which
Lowell was invited. He initially accepted but almost immediately
changed his mind. His letter to Johnson was published in the front
page of the *New York Times* on 3 June 1965, followed the next day by
another headline: "Twenty Writers and Artists Endorse Poet's Rebuff
of President."[32] This article featured a telegram signed by some of
the nation's most prominent intellectuals: Hannah Arendt, John Berry-
man, Alan Dugan, Jules Feiffer, Philip Guston, Lillian Hellman, Alfred
Kazin, Stanley Kunitz, Dwight Macdonald, Bernard Malamud, Mary
McCarthy, Larry Rivers, Philip Roth, Mark Rothko, Louis Simpson,
W. D. Snodgrass, William Styron, Peter Taylor, Edgar Varese, and
Robert Penn Warren.[33] It was one of the most memorable public embar-
rassments for Johnson, a minor incident that spun completely out of
control. Lowell's letter started it all:

> Although I am very enthusiastic about most of your domestic legis-
> lation and intentions, I nevertheless can only follow our present for-
> eign policy with the greatest dismay and distrust. What we will do
> and what we ought to do as a sovereign nation facing other sover-
> eign nations seem now to hang in the balance between the better
> and the worse possibilities. . . . At this anguished, delicate and per-
> haps determining moment, I feel I am serving you and our country
> by not taking part in the White House Festival of the Arts.[34]

Lowell had no quarrel with Johnson's "great society" program. He did
have a quarrel with Johnson's foreign policy, specifically, the escalat-
ing use of force in Vietnam and the shotgun time frame of military
action. As a nation in combat, the United States needed to have all

its citizens marching in the same direction, to the rhythm of national chronology. But some of its citizens were obviously out of step.

Lowell dramatizes this rupture of the national chronology by creating a poetic time frame also deliberately out of sync. To talk about the Roman empire at all, to present it as somehow pertinent to the United States and to the year 1965, is to have taken one's stand against the war. Allegory—with its juxtaposing of two time frames, projecting the twentieth century to the deep time of the first century—is Lowell's style of politics.[35] "I have never been New Left, Old Left, or liberal," he says in his acid exchange with Diana Trilling. "I wish to turn the clock back with every breath I draw, but I hope I have the courage to occasionally cry out against those who wrongly rule us."[36] Turning back the clock is one form of antiwar protest, the one most congenial to Lowell. And nothing turns back the clock more eloquently than translating from Latin. "The theme that connects my translations is Rome, the greatness and horror of her Empire," Lowell says in his note to *Near the Ocean*, a collection that features not only his antiwar poem "Waking Early Sunday Morning" but also his translations of Horace and Juvenal. The volume came out in 1967, the same year that Lowell took part in the March on the Pentagon. These translations are indeed written in the "alive English" he wants, as if the Latin authors were living in the 1960s. They are bits of Roman history written over by Vietnam. Lowell needs these uneasy conjunctions— needs the relativity effect they create—in order to keep his alternate time alive. He needs the tenth satire of Juvenal, "The Vanity of Human Wishes," in order to put himself, however briefly, outside the national timetable:

> And yet the boy will never be a man.
> Some prodigal seducer will seduce
> the parents—money never fails its giver.
> No overweight tyrant castrates the deformed.
> Trust Nero, Nero had an eye for beauty:
> he never picked a spastic or a lout.[37]

Lowell is translating Roman history, talking about the fate of boys who, under the reign of Nero, never reach manhood. But he is talking of course about something else as well: the fate of boys who live under the draft, who never reach manhood either, because the draft, too, has a peculiar way of cutting short the lives of the handpicked. Nero, in this sense, is not the last Nero either.[38] Like Caligula, he too has a long afterlife, a ghostly hand extended murderously into the twentieth century.

But to recall Nero, his roving eye, his "overweight" body, in turn exposed to our eye, is to be struck by the difference between what this namable Roman tyrant can do and what can be done by his modern counterpart without a name, without a body, and not called tyrant at all. The yoking of ancient and modern history once again generates a repulsive force, a double alienation, a sundering of these historical moments each from the other, and each from its own synchronic plane. To experience the Vietnam War inflected through the history of the Roman empire is to be jolted out of any secure temporal mooring. It is to see the United States in the light of a distant empire: summoned, brought forward, but not domesticated, not unified by a serial number. What, then, does the year 1965 mean for Lowell? This was the year in which he refused to take part in the White House Festival of the Arts. It was the year in which he wrote "Waking Early Sunday Morning." And it was also a year that was both near and far from the year 65, when Nero was approaching the end of his reign as Roman emperor and getting ready to move on, or so it seems, winding up in the United States, becoming a nonresident alien in the midst of the Vietnam War. 65, 1965 — what exactly is the distance between these two dates? No one can say for sure. All we know is that it is non-Newtonian time. Not quantified by chronology, not quantified by serial numbers, it gives literary studies an analytic domain the full significance of which we have yet to explore.

Yale University

Notes

1   Wai Chee Dimock, "Deep Time: American Literature and World History," *American Literary History* (December 2001): 755–75.
2   Plato, *Timaeus*, trans. Benjamin Jowett (Indianapolis: Bobbs-Merrill, 1949), 19–20. The full passage is as follows: "Now the nature of the ideal being was everlasting, but to bestow this attribute in its fullness upon a creature was impossible. Wherefore he resolved to have a moving image of eternity, and when he set in order the heaven, he made this image eternal but moving according to number, while eternity itself rests in unity; and this image we call time."
3   Aristotle, *Physics*, ed. W. D. Ross (Oxford: Clarendon Press, 1936), book 4,

219b.5–7, 386; further references to this source will be cited parenthetically in the text as *P*.

4   For the centrality of Newton to the Enlightenment, see Peter Gay, *The Enlightenment: The Science of Freedom* (New York: Norton, 1977), 126–87. For the importance of Newton to seventeenth- and eighteenth-century English political culture, see Margaret C. Jacob, *The Newtonians and the English Revolution, 1689–1720* (Ithaca, N.Y.: Cornell Univ. Press, 1976); and Betty Jo Teeter Dobbs and Margaret C. Jacob, *Newton and the Culture of Newtonianism* (Atlantic Highlands, N.J.: Humanities Press, 1995). For the importance of Newton to political culture in the United States, see Garry Wills, *Inventing America: Jefferson's Declaration of Independence* (New York: Vintage, 1979), 93–110; and I. Bernard Cohen, *Science and the Founding Fathers* (New York: Norton, 1995).

5   Isaac Newton, *Philosophiae Naturalis Principia Mathematica* (1686), trans. by Andrew Motte as *Mathematical Principles of Natural Philosophy*, rev. by Florian Cajori (1729; Berkeley and Los Angeles: Univ. of California Press, 1934), 6, 8.

6   It should be pointed out that this numerical regime was hardly Newton's alone. Seventeenth-century science was founded upon it. For the importance of numerical reasoning not only to the physical sciences but also to the biological sciences, see I. Bernard Cohen, *The Newtonian Revolution* (Cambridge, Eng.: Cambridge Univ. Press, 1980), 15–38.

7   On space in Newton, see Lawrence Sklar, *Space, Time, and Spacetime* (Berkeley and Los Angeles: Univ. of California Press, 1977), 182–93. For an emphatic argument about the centrality in Newton of "an absolutely immobile space, distinct from body, extending from infinity to infinity," see Robert Rynasiewicz, "By Their Properties, Causes, and Effects: Newton's Scholium on Time, Space, Place, and Motion," *Studies in History and Philosophy of Science* 26 (March and June 1995): 135; also 133–53, 295–321.

8   "Simultaneity" remains an important (if thorny) concept for the physical sciences even after Newton; see Hans Reichenbach, *The Philosophy of Space and Time*, trans. Maria Reichenbach and John Freund (New York: Dover, 1958), 123–35.

9   Homi K. Bhabha, "DissemiNation: Time, Narrative, and the Margins of the Modern Nation," in *The Location of Culture* (London: Routledge, 1994), 139–70.

10   Benedict Anderson, *Imagined Communities: Reflections on the Origin and Spread of Nationalism* (London: Verso, 1983), 30.

11   Bhabha here draws on Julia Kristeva, "Women's Time," in *The Kristeva Reader*, ed. Toril Moi (Oxford: Blackwell, 1986), 187–213.

12   Bhabha, "DissemiNation," 153.

13   J. M. Coetzee, "Newton and the Ideal of a Transparent Scientific Language," *Journal of Literary Semantics* 11 (April 1982): 3–13; reprinted in

Doubling the Point: Essays and Interviews, ed. David Attwell (Cambridge: Harvard Univ. Press, 1992), 181–94.

14 Albert Einstein, "Autobiographical Notes," in *Albert Einstein: Philosopher-Scientist*, ed. Paul Arthur Schilpp (La Salle, Ill.: Open Court, 1969), 33.

15 Albert Einstein, *Relativity: The Special and the General Theory*, trans. Robert W. Lawson (New York: Crown, 1961), 26; further references to this source will be cited parenthetically in the text as *R*.

16 For a useful account of Einstein and non–Euclidean geometry, see Rudolf Carnap, *An Introduction to the Philosophy of Science*, ed. Martin Gardner (New York: Dover, 1995), 132–76.

17 Einstein's commitment to mathematical formalization is steadfast; see, for instance, Abraham Pais, *"Subtle Is the Lord": The Science and Life of Albert Einstein* (New York: Oxford Univ. Press, 1982), 111–291.

18 I follow Hans Robert Jauss in seeing literary history as a "dialectic" between text and reader, but whereas Jauss explores that dialectic as a history of changing "horizons of expectation," I explore it as a history of incomplete domestication; see Jauss, *Toward an Aesthetic of Reception*, trans. Timothy Bahti (Minneapolis: Univ. of Minnesota Press, 1982).

19 Roger Chartier, *The Order of Books: Readers, Authors, and Libraries in Europe between the Fourteenth and Eighteenth Centuries*, trans. Lydia G. Cochrane (Stanford, Calif.: Stanford Univ. Press, 1994), viii.

20 For an earlier critique of Anderson, see my "Literature for the Planet," *PMLA* 116 (January 2001): 173–88, especially 175–76. See also Jonathan Culler's important essay, "Anderson and the Novel," *Diacritics* 29 (winter 1999): 20–39.

21 For theories and practices of translation, by Lowell himself and by others, see D. S. Carne-Ross, "Conversation with Robert Lowell," in *Robert Lowell: Interviews and Memoirs*, ed. Jeffrey Meyers (Ann Arbor: Univ. of Michigan Press, 1988), 129–40.

22 Robert Lowell, introduction to *Imitations* (New York: Farrar, Straus, and Giroux, 1961), xi.

23 Ibid., xi.

24 Gaius Julius Caesar Germanicus (12–41), nicknamed Caligula (literally, "baby boot"), was Roman Emperor from 37 to 41. His short reign, which ended with his assassination, was synonymous with tyranny.

25 Actually "Cal" is even more complicated than that—"part Caligula and part Caliban," as Ian Hamilton points out. Hamilton quotes this interesting recollection from one of Lowell's St. Mark's classmates: "He was called Caliban. He was also called Caligula—the least popular Roman emperor with all the disgusting traits, the depravity that everyone assumed Cal had" (see Hamilton, *Robert Lowell: A Biography* [London: Faber and Faber, 1982], 20).

26 Lowell, "Caligula," in *For the Union Dead* (New York: Farrar, Straus, and Giroux, 1964), 49.

27   Helen Vendler, *The Given and the Made: Strategies of Poetic Redefinition* (Cambridge: Harvard Univ. Press, 1995), 20–21.

28   Lowell, "Caligula," in *For the Union Dead,* 51.

29   This much abbreviated version in *Notebook* (New York: Farrar, Straus, and Giroux, 1967) reads as follows:

> My sake, Little Boots, Caligula,
> you disappoint me. Tell me what you saw—
> Item: your body hairy, badly made,
> head hairless, smoother than your marble head;
> Item: eyes hollow, hollow temples, red
> cheeks roughed with rouge, legs spindly, hands that leave
> a clammy snail's trail on your wilting sleeve,
> your hand no hand can hold . . . bald head, thin neck—you wished
>   the Romans had a single neck.
> That was no artist's bubble. Animals
> ripened for your arenas suffered less
> than you when slaughtered—yours the lawlessness
> of something simple that has lost its law,
> my namesake, not the last Caligula. (176)

30   Lowell, "Waking Early Sunday Morning," in *Near the Ocean* (New York: Farrar, Straus, and Giroux, 1967), 24.

31   See Hamilton, *Robert Lowell: A Biography,* 327; see also Paul Mariani, *Lost Puritan: A Life of Robert Lowell* (New York: Norton, 1994), 336. For the several drafts of "Waking Early Sunday Morning," see Alan Williamson, *Pity the Monsters: The Political Vision of Robert Lowell* (New Haven: Yale Univ. Press, 1974), 119; and Williamson, "The Reshaping of 'Waking Early Sunday Morning,'" in his *Eloquence and Mere Life* (Ann Arbor: Univ. of Michigan Press, 1994), 3–28.

32   As Robert von Hallberg points out, the letter went through at least five drafts (see *American Poetry and Culture, 1944–1980* [Cambridge: Harvard Univ. Press, 1985], 170). The drafts are in the Houghton Library, Harvard University.

33   See Hamilton, *Robert Lowell,* 323.

34   Robert Lowell to President Lyndon Johnson, *New York Times,* 3 June 1965, 1; reprinted in *Robert Lowell: Collected Prose,* ed. Robert Giroux (New York: Farrar, Straus, and Giroux, 1987), 371.

35   Paul de Man argues that "in the world of allegory, time is the originary constitutive category. . . . It remains necessary, if there is to be allegory, that the allegorical sign refer to another sign that precedes it, . . . a previous sign with which it can never coincide, since it is of the essence of this previous sign to be pure anteriority" ("The Rhetoric of Temporality," in *Interpretation: Theory and Practice,* ed. Charles S. Singleton [Baltimore: Johns Hopkins Univ. Press, 1969], 190; see also 173–209).

36 Lowell, "Liberalism and Activism," *Commentary* 47 (April 1969), 19. This was the second exchange between Lowell and Diana Trilling, starting with Trilling's long essay, "On the Steps of Low Library," *Commentary* 46 (November 1968): 29–55.

37 Lowell's translation of Juvenal, "The Vanity of Human Wishes," in *Near the Ocean*, 98.

38 Nero Claudius Caesar (15–68), Roman emperor, 54–68. During the great fire that destroyed half of Rome in 64, he was rumored to have used the fire as a backdrop to recite his own poem on the fall of Troy. Widespread public unrest in 68 led to his flight from Rome and to suicide.

Announcements

Massachusetts Historical Society: Emerson Bicentennial Conference

The Massachusetts Historical Society will host "Spires of Form": The Emerson Bicentennial Conference, 24–26 April 2003, in Boston, Massachusetts, 1154 Boylston Street. Organized by Joel Myerson (University of South Carolina) and Ronald Bosco (SUNY-Albany), the conference events will include papers and panels, a visit to Concord to see the Emerson house, an exhibition at the Concord Free Public Library, and a reception at the Concord Museum. For information, see the Society's Web site: www.masshist.org/conference/emerson.html; for answers to questions, send e-mail to conference@masshist.org, or call 617-646-0542.

American Literature
Index to Volume 74 (December 2002)

Board of Editors

Authors of Articles and Reviews

Abraham, Julie. Review: Rohy, *Impossible Women: Lesbian Figures and American Literature*, 679–80.

Albrecht, James M. Review: Warren, *Culture of Eloquence: Oratory and Reform in Antebellum America*, 142–43.

Aldama, Frederick Luis. Review: Goldman, *Continental Divides: Revisioning American Literature*, 192–94.

Andrews, Scott. Review: Wyss, *Writing Indians: Literacy, Christianity, and Native Community in Early America*, 140–42.

Argersinger, Jana. "Family Embraces: The Unholy Kiss and Authorial Relations in *The Wide, Wide World*," 251–85.

Baum, Rosalie Murphy. Review: Hammond, *The American Puritan Elegy: A Literary and Cultural Study*, 635–37.

Baym, Nina. Review: Cameron, *Beautiful Work: A Meditation on Pain*, 441–43.
———. Review: Scarry, *Dreaming by the Book*, 441–43.

Beasley, Rebecca, "Ezra Pound's Whistler," 485–516.

Browne, Cornelius. Review: Mazel, *American Literary Environmentalism*, 433–35.

Burns, Allan. Review: Will, *Gertrude Stein, Modernism, and the Problem of "Genius,"* 165–67.

Byers, Thomas B. Review: Springer, *Hollywood Fictions: The Dream Factory in American Popular Literature*, 660–62.

Carlson, Larry. Review: Doyle: *Louisa May Alcott and Charlotte Brontë: Transatlantic Translations*, 151–52.

Charles, Anne. Review: Winning, *The Pilgrimage of Dorothy Richardson*, 167–69.

Clayton, Jay. "Convergence of the Two Cultures: A Geek's Guide to Contemporary Literature," 807–31.

Clendenning, John. Review: Brown, *The Material Unconscious: American Amusement, Stephen Crane, and the Economies of Play*, 411–13.
———. Review: Monteiro, *Stephen Crane's Blue Badge of Courage*, 411–13.

Coe, Theodore A. Review: Simon, *Trash Culture: Popular Culture and the Great Tradition*, 439–41.

Cook, Don L. Review: Herman, ed., *Pynchon Notes 42–43: Approach and Avoid: Essays on "Gravity's Rainbow,"* 668–70.
———. Review: Patell, *Negative Liberties: Morrison, Pynchon, and the Problem of Liberal Ideology*, 668–70.

Damon, Maria. Review: Finkelstein, *Not One of Them in Place: Modern Poetry and Jewish American Identity*, 674–77.
———. Review: Fredman, *A Menorah for Athena: Charles Reznikoff and the Jewish Dilemmas of Objectivist Poetry*, 674–77.
———. Review: Mintz, *Translating Israel: Contemporary Hebrew Literature and Its Reception in America*, 674–77.

Harris, Sharon M. Review Essay: "'A New Era in Female History': Nineteenth-Century U.S. Women Writers," 603–18.

Hatten, Charles. Review: Horvitz, *Literary Trauma: Sadism, Memory, and Sexual Violence in American Women's Fiction*, 677–79.

Hayles, N. Katherine. "Saving the Subject: Remediation in *House of Leaves*," 779–806.

Heise, Ursula K. "Toxins, Drugs, and Global Systems: Risk and Narrative in the Contemporary Novel," 747–78.

Helle, Anita Plath. Review: Hejinian, *The Language of Inquiry*, 430–33.

———. Review: Rifkin, *Career Moves: Olson, Creely, Zukofsky, Berrigan, and the American Avant-Garde*, 430–33.

———. Review: Vickery, *Leaving Lines of Gender: A Feminist Genealogy of Language Writing*, 430–33.

Henigman, Laura. Review: Bach, *Colonial Transformations: The Cultural Production of the New Atlantic World, 1580–1640*, 403–5.

———. Review: Brown, *The Consent of the Governed: The Lockean Legacy in Early American Culture*, 403–5.

———. Review: Crain, *The Story of A: The Alphabetization of America from "The New England Primer" to "The Scarlet Letter,"* 403–5.

Hepburn, Allan. Review: Hoople, *In Darkest James: Reviewing Impressionism, 1900–1905*, 152–54.

Hochman, Barbara. "The Reading Habit and 'The Yellow Wallpaper,'" 89–110.

Hoffman, Michael J. Review: DuPlessis, *Genders, Races, and Religious Cultures in Modern American Poetry, 1908–1934*, 662–64.

———. Review: Morrisson, *The Public Face of Modernism: Little Magazines, Audiences, and Reception, 1905–1920*, 164–65.

Hotek, Adam. Review: Favor, *Authentic Blackness: The Folk in the New Negro Renaissance*, 419–21.

Jarraway, David. Review: Gunn, *Beyond Solidarity: Pragmatism and Difference in a Globalized World*, 652–54.

———. Review: Kadlec, *Mosaic Modernism: Anarchism, Pragmatism, Culture*, 652–54.

Johnson, Thomas C. Review: Van Allen, *James Whitcomb Riley: A Life*, 410–11.

Johnson, Kendall. "'Dark Spot' in the Picturesque: The Aesthetics of Polygenism and Henry James's 'A Landscape-Painter,'" 59–87.

Joseph, Philip. "The Verdict from the Porch: Zora Neale Hurston and Reparative Justice," 455–83.

Kessler, Carol Farley. Review: Batker, *Reforming Fictions: Native, African, and Jewish American Women's Literature and Journalism in the Progressive Era*, 162–64.

Klimasmith, Betsy. Review: Rosowski, *Birthing a Nation: Gender, Creativity, and the West in American Literature*, 179–81.

Knadler, Stephen. Review: Middleton and Woods, *Literatures of Memory: History, Time, and Space in Postwar Writing*, 426–28.

Newfield, Christopher. Review: Douglass, *The California Idea and American Higher Education: 1850 to the 1960 Master Plan*, 196–98.

Ngai, Sianne. "'A Foul Lump Started Making Promises in My Voice': Race, Affect, and the Animated Subject," 571–601.

Osteen, Mark. Review: Seguin, *Around Quitting Time: Work and Middle-Class Fantasy in American Fiction*, 680–82.

Packer, Barbara. Review: Foster Jr. and Foster, *Beechers, Stowes, and Yankee Strangers: The Transformation of Florida*, 147–48.

Perkins, Priscilla. Review: Pollak, *The Erotic Whitman*, 640–42.

Powell, Timothy. Review: Douglass-Chin, *Preacher Woman Sings the Blues: The Autobiographies of Nineteenth-Century African American Evangelists*, 645–47.

———. Review: Moody, *Sentimental Confessions: Spiritual Narratives of Nineteenth-Century African American Women*, 645–47.

Prebel, Julie. Review: Russell, *Crossing Boundaries: Postmodern Travel Literature*, 406–8.

———. Review: Ziff, *Return Passages: Great American Travel Writing, 1780–1910*, 406–8.

Rodríguez, Ana Patricia. Review: Saldívar-Hull, *Feminism on the Border: Chicana Gender Politics and Literature*, 190–91.

Ryan, Barbara. Review: Crain, *American Sympathy: Men, Friendship, and Literature in the New Nation*, 408–10.

———. Review: Williams, *Not in Sisterhood: Edith Wharton, Willa Cather, Zona Gale, and the Politics of Female Authorship*, 408–10.

Sadowski-Smith, Claudia. Review: Fox, *The Fence and the River: Culture and Politics at the U.S.–Mexico Border*, 185–87.

Scheckel, Susan. "Home on the Train: Race and Mobility in *The Life and Adventures of Nat Love*," 219–50.

Schulz, Jennifer L. "Restaging the Racial Contract: James Weldon Johnson's Signatory Strategies," 31–58.

Scott, Bonnie Kime. Review: Boone et al., eds., *Queer Frontiers: Millennial Geographies, Genders, and Generations*, 654–56.

———. Review: Scandura and Thurston, eds., *Modernism, Inc.: Body, Memory, Capital*, 654–56.

Shockley, Evie. Review: Castronovo, *Necro Citizenship: Death, Eroticism, and the Public Sphere in the Nineteenth-Century United States*, 683–85.

———. Review: Holland, *Raising the Dead: Readings of Death and (Black) Subjectivity*, 683–85.

Silverman, Gillian. "Textual Sentimentalism: Incest and Authorship in *Pierre*," 345–72.

Smith, Martha Nell. "Computing: What's American Literary Study Got to Do with IT?" 833–57.

Solomon, Melissa. Review: Delany, *Shorter Views: Queer Thoughts and the Politics of the Paraliterary*, 437–39.

Articles as Subject Matter

Transnationalism. "Filibustering Cuba: *Cecilia Valdéz* and a Memory of Nation in the Americas," by Rodrigo Lazo, 1–30.

True Crime Narratives. "'Indelicate Exposure': Sentiment and Law in *Fall River: An Authentic Narrative*," by Jeanne Elders DeWaard, 373–401.

Twain, Mark. "American Literary Realism and Nervous 'Reflexion,'" by Randall Knoper, 715–45.

Two Cultures. "Convergence of the Two Cultures: A Geek's Guide to Contemporary Literature," by Jay Clayton, 807–31.

———. "Preface: Literature and Science: Cultural Forms, Conceptual Exchanges," by Wai Chee Dimock and Priscilla Wald, 705–14.

Verdad, La. "Filibustering Cuba: *Cecilia Valdéz* and a Memory of Nation in the Americas," by Rodrigo Lazo, 1–30.

Vietnam War. "Non-Newtonian Time: Robert Lowell, Roman History, Vietnam War," by Wai Chee Dimock, 911–31.

Warner, Susan. "Family Embraces: The Unholy Kiss and Authorial Relations in *The Wide, Wide World*," by Jana Argersinger, 251–85.

Washington, Booker T. "Home on the Train: Race and Mobility in *The Life and Adventures of Nat Love*," by Susan Scheckel, 219–50.

Western Fiction. "Home on the Train: Race and Mobility in *The Life and Adventures of Nat Love*," by Susan Scheckel, 219–50.

Whistler, James McNeill. "Ezra Pound's Whistler," by Rebecca Beasley, 485–516.

Williams, Catharine. "'Indelicate Exposure': Sentiment and Law in *Fall River: An Authentic Narrative*," by Jeanne Elders DeWaard, 373–401.

Yau, John. "'A Foul Lump Started Making Promises in My Voice': Race, Affect, and the Animated Subject," by Sianne Ngai, 571–601.

Books Reviewed

Adams, Katherine H. *A Group of Their Own: College Writing Courses and American Women Writers, 1880–1940*, reviewed by Stephanie Foote, 158–59.

Anderson, Paul Allen. *Deep River: Music and Memory in Harlem Renaissance Thought*, reviewed by John Gennari, 649–52.

Bach, Rebecca Ann. *Colonial Transformations: The Cultural Production of the New Atlantic World, 1580–1640*, reviewed by Laura Henigman, 403–5.

Batker, Carol J. *Reforming Fictions: Native, African, and Jewish American Women's Literature and Journalism in the Progressive Era*, reviewed by Carol Farley Kessler, 162–64.

Bell, Michael Davitt. *Culture, Genre, and Literary Vocation: Selected Essays on American Literature*, reviewed by Ian Frederick Finseth, 194–96.

Boone, Joseph et al., eds. *Queer Frontiers: Millennial Geographies, Genders, and Generations*, reviewed by Bonnie Kime Scott, 654–56.

Foster Jr., John T. and Sarah Whitmer Foster. *Beechers, Stowes, and Yankee Strangers: The Transformation of Florida*, reviewed by Barbara Packer, 147–48.

Fox, Claire F. *The Fence and the River: Culture and Politics at the U.S.–Mexico Border*, reviewed by Claudia Sadowski–Smith, 185–87.

Fredman, Stephen. *A Menorah for Athena: Charles Reznikoff and the Jewish Dilemmas of Objectivist Poetry*, reviewed by Maria Damon, 674–77.

Freedman, Jonathan. *The Temple of Culture: Assimilation and Anti-Semitism in Literary Anglo-America*, reviewed by Thomas J. Ferraro, 155.

Gaines, Jane. *Fire and Desire: Mixed Raced Movies in the Silent Era*, reviewed by Linda Williams, 160–61.

Goldberg, Jonathan. *Willa Cather and Others*, reviewed by Lisa Marcus, 656–58.

Goldman, Anne E. *Continental Divides: Revisioning American Literature*, reviewed by Frederick Luis Aldama, 192–94.

Gray, Richard. *Southern Aberrations: Writers of the American South and the Problems of Regionalism*, reviewed by Jennifer Rae Greeson and Candace Waid, 176–77.

Gunn, Giles. *Beyond Solidarity: Pragmatism and Difference in a Globalized World*, reviewed by David Jarraway, 652–54.

Hall, Roger A. *Performing the American Frontier, 1870–1906*, reviewed by Gretchen Murphy, 647–49.

Hammond, Jeffrey A. *The American Puritan Elegy: A Literary and Cultural Study*, reviewed by Rosalie Murphy Baum, 635–37.

Hejinian, Lyn. *The Language of Inquiry*, reviewed by Anita Plath Helle, 430–33.

Hendler, Glenn. *Public Sentiments: Structures of Feeling in Nineteenth–Century American Literature*, reviewed by Joycelyn Moody, 156–58.

Henigman, Laura. *Coming into Communion: Pastoral Dialogues in Colonial New England*, reviewed by Fritz Fleishmann, 139–40.

Herman, Luc, ed. *Pynchon Notes 42–43: Approach and Avoid: Essays on "Gravity's Rainbow,"* reviewed by Don L. Cook, 668–70.

Holland, Sharon Patricia. *Raising the Dead: Readings of Death and (Black) Subjectivity*, reviewed by Evie Shockley, 683–85.

Hoople, Robin. *In Darkest James: Reviewing Impressionism, 1900–1905*, reviewed by Allan Hepburn, 152–54.

Horvitz, Deborah M. *Literary Trauma: Sadism, Memory, and Sexual Violence in American Women's Fiction*, reviewed by Charles Hatten, 677–79.

Huhndorf, Shari M. *Going Native: Indians in the American Cultural Imagination*, reviewed by Michael A. Elliott, 183–85.

Hunt, Peter, ed. *Understanding Children's Literature*, reviewed by Bonnie Gaarden, 191–92.

Jacobs, Karen. *The Eye's Mind: Literary Modernism and Visual Culture*, reviewed by Laura Doyle, 418–19.

Statement of Ownership and Management

American Literature (ISSN 0002-9831) is published four times a year in March, June, September, and December by Duke University Press. The Office of Publication and General Business Office are located at 905 W. Main St., Suite 18-B, Durham, NC 27701. The editor is Houston A. Baker Jr., Duke University, P.O. Box 90020, Durham, NC 27708-0020. The owner is Duke University Press, Durham, NC. There are no bondholders, mortgagees, or other security holders.

Extent and Nature of Circulation

Average number of copies of each issue published during the preceding twelve months; (A) total number of copies printed, 4100; (B.1) sales through dealers and carriers, street vendors and counter sales, 0; (B.2) paid mail subscriptions, 3750; (C) total paid circulation, 3750; (D) samples, complimentary, and other free copies, 40; (E) free distribution outside the mail (carriers or other means), 10; (F) total free distribution (sum of D & E), 50; (G) total distribution (sum of C & F), 3800; (H.1) office use, leftover, unaccounted, spoiled after printing, 300; (H.2) returns from news agents, 0; (I) total, 4100.

Actual number of copies of a single issue published nearest to filing date: (A) total number of copies printed, 3997; (B.1) sales through dealers and carriers, street vendors and counter sales, 0; (B.2) paid mail subscriptions, 3837; (C) total paid circulation, 3837; (D) samples, complimentary, and other free copies, 15; (E) free distribution outside the mail (carriers or other means), 12; (F) total free distribution (sum of D & E), 27; (G) total distribution (sum of C & F), 3864; (H.1) office use, leftover, unaccounted, spoiled after printing, 133; (H.2) returns from news agents, 0; (I) total, 3997.

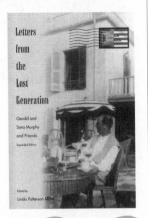

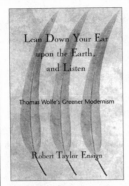

WEST OF EMERSON
The Design of Manifest Destiny
KRIS FRESONKE

Where did American literature start? Fresonke tracks down the texts by explorers of the far West that informed *Nature*, Emerson's most famous essay, and proceeds to uncover the parodic Western politics at play in classic New England works of Romanticism. Westerns, this book shows, helped create "Easterns."
$49.95 hardcover, $19.95 paperback

Captain Lewis shooting an Indian.

From *West of Emerson*

"The Mark Twain Project looms over the landscape of literary scholarship like Mount Everest."
—*San Francisco Chronicle*

MARK TWAIN'S LETTERS, VOLUME 6: 1874-1875
EDITED BY MICHAEL B.FRANK & HARRIET ELINOR SMITH

Twain's letters for 1874 and 1875 encompass one of his most productive and rewarding periods as author, husband and father, and man of property. All of these accomplishments and events are vividly captured, in his inimitable language and with his unmatched humor, in letters to family and friends, among them some of the leading writers of the day. The comprehensive editorial annotation supplies the historical and social context that helps make these letters as fresh and immediate to a modern audience as they were to their original readers.

Mark Twain Papers
$85.00 hardcover

At bookstores or order
(800) 822-6657   www.ucpress.edu

ADVENTURES OF HUCKLEBERRY FINN
MARK TWAIN
Edited by Victor Fischer and Lin Salamo

The text of this new scholarly edition of *Adventures of Huckleberry Finn* is the first ever to be based on Mark Twain's complete, original manuscript—including its first 665 pages, which had been lost for over a hundred years.
$75.00 hardcover

UNIVERSITY OF CALIFORNIA PRESS

LITERARY STUDIES

from LSU Press

HEARTS OF DARKNESS
Wellsprings of a Southern Literary Tradition
Bertram Wyatt-Brown

The role of melancholy and alienation in the evolution of nineteenth-century southern letters

WALTER LYNWOOD FLEMING LECTURES IN SOUTHERN HISTORY
Illustrated, $59.95 cloth, $24.95 paper

THE FREE FLAG OF CUBA
The Lost Novel of Lucy Holcombe Pickens
Edited, with an Introduction, by Orville Vernon Burton and Georganne B. Burton

A forgotten novel gains historical significance when its author is revealed

THE LIBRARY OF SOUTHERN CIVILIZATION
Lewis P. Simpson, *Editor*
$59.95 cloth, $29.95 paper

GOING THE DISTANCE
Dissident Subjectivity in Modernist American Literature
David R. Jarraway

An illuminating perusal of five major American modernist poets and their constructed identities

HORIZONS IN THEORY AND AMERICAN CULTURE
Bainard Cowan and Joseph G. Kronick, *Editors*
$69.95 cloth, $24.95 paper

SOUTHERN LITERARY STUDIES
Fred Hobson, *Editor*

ONE WRITER'S IMAGINATION
The Fiction of Eudora Welty
Suzanne Marrs

An illuminating investigation of Eudora Welty's creative process

Illustrated, $59.95 cloth, $24.95 paper

SOUTH TO A NEW PLACE
Region, Literature, Culture
Edited by Suzanne W. Jones and Sharon Monteith
Foreword by Richard Gray

Innovative scholars answer the perennial question "What is southern?"
Illustrated, $85.00 cloth, $34.95 paper

THE BELLE GONE BAD
White Southern Women Writers and the Dark Seductress
Betina Entzminger

A study of the spellbinding character type that has shaken southern society for two centuries
Illustrated, $59.95 cloth, $24.95 paper

LOUISIANA STATE UNIVERSITY PRESS
Baton Rouge 70803 • (800) 861-3477 • www.lsu.edu/lsupress

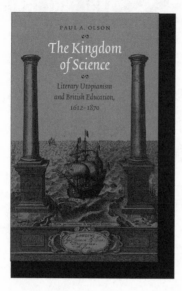

The Kingdom of Science
Literary Utopianism and British
Education, 1612–1870
By Paul A. Olson
The Kingdom of Science examines Baconian
utopias as blueprints for a scientific
sociology of knowledge that founded a
new social and economic world in the
seventeenth century.
$65 cloth

Willa Cather Remembered
Edited by Sharon Hoover
Compiled by L. Brent Bohlke and
Sharon Hoover
Willa Cather Remembered comprises
reminiscences of the author written
between the 1920s and 1980s by people
ranging from close friends to journalistic
observers and acquaintances.
$19.95 paper/ $45 cloth

Designs of the Night Sky
By Diane Glancy
"Voices and stories fill the pages of prolific
Native American writer Glancy's
latest . . . as a middle-aged Cherokee woman
faces conflicts at work, in her fractured
family, and in her faith."—*Kirkus*
$24.95 cloth

Memorial Fictions
Willa Cather and the First World War
By Steven Trout
Memorial Fictions offers a major
reassessment of Willa Cather's artistic
achievements, provides information on
popular culture, and demonstrates the
importance of literature as a forum for
addressing American culture.
$40 cloth

University of Nebraska Press
publishers of Bison Books / www.nebraskapress.unl.edu / 800.755.1105

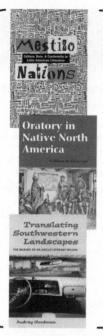
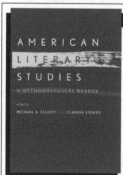

UNIVERSITY OF MISSOURI PRESS

Scarring the Black Body
Race and Representation in African American Literature
Carol E. Henderson

In *Scarring the Black Body,* Carol E. Henderson analyzes the cultural and historical implications of scarring in a number of African American texts that feature the trope of the scar, including works by Sherley Anne Williams, Toni Morrison, Ann Petry, Ralph Ellison, and Richard Wright.
216 pages, $32.50

The Souls of Black Folk
One Hundred Years Later
Edited with an Introduction
by Dolan Hubbard

One hundred years later, Du Bois's classic from a variety of disciplines remains a pivotal text in the American understanding of the black experience, and this important collection investigates this indispensable text.
February, 328 pages, $39.95

Toni Morrison's *Beloved* and The Apotropaic Imagination
Kathleen Marks

Kathleen Marks investigates Toni Morrison's *Beloved* in light of ancient Greek influences, arguing that the African American experience depicted in the novel can be set in a broader context than is usually allowed.
192 pages, $29.95

Mark Twain
The Fate of Humor
James M. Cox

Instead of seeking the seriousness behind the humor, Cox concentrates upon the humor itself as the transfiguring power that converted all the "serious" issues and emotions of Mark Twain's life and time into narratives designed to evoke helpless laughter.
376 pages, $24.95

Wallace Steven and the Limits of Reading and Writing
Bart Eeckhout

Arguing that a concern with the establishment and transgression of limits goes to the heart of Stevens's work, Bart Eeckhout traces both the limits of his poetry and the limits of writing as they are explored by that poetry.
January, 344 pages, $42.50

The One Voice of James Dickey
His Letters and Life, 1942–1969
Edited with an Introduction
by Gordon Van Ness

In *The One Voice of James Dickey,* Gordon Van Ness skillfully documents James Dickey's growth from a callow teen interested primarily in sports to a mature poet who possessed literary genius and who deliberately advanced himself and his career.
January, 560 pages, 12 illustrations, $49.95

THE COLLECTED WORKS OF LANGSTON HUGHES

VOLUME 14
Autobiography
I Wonder As I Wander
Edited with an Introduction
by Joseph McLaren
January, 408 pages, $34.95

VOLUME 16
The Translations
Frederico García Lorca, Nicolás Guillén, and Jacques Roumain
Edited with an Introduction
by Dellita Martin-Ogusola
January, 240 pages, $29.95

1–800–828–1894   www.system.missouri.edu/upress